ENLIGHTENING
THE WORLD

ENLIGHTENING THE WORLD

THE
CREATION
OF THE
STATUE
OF LIBERTY

Yasmin Sabina Khan

Cornell University Press
Ithaca and London

First published 2010 by Cornell University Press
Printed in the United States of America

Library of Congress Cataloging-in-Publication Data
Khan, Yasmin Sabina.
  Enlightening the world : the creation of the Statue of Liberty /
Yasmin Sabina Khan.
      p. cm.
  Includes bibliographical references and index.
  ISBN 978-0-8014-4851-5 (cloth : alk. paper)
  1. Statue of Liberty (New York, N.Y.)—History. 2. Monuments—
New York (State)—New York—Design and construction. 3. Bartholdi,
Frédéric Auguste, 1834–1904. 4. New York (N.Y.)—Buildings, structures,
etc.—History. 5. United States—Relations—France. 6. France—
Relations—United States. I. Title.
  F128.64.L6K53 2010
  974.7′1—dc22   2009035711

Cornell University Press strives to use environmentally responsible suppliers and materials to the fullest extent possible in the publishing of its books. Such materials include vegetable-based, low-VOC inks and acid-free papers that are recycled, totally chlorine-free, or partly composed of nonwood fibers. For further information, visit our website at www.cornellpress.cornell.edu.

Cloth printing   10 9 8 7 6 5 4 3 2 1

Contents

Acknowledgments

Half a year before his death Allan Temko recommended that I read his book. I already had *Notre Dame of Paris* on my bookshelf, so I started it immediately. I was thinking much about liberty at the time, both grateful for a system of government based on respect for individual liberty and worried that our unique inheritance might, out of fear, be diminished by our own government. Allan Temko's sensitive book about how and why Notre Dame was built encouraged me to explore a monument as meaningful to our nation as Notre Dame is to France, and as universally cherished. Thus began my work on this book.

A book of course is never the work of an individual, and many people have supported me in various ways over the years as I thought about and prepared this text. Nicole Fronteau, Sergio Coelho, and Beatriz Lienhard-Fernandez helped with translations, and my brother Martin Reifschneider with the illustrations. Kathleen Coleman and Maria Luisa Mansfield offered valuable suggestions on individual chapters of the manuscript as it developed; Sr. Virginia Daniels, Carmella Yager, Msgr. Dennis Sheehan, Liliane Chase, Adam Chase, and Zillur R. and Tanjina Khan also read portions of the text. John Mansfield, Arlene Polonsky, Marlies Mueller, Beatriz Espinosa de Fernandez, and Chin-Chin Yeh generously offered their thoughts and advice on the full manuscript, and two anonymous readers shared their knowledge of the topic and the literature on the statue. A number of people at libraries, museums, and collections greatly assisted my research, including Marie-Sophie Corcy at the Conservatoire national des arts et métiers near Paris, Françoise Gademann and Régis Hueber at the Musée Bartholdi, the photographer Christian Kempf in Colmar, Sherry Birk and Mari Nakahara at the Richard Morris Hunt Collection of the American Architectural Foundation in Washington, D.C., Barbara Wolanin and Jennifer Pullara Blancato at the Office of the Architect of the Capitol, Catharina Slautterback at the Boston Athenaeum, and David Cassedy of the Union League of Philadelphia. Diane Windham Shaw at Lafayette College, Alan Hoffman, and other admirers of the Marquis de Lafayette helped me appreciate the involvement of France in the American War for Independence; many others clarified my thoughts by discussing the statue and my ideas for the book. I sincerely thank everyone who shared in some way in this project.

Michael J. McGandy, my editor at Cornell University Press, worked with me for close to a year to shape the manuscript, and his background and guidance are reflected in this text. With his help I have been better able to express my wonder at the statue's story and at how the inspired efforts of individuals can affect the course of history.

My husband, Stephen D. Byron, encouraged me to pursue my idea for a book when it was yet a vague concept. Aware of the intense research and focus that a book demands, he supported me as this idea began to take form and assisted me in innumerable ways, from finding sources to traveling to France to visit collections. I am thankful for his companionship and count on his support for all of my efforts.

INTRODUCTION

Five days before the official unveiling of the Statue of Liberty on October 28, 1886, workmen riveted the last sculpted sheet of thin copper into position. With the placement of this copper sheet at the heel of the statue, a twenty-one-year journey from conception to completion came to a close. Standing high on her pedestal, the statue rose 305 feet 11 inches (94 m) above mean low water level, higher than the piers of the Brooklyn Bridge and the office towers of New York. The entire copper skin and iron support frame had arrived from France in pieces the previous year, packed in over two hundred large wooden crates. Preassembled in Paris to ensure it would be complete and ready for erection in its permanent setting, the structure had taken nearly three years to construct. Starting with the sculptor's four-foot-high (1.2 m) terra-cotta model, plaster models progressively enlarged the design until the statue reached 151 feet 1 inch (46 m). Three hundred and ten sheets of copper were hammered into shape, forming the sculptural skin of the figure, and fastened to a truss tower designed to support this colossal work of art. The finished statue remained standing in the 17th arrondissement in Paris for over half a year as preparations were made for her arrival at Bedloe's Island (today Liberty Island) in New York Harbor.

Completion of this record-setting monument in 1886 repre-

The sculptor Auguste Bartholdi at the foot of the statue in Paris on July 4, 1884, the day it was presented to the U.S. minister to France. The statue was disassembled and shipped to the United States for erection on Bedloe's Island. © Musée des arts et métiers–Cnam, Paris. Photograph by S. Pelly.

sented a stunning technical achievement. The statue was immediately hailed as the eighth wonder of the world and the first modern wonder. The designers who joined the French sculptor Frédéric Auguste Bartholdi to create this work, the American architect Richard Morris Hunt and the French engineer Alexandre-Gustave Eiffel, were both accomplished in their fields and well-equipped to undertake a project of such grand, even unprecedented, scale. It was not to challenge the skills of her designers and builders, however, that the statue assumed exceptional proportions. What motivated the sculptor and the architect was instead the significance of the ideas and achievements that the monument portrays.

Liberty Enlightening the World (*La Liberté éclairant le monde*), as the statue was initially called, was conceived by an ardent admirer of the United States, Édouard-René Lefebvre de Laboulaye. A French scholar of legal and political institutions, Laboulaye found inspiration in America's founding history and in her people's commitment to liberty and representative government. The United States had served as an exemplary republic since its founding; the founders themselves believed that they were a part of something larger even than the nation. In this new government, they prophesied, "lay a foundation for erecting temples of liberty in every part of the earth."

Yet by the middle of the nineteenth century, the influence of the American system of government based on respect for individual liberty and dignity was heavily burdened by the abhorrent enslavement of the African American people. When the American Civil War commenced in 1861, Laboulaye, along with many people around the world, followed events closely. Laboulaye felt strongly that the resolution of the issues that fueled the war, the authority of the federal government and the future of slavery, held global importance. The Civil War asked, and would answer, the question, Can "a constitutional republic, or democracy—a government of the people, by the same people," withstand this grave threat to its existence while honoring its principles? If the Union failed, President Abraham Lincoln warned the U.S. Congress and the rest of the world in 1861, such failure would "thus practically put an end to free government upon the earth." In this light, the preservation of the American republic was perceived to carry immense importance beyond national borders.

When the war came to an end, Laboulaye and other admirers of the American form of government enjoyed great relief. The devastating news that followed shortly thereafter, however, shattered this sense of ease and imbued the Union's victory with heightened significance. Less than a week after the surrender of the Confederate army under Robert E. Lee and the cessation of the brutal four-year-long war, Abraham Lincoln, whose words and deeds had come to represent his nation's commitment to liberty, was mortally wounded in Ford's Theatre in Washington, D.C.

"How great is the emotion in Paris," observed Laboulaye. People in France reacted to the tragedy of Lincoln's death with declarations of goodwill toward the American people. For Laboulaye, this response demonstrated a rekindling of the bonds of friendship that had been established during the American War for Independence, personified by the Marquis de Lafayette. The French military had participated in the American Revolutionary War and the French people had watched with interest as the young nation developed. They admired the founding ideals of the American Republic and rejoiced in the survival of the Union. A monument to liberty and the independence of the United States, Laboulaye now proposed, built as a collaborative effort by the two peoples, would celebrate their friendship and express the aspirations and ideals they shared.

The Statue of Liberty was thus conceived, in the words of the sculptor, Auguste Bartholdi, "grand as the idea which it embodies." In size and in composition, the statue's grand design was perfectly suited to her island setting in New York Harbor and to her identification with the United States. As one of the statue's supporters, a young Theodore Roosevelt, assured his listeners during a Fourth of July celebration the same year the statue was unveiled: "Like all Americans, I like big things; big prairies, big forests and mountains, big wheatfields, railroads, and herds of cattle, too." The statue's symbols of liberty and independence seem to emerge spontaneously from the history of the nation's birth. In her left arm she carries a tablet of the law marked with the date of the Declaration of Independence; in her right hand she raises a torch of enlightenment; and with her left foot she tramples a broken chain. The diverse yet complementary moods she conveys are also drawn from America's history: triumph at having achieved independence from oppression, delight in liberty, eagerness to progress rather than remain fixed in time, an understanding of the struggles inherent in liberty, and the determination to maintain stability and uphold justice.

It is indeed a measure of the sculptor's talent that the statue embodies such a range of meaning. Bartholdi sensed that his design might become an emblem of national identity. In preparation for his work he toured the United States with an attentive eye, aiming to understand American values and character. He observed the classical traditions in the design of the Capitol in Washington, D.C., which commemorates the nation's accomplishments within the context of civilization. The founders of the nation sought to associate the new republic with "models of antiquity," Thomas Jefferson explained, "which have had the approbation of thousands of years." Bartholdi similarly reached back in history, taking as models structures that were the pride of the ancient world.

As a work of art and a feat of large-scale construction, the Statue of Liberty commands attention from her pedestal on Bedloe's Island. Confidently offering reassurance and hope, her strong presence in New York Harbor invariably causes visitors to marvel at her. Her vitality as a visionary monument and iconographic symbol further distinguishes this statue from all others. Whether one glimpses only her uplifted torch, crown of rays, or inscribed tablet, one can immediately identify the statue and respond intuitively to her meanings. Today, over a century after the statue's completion, her image is honored across the globe by those who champion freedom, whether it be political, religious, or economic, philosophical or practical. Americans have embraced the statue as their own, making her the representative of a people bound together by common beliefs about liberty, opportunity, and justice.

Symbolizing a people's commitment to liberate the spirit of the individual, the statue inspires with the ideas she embodies and illuminates a vision of life and hope with the blaze of light she raises. Cradling the tablet of the law in her left arm, she reminds us that the American founders blended revolutionary idealism with practical realism. The zeal that brought about the American Revolution was shaped into a commitment to stable democracy by way of a Constitution.

Discussing the statue's meanings at a meeting of the New England Society in 1876, Bartholdi referred to America's tradition of providing, as the revolutionary Thomas Paine exulted one hundred years earlier, an "asylum for the persecuted lovers of civil and religious liberty." The Statue of Liberty, Bartholdi believed, would fit in this tradition and manifest the exceptional character of the New World. And so she did. Her presence in the harbor transformed a faceless shoreline, offering to weary travelers a powerful image of welcome and the marker of a new beginning. This was the sense of anticipation that Emma Lazarus captured in her sonnet "The New Colossus," the closing lines of which have become most familiar:

> "Keep, ancient lands, your storied pomp!" cries she
> With silent lips. "Give me your tired, your poor,
> Your huddled masses yearning to breathe free,
> The wretched refuse of your teeming shore.
> Send these, the homeless, tempest-tost to me,
> I lift my lamp beside the golden door!"

How we interpret the statue's meanings depends on our own personal history, along with the mood of the country at any given moment. In the 1870s and 1880s, the nation's reputation was blossoming into one of vitality derived from its unique blend of people and its "open gates," in the words of U.S. president Stephen Grover Cleveland at the unveiling ceremony. Over the next century millions of new immigrants—people like my own parents—would find inspiration and opportunity in their new home and eagerly fulfill the promise of a better life. Some would become world leaders in their fields, heightening international respect for their adopted home. During World War I, the government reinforced the nation's association with the statue by issuing liberty bonds with an image of the statue. Individuals, on the contrary, have looked to her to bolster their cause, often in opposition to the government. Since her design was announced in France the statue has been employed in commerce, advertising a surprising range of merchandise and services. Indeed, the uses of her image can seem disgraceful at times. But no one fears for her; her identity is firmly grounded. From political debate to commerce, she can support protest and humor without loss of dignity.

"Such a work as this gift of one people to another has never yet been thought of, much less achieved," wrote the New York *Independent* at the time of the statue's unveiling. The depth of feeling that caused the French people to partake in this exceptional enterprise was founded in a sense of pride in their involvement in the American Revolutionary War. Equally important, the people of France esteemed the stable democracy that had been crafted in the United States. They knew the difficulty of balancing revolution and reaction, liberty and order. In the 1860s and 1870s they were struggling to secure a representative government and individual liberties in France. For the people who felt drawn to the Statue of Liberty and contributed to her making, she represented aspirations that neither geographical boundaries nor political jurisdictions could constrain.

The French sponsors of the statue looked to the United States for evidence that ideas of liberty and constitutional government could be shaped into a practical system, melding foundational stability with openness to change as the life of the people changes. In 1875, the year plans for the statue were announced, France still felt the effects of monarchic and hereditary privilege even as the Third Republic sought to secure its own foundations. The French people knew too well that "liberty and peace are living things," as U.S. president Franklin D. Roosevelt remarked during the statue's fiftieth anniversary celebration; "in each generation . . . they must be guarded and vitalized anew." In the 1870s and 1880s, the statue was one element of the French people's efforts to vitalize liberty, affirming their admiration for the achievements of the American republic. As Édouard Laboulaye put it, "One is never cured of a yearning for freedom."

The story of the statue that unfolds in the following pages is familiar in its outline—the French sculptor, the oft-repeated sonnet, the *New York World*'s fundraising drive—but not in its details. It is in the details of the statue's design and the individuals who make up her story that one discovers the fascinating nature of her creation. For the statue did not emerge simply out of the founding history of the United States or as an example of heroic sculpture. Instead, twenty-one years passed as the creators and sponsors of this monument struggled within the framework of their own lives to bring it to fruition. By looking more closely at the driving events of the period and the personal motivations of the main characters in this story, we can begin to understand the circumstances and extraordinary effort that guided the monument from its conception in 1865 to its unveiling in New York Harbor in 1886.

Let us begin at Gettysburg, Pennsylvania, in 1863, when the words of President Lincoln bound the fate of the Union with that of people around the world.

1

·❖·

THE IDEA

Four score and seven years ago our fathers brought forth, upon this continent, a new nation, conceived in Liberty, and dedicated to the proposition that all men are created equal.

Now we are engaged in a great civil war, testing whether that nation, or any nation, so conceived, and so dedicated, can long endure. . . .

. . . It is rather for us to be here dedicated to the great task remaining before us . . . that we here highly resolve that these dead shall not have died in vain; that this nation shall have a new birth of freedom; and that this government of the people, by the people, for the people, shall not perish from the earth.

When President Abraham Lincoln spoke at the cemetery in Gettysburg on November 19, 1863, he defined the Civil War for Americans and the world. In a powerful address that lasted a mere three minutes, he confirmed the moral issue that underlay the division between North and South, assumed for his cause the authority of America's founders, and asserted the global significance of the outcome of the war. By focusing on the abstract ideal of equality rather than the political implications of secession by the Confederate states, Lincoln began the process of transforming the conflict. Imbued with moral weight, the threatened dismantlement of the Union involved people in the conflict on an emotional and philosophical level. At the same time, in linking it with the political future of all nations, he secured the support of people around the world who looked to the success of America's "experiment of self-government" to provide a modern precedent for their own governments.

Lincoln consistently emphasized the important role of the United States in assisting aspiring republics. As Thomas Jefferson had cast the cause of liberty, proclaimed in the Declaration of Independence, in universal terms, highlighting the laws of nature as the basis for individual liberty rather than the rights specific to British subjects, so too did Lincoln cast the issues now confronting the Union in global terms. When arguing against a policy permitting the expansion of slavery into new territories, he declared that such a policy extends the "monstrous injustice" of slavery in American society. It "deprives our republican example of its just influence in the world—enables the enemies of free institutions, with plausibility, to taunt us as hypocrites—causes the real friends of freedom to doubt our sincerity." Addressing Congress shortly after the commencement of the war, Lincoln dramatically tied the North's commitment to preserving the Union to the fate of the world, "the whole family of man."

Lincoln knew that the time was right to frame the Civil War in international terms. Events in the United States were of great import to those in Europe who longed for a "new birth of freedom" in their own countries. Societies, they believed, could strengthen one another as each struggled to shape its own political system, and they assured Lincoln of their support. From Italy Lincoln received a declaration signed by the legendary leader of the independence fighters, Giuseppe Garibaldi, together with others who worked for the establishment of a republic. Garibaldi had fought during the revolution of 1848–49 to liberate the Italian people, living "as slaves of the foreigner" in their own land, from repressive governments and foreign domination, primarily that of the Austrians and the French. Unshaken by defeat, Garibaldi took up his sword again in 1860. Leading an army of volunteers, he astounded the world with the liberation of Sicily and subsequent victories that furthered efforts to unify Italy and remove foreign armies. In 1870, the last forces to remain in Italy, the French, returned to their homeland at the start of the Franco-Prussian War. "Let free men religiously keep sacred the day of the fall of slavery," the Italians declared in their letter, written in the middle of the four-year-long American Civil War. "Prosperity to you, Abraham Lincoln, pilot of liberty; hail to all you who for two years have fought and died around her regenerating banner." From France Lincoln also received assurances of support. Despite a reprieve from monarchical rule following France's revolution of 1848, a coup d'état in 1851 had preceded the declaration in 1852 of an empire under Emperor Napoleon III. Those who desired a change from autocratic to representative government based on respect for individual liberty, the "liberals," looked to the United States for confirmation that a stable modern republic could be achieved. Among the anxious observers of events in the United States was Édouard Laboulaye. Following the path of the Marquis de Lafayette, Laboulaye had, by the early 1860s, established a reputation as a mediator between France and the United States. He aimed to maintain the friendship between the two countries that dated back to the American War for Independence and was personified by Lafayette. Laboulaye greatly admired the young nation and had carefully studied the history of America's founding and political institutions, publishing his three-volume *History of the United States* (*Histoire des États-Unis*) in 1855–66. The battle he waged for change in France was carried out in lectures, books, and articles, in his support for social justice organizations, and, in the 1870s, in helping to define the form and the constitution of the Third Republic.

At the outbreak of the American Civil War Laboulaye summarized France's historical commitment to the United States in an article titled "The United States and France" ("Les États-Unis et la France"). His concise analysis so impressed the American consul-general in Paris, John Bigelow, that Bigelow asked Laboulaye's permission to reproduce the article as a pamphlet, for distribution "to the two hundred members of the institute, to most of the Paris bar, to the diplomatic representatives residing at Paris, and most of the prominent statesmen and journals of Europe." Its favorable effect, Bigelow noted, "was far greater than I had ventured to anticipate." A translated, abridged version also made its way into American newspapers. Although Laboulaye never crossed the Atlantic, his reputation as a friend of America flourished during these years and earned him high honors, including an honorary doctorate awarded by Harvard University in June 1864.

Laboulaye remained a firm supporter of the Union cause and Lincoln's pursuit of the war, despite complaints on both sides of the Atlantic about the war's duration and calls for compromise to achieve peace. Lincoln's announcement of the Emancipation Proclamation in September 1862 (to take effect January 1, 1863) and important, though occasional, battlefield victories indicated that the war could be won, the Union preserved, and slavery abolished. Laboulaye considered the reelection of Lincoln in 1864 vital to the future of the Union and offered his assistance to his friends in America. He wrote letters and articles for publication in the United States and proved a spirited campaigner. In a pamphlet published by the Union Congressional Committee, Laboulaye concluded: "Therefore we wait with impatience the result of the presidential election, praying God that the name which shall stand first on the ballot shall be that of honest and upright Abraham Lincoln; for that name will be a presage of victory, the triumph of Justice and of Law. . . . To vote for Lincoln, is to vote for Union and for Liberty." Laboulaye, along with many people in France as well as in the United States, perceived Lincoln as a successor to George Washington in spirit, a man devoted to the Union who sacrificed personal and party interests to the interests of the nation.

Known for his humanitarian efforts, Laboulaye was also asked to assist the United States Sanitary Commission, the predecessor of the Red Cross in America. Francis Lieber, whose 1863 *Instructions for the Government of Armies of the United States in the Field* was the basis for international conventions of conduct during war, maintained an active correspondence with Laboulaye in the 1860s and suggested Laboulaye's involvement. The Sanitary Commission sponsored fairs to raise funds to care for wounded troops. Laboulaye agreed to gather autographed manuscripts and other items that could be auctioned for sale at the fairs, a customary method of fundraising.

The reelection of Lincoln in November 1864 was followed by two other events of considerable importance to Laboulaye and others in France who supported the government of the United States. First, both houses of the U.S. Congress voted to commit the federal government to the protection of personal liberties. Passed in January 1865 and ratified by the end of the year, the Thirteenth Amendment to the Constitution abolished slavery in every state of the Union. A few months later, on April 9, 1865, Robert E. Lee's

Following the Civil War, Lincoln and Washington were frequently paired as pillars of the Union: Lincoln saved the Union, which Washington had made. In this lithograph by Charles Shober, Washington holds the Constitution and Lincoln the Proclamation of Emancipation. Library of Congress, Prints and Photographs Division, LC-USZ62-13959.

surrender to Ulysses S. Grant brought the war to an end. An atmosphere of rejoicing lasted only a few days, however. On Good Friday, a day rife with symbolism for a man whom some considered a savior, President Lincoln was critically wounded by an assassin's bullet. The next day, April 15, four years from the start of the Civil War, Abraham Lincoln was pronounced dead.

The shocking news of Lincoln's death precipitated an outpouring of grief in France and around the world. "Mr. Lincoln had come to symbolize the republic in all its attributes of the liberty and equality of all men," the U.S. minister to Prussia, Norman B. Judd, wrote to U.S. secretary of state William H. Seward. A large number of the German people, Judd continued, "feel that in [Lincoln] all humanity has lost a pure and noble champion." In a letter of condolence, members of the Prussian House of Deputies reiterated the "heart-felt sympathy" that the people of Prussia had "preserved for the people of the United States during this long and severe conflict." Adding their signatures to those of their German colleagues, the Polish members of the Prussian House of Deputies expressed their grief at the death of Lincoln, "a martyr of the great cause of the abolition of slavery."

In France, reported the *New York Times* Paris correspondent, reaction to the news "has assumed proportions which are the astonishment of everybody. Nothing like it has ever before been seen." John Bigelow, who occupied the position of U.S. Minister in Paris since March 1865, was overwhelmed by "expressions of sympathy . . . from every quarter," many of which were collective letters from groups or communities. By the end of May he received letters from twenty-nine Masonic lodges "struck with stupor by the horrid news," in the words of one letter from Charente. America's sorrow, a letter from the people of Caen declared, "is the sorrow of all good men."

Large numbers of students also conveyed their distress to Bigelow. One letter circulated in the Latin Quarter in Paris, where Laboulaye taught at the Collège de France. "At the termination of Prof[essor] Laboulaye's lecture, which was devoted in part to a biography of Mr. Lincoln," the *New York Times* reported, "the students congregated at the Pont St. Michael [*sic*] . . . to the number of about 1,500, to proceed in a body to Mr. Bigelow's house. But the police turned out hastily in great force . . . and, unsheathing their swords, managed in dispersing the greater part of the crowd." Nevertheless, a handful of students reached Bigelow's house and slipped past a police barricade at the front door to deliver their message of condolence. "I had no idea," Bigelow wrote to Seward, who had been attacked the same evening as Lincoln, "that Mr. Lincoln had such a hold upon the heart of the young gentlemen of France, or that his loss would be so properly appreciated."

A national subscription was initiated for a commemorative gold medal to be presented to Mary Todd Lincoln from the people of France. More than forty thousand French citizens contributed to the making of the medal, which was completed in 1866. The design selected for its reverse (Lincoln's portrait is on the front) depicts an altar with the words "Lincoln, honest man, abolished slavery, restored the union, and saved the Republic, without veiling the statue of liberty." The lettering is small, making most of the text barely legible, but the words "saved the Republic" ("Sauva la Republique") are enlarged. This emphasis on the fate of the Union reveals the anxiety felt by people in France, as they wondered whether a modern republic could last. Compounding worries about the future of the American community, the fundamental principles of civil liberty, including freedom of speech, suffered as a result of the conflict. In both the North and the South, discussion and dissent had been restricted, even entirely suspended in some places. To have saved the republic but sacrificed liberty would have been the equivalent of ceding defeat, for the system of government attempted in the United States and for the aspirations of people in France and across the globe. This is the meaning of the concluding qualification on the medal, "without veiling the statue of liberty."

This poetic turn of phrase was not unknown in France; Laboulaye had used a similar phrase in his writings. In *Paris in America* (*Paris en Amérique*) he referred to disregard for, as opposed to disavowal of, the law as "veil[ing] the statue of the law." The phrase may have derived from the tradition in art of personifying abstract concepts as allegorical figures. Liberty and the Republic were often personified as a single figure. They were also portrayed individually, with the Republic accompanied by symbols of the principles on which it was founded, among them liberty. An entry in the 1848 competition for the design of a symbolic figure for the Second Republic, for instance, depicted the Republic as a female figure raising in her hand a statue representing liberty.

Could the reference on the medal to a statue have been motivated by the anticipation of a proposed liberty gift? It is improbable; and yet, the idea of a statue for America was conceived in this same period.

During the Second Empire, Napoleon III forbade political rallies and other forms of political gatherings. Debate among the French, however, was not so easily silenced. In place of formal gatherings, dinner parties brought together people who shared political concerns. Laboulaye, a central figure in much of the political discussion in France at the time, frequently invited colleagues to dinner at his home in Glatigny, near Versailles. In 1865, the sculptor Frédéric Auguste Bartholdi was at one such gathering. In the course of the evening the discussion turned to Lincoln's assassination and the events in America. Laboulaye and his colleagues fully agreed with Lincoln's assertion that "the whole family of man" shared an interest in the success of the United States. The French people valued similar ideas, and they, too, desired a government that upheld the political and civil rights of the individual. Beneath the calm of the Second Empire a movement for change was brewing. The level of popular support for the Lincoln medal demonstrated the sentiments of many in France.

The American experience had shown the fragility of liberty, even in a political system founded on its cause. Lincoln's Emancipation Proclamation, the Thirteenth Amendment to the Constitution, and the triumph of the Union in the Civil War had unequivocally confirmed the commitment of the United States to the "principle of 'liberty to all.'" It would be appropriate, Laboulaye suggested, to commemorate this commitment in a public monument. The building of monuments was a common means of expression. Nations asserted their identity and commemorated national heroes; groups proclaimed their particular interests. Allegorical personification was used to depict abstract concepts, of which liberty was a favored theme. Liberty figures were familiar in the United States as well as in France; they appeared in government settings, such as the Capitol in Washington, D.C., and in private homes as decoration and on furniture. The first coins regulated by an act of Congress in 1792, which concurrently established the U.S. Mint, had featured a design "emblematic of Liberty, with an inscription of the word Liberty."

The monument Laboulaye suggested in 1865 would represent liberty and the establishment of the United States in a manner that only a friend could achieve. As Bartholdi later recalled, Laboulaye proposed to his dinner guests that it would be "very natural" for a monument to be "built by united effort . . . [as] a common work of both nations." It would be built in the same spirit of kinship that led Lafayette to America and characterized the collaboration between the two peoples during the American War for Independence.

Laboulaye's proposal signified a project of considerable ambition. It is unlikely that he considered the details of a design or the complexity of the process. Nor could he have imagined that his idea would ultimately lead to the creation of a magnificent colossal statue. As the design for a monument developed in the years from its conception to its public announcement in 1875, it grew both in size and in significance. Laboulaye, the primary sponsor of the project, offered Bartholdi occasional direction as Bartholdi contemplated a variety of liberty emblems for his composition; the decision to include a tablet of the law, for example, was probably Laboulaye's. The figure that coalesced for Liberty Enlightening the World, the name by which the statue was initially known, gave form to Abraham Lincoln's words at Gettysburg describing the creation of the nation "conceived in Liberty." It blended traditional symbols with signs particularly relevant to the history of the United States. This monument of national yet universal meaning would celebrate America's founding ideals and unprecedented accomplishments. It would acknowledge the roots of democracy in antiquity and offer optimism about the future to people around the world.

In the years following Laboulaye's proposal, the careers of the monument's three main designers suitably prepared each of them for this project. Auguste Bartholdi developed a perspective on life that would guide his design and sustain his long, at times seemingly unrewarding, commitment to the effort; Richard Morris Hunt established his reputation as the dean of American architecture and gained experience designing patriotic public monuments; and Gustave Eiffel built his business in engineering and construction to become a leader in the field of metal bridge and viaduct design, pushing the limits of large-scale construction. Laboulaye, too, needed time to prepare for this monumental undertaking, which would mirror the fulfillment of his dream to contribute to his nation's embrace of justice and liberty.

2

A CHAMPION
OF LIBERTY

In the early 1860s Édouard Laboulaye was consumed with frustration over the political situation in France. Born in 1811, when the country was still roiling from the effects of the French Revolution, he knew both the anticipation and disappointment long felt by the French people. Since 1789 France had experienced brief moments of free political expression between long periods of authoritarian rule. When Parisians marched on the Bastille on July 14, 1789, attacking and destroying the fortress and its keepers, they offered a glimpse of the upheaval France would endure in the years ahead. During the early days of the French Revolution optimism about the future prevailed. The transition from Louis XVI's absolute monarchy to a system of constitutional monarchy suggested that a form of government based on the acclaimed principles of *liberté, égalité, fraternité* would be established. Many people, including Americans such as Thomas Jefferson, believed that the revolution in France would foster the spread of liberty across Europe. "Bliss was it in that dawn to be alive," the English poet William Wordsworth wrote in 1805, recalling the sense of expectation that prevailed.

As the revolutionaries struggled to shape a new system of government, however, they lost control of the country and of the escalating revolutionary passion. Tensions rose when Louis XVI and

Marie Antoinette were caught attempting to escape Paris in June 1791. The king of Prussia and the German emperor declared that they might act to aid the French king; Prussia also formed an alliance with Austria against France. These events, in addition to reports that popular movements across Europe needed the support of France to oppose authoritarian rulers, led the French Legislative Assembly to declare war on Austria in 1792 and subsequently on much of Europe. Initial defeats suffered by the French army heightened the distress already felt in France. A deteriorating economy and food shortages, internal revolts, and intense rivalries between factions contributed to mounting unrest. The French king was executed in January 1793, the queen in October. A series of executions that year began the slide of the First French Republic, only just announced in 1792, into the period known as the Reign of Terror, the pinnacle of revolutionary extremism. Central authority was strengthened, but individual liberties—the cornerstone of the revolution in its first years—were lost. Political discussion was seen as subversive, and moderates, such as Lafayette, were denounced for counterrevolutionary tendencies; some were deprived of their possessions, forced to flee, or guillotined.

The end of the Terror in 1794 following the execution of Maximilien Robespierre brought relative calm but not stability. Characterized as a "régime of improvisations" during these years, the five-member governing body of the Directory was unable to determine an effective mode of governance. The country remained at war and an ambitious young general, Napoleon Bonaparte, gained influence as he fought the Austrians in Italy in 1796 and 1797 and set sail for his Egyptian expedition in 1798, taking with him close to forty thousand troops and a corps of scientists and scholars. When two of the directors acted on the idea of replacing their governing body with a strong executive to establish authority and stabilize the government, little did they anticipate that the man to whom this proposition was extended, General Napoleon Bonaparte, would thereupon found an empire.

With the help of one director in particular, Abbé Emmanuel Joseph Sieyès, Napoleon returned to Paris in November 1799 to initiate a new government through a coup d'état. Napoleon was named the First Consul of a tripartite Consulate; the two other consuls were appointed by him. In this position, Napoleon concentrated power, reshaping the political bodies instituted during the revolutionary period. Within a few years he found an opportunity to take a further step. When his life was threatened in 1804, Napoleon declared that circumstances necessitated the continuity that an empire offered. Although he maintained some of the gains of the revolution in his comprehensive and widely influential codes of law and espoused the "liberation" of people across Europe, the First Republic came to a close. In 1804 Napoleon set the crown on his head, now emperor of the French.

War in Europe continued during the next decade. In 1811, the year of Édouard Laboulaye's birth, France enjoyed the success of Napoleon's military campaigns and his building program, in particular in Paris. But Napoleon's ambitious rise eventually faltered, and in 1815 at Waterloo he suffered his second, and final, defeat at the hands of the European powers. Napoleon was forced to abdicate, punitive measures were enacted against the country, and the rulers of Europe agreed on the return of monarchical rule to France. Louis XVIII, brother of Louis XVI, rushed back to Paris to claim the throne.

For those in France who yearned for peace after years of upheaval and war, Louis XVIII's form of quasi-parliamentary monarchy was acceptable, at least for a time. Nonetheless, a desire for political and social reform persisted in the subsequent decades and manifested itself as recurrent political instability. Since the days of the Revolution of 1789, Alexis de Tocqueville wrote of France in 1856, "We find the desire for freedom reviving, succumbing, then returning, only to die out once more and presently blaze up again." Following the end of Napoleon's reign a period of Restoration, during which kings Louis XVIII and Charles X ruled, was followed by an uprising in 1830 and the installation of the Duc d'Orleans, which promised a change to a progressive constitutional monarchy. Disappointment set in during the first decade of his reign as King Louis-Philippe, and in the 1840s calls for economic and social reform strengthened the position of those opposed to his government. This was due, in part, to rapid industrialization and development; a railway act of 1842, for instance, hastened construction of railway bridges, among other facilities. When the government ordered the cancellation of a large banquet in February 1848, at which members of the opposition planned to meet, a street demonstration formed. The demonstration gained momentum, barricades went up in the streets, and the Revolution of 1848 began.

The abdication of King Louis-Philippe ushered in a second attempt at a republic and the end of authoritarian rule. Once again, disillusion followed. The nephew of Emperor Napolean I, Louis Napoleon Bonaparte, who had been elected president in large part by way of name recognition, followed his uncle's example. Claiming that a stronger authority was necessary for the maintenance of public order and the good of the country, he consolidated his power with a coup d'état in 1851. "In one night," exclaimed Victor Hugo, who was forced into exile as a consequence, "liberty was struck down by a hand sworn to support it." Shortly thereafter Louis Napoleon declared himself Emperor Napoleon III. For the nearly twenty years that followed, those who opposed autocratic government continued to be repressed. "Although the political horizon looks clear at present," predicted the *New York Times* Paris correspondent, "there is yet a deep under-current perceptible in the faces of the people. . . . Whenever passing events shall develop a weak place in the Government, then will a deep revenge be gratified."

"Liberty and public order!" grieved Laboulaye in the early 1860s. These two conditions were claimed by extremists as justification for either revolution or reaction, as if they were mutually exclusive. "One might see them as two immortal enemies who, by turn conquering and conquered, wage against each other an endless combat, of which we are the stake. One day liberty prevails, the sky resounds with cries of joy and hope; but under the mask of this serene divinity, it is anarchy that triumphs, drawing after it civil war, attacking all rights, menacing all interests, making a frightened people recoil in horror. The next day public order is installed, sabre in hand: giving peace, imposing silence." When, he asked, would the French people bring together their political aspirations to construct a durable and practical system of participatory government?

The decades of Laboulaye's youth, from Louis XVIII to the Revolution of 1848, have been called a "time of ferment," when intellectuals and politicians debated the future social and political order of France. Laboulaye's personal experience followed this pattern. Early in his career, his interests centered on the legal and political doctrines and practices since antiquity. He was a prolific writer and by the age of thirty-four his numerous publications earned him election to the prestigious society of scholars, the Académie des inscriptions et belles-lettres of the Institut de France. His writing addressed topics ranging from English criminal procedure to religious liberty and was further broadened by his concern for the treatment of individuals, encompassing the establishment of guidelines for the treatment of enemies during war and the civil and political condition of women since Roman times.

The year 1848 and the start of the Second Republic marked a turning point for Laboulaye. Focusing his attention on contemporary politics, he now dedicated his career to realizing a moderate system of representative government in France. When Napoleon III's coup d'état "yoked" France, in Tocqueville's words, "to the despotic monarchies of the Continent," Laboulaye became a leading figure in the opposition. His ambition was not simply to depose the emperor but to establish a lasting form of democratic government.

The successive constitutions of France had failed to institutionalize the ideals of liberty, equality, and fraternity. The constitutions—written to meet the needs of each new form of government—were unworkable, in Laboulaye's view. As Laboulaye contemplated the necessary ingredients for a balanced system of government and a constitution for France, he looked to the United States for guidance. He appreciated the equilibrium that characterized the nation's formative years, making possible the creation of an enduring democracy. An essential achievement of America's founders, he recognized, was their negotiation of a middle path between reform and stability.

Two of the Frenchmen who most influenced Laboulaye's interest in the United States were the Marquis de Lafayette and Alexis de Tocqueville. Lafayette was a hero from the American War for Independence and considered to be the "connecting link" between France and the United States. During the Restoration monarchy of the 1820s, Lafayette had actively opposed authoritarian rule in France. Laboulaye, still a youth at the time, had heard Lafayette speak about America on a few occasions. Lafayette also provided a venue for political discussion. His home in the country was regularly filled with visitors, from politicians to artists, who supported a change in government, and his apartment in Paris was the setting for a weekly salon, frequented by a similar crowd. Lafayette encouraged an American writer living in France, James Fenimore Cooper, to convey the positive aspects of American institutions and culture in a novel for a European audience. Throughout his life, Lafayette maintained correspondence with his friends in America. Alexis de Tocqueville was closer in age to Laboulaye, born only six years before. He had visited the United States shortly after the Revolution of 1830 and the beginning of Louis-Philippe's reign. He traveled in the United States for nine months, with the purpose of learning about the American democracy and understanding the influence of its political institutions on the nature of society. The two-part book in which he examined the character of American society in the early 1830s, *Democracy in America* (*De la démocratie en Amérique*), published in 1835 and 1840, was highly regarded in France and maintained attention on the form of government in the United States. Tocqueville served in the French National Assembly in the 1840s, and in 1856 he published a study of the ancien régime and the French Revolution. In his writings he emphasized the importance of individual liberty and freedom of association to the public good; "for only freedom," he wrote in 1856, "can deliver the members of a community from that isolation which is the lot of the individual . . . and, compelling them to get in touch with each other, promote an active sense of fellowship." Tocqueville's historical work was imbued with contemporary meaning. "He considered the past only as it affected the present," observed Gustave de Beaumont, Tocqueville's close colleague and companion on his American tour. Laboulaye would follow a similar approach and similarly promote the United States as a model democracy for other nations, in particular France.

In 1849, during the brief Second Republic, Laboulaye was appointed chair of comparative law at the Collège de France. He immediately made use of his courses to explore and inform others about the history and institutions of the United States, an area not yet included in most history departments because the founding of the United States was too recent to qualify as a topic of study. In his lectures Laboulaye focused on the Constitution and the formation of political institutions dedicated to maintaining civil and political liberty, including religious liberty, "the spirit of modern societies." His special interest was the central role of the courts in protecting liberties, notably the presumption of innocence until proven otherwise. The founders and framers of the Constitution, he believed, whatever their disagreements and imperfections, had crafted a remarkable system of government for the new federal

Union. Adding to the significance of the American system of government was the conviction that America's achievement strengthened other aspiring republics. As the "repository of the sacred fire of freedom and self government," Thomas Jefferson proudly said of the United States, the nation offered a source from which companion flames of enlightenment might "be lighted up in other regions of the earth."

When censorship tightened under the Second Empire, Laboulaye was alerted by the dismissal of fellow academics to suspend his lectures. Their implied meaning—that the government of France should adopt the principles of individual liberty from the United States—was easily perceptible and no longer tenable. Government censorship in these years extended from professors' lectures and public gatherings to the posting of handbills. The police expended considerable effort preventing the posting of "incendiary" handbills, noted the Paris correspondent for the *New-York Daily Times,* who was irritated by the government's attempt to silence public discourse. Despite many arrests and constant surveillance in the streets, the police were unable to ascertain how handbills continued to appear on building walls. "At last," he reported, they "made the discovery." A *chiffonnier* (ragman) carrying on his back a large basket of rags and other articles of his trade would lean against a wall to take a rest. While in this position, a young boy hidden inside the heavy basket opened a secret sliding door and posted one of these incendiary handbills. Having no other means to voice their complaints, people persevered thus, at the risk of arrest.

Napoleon III was not alone in restricting the study of the United States. Traditionalists throughout Europe felt threatened by the concept of a democratic republic and sought to limit its influence. *Democracy* brought forth images of the raucous assemblies of ancient Athens, and *republic* was by now associated with European scenes of upheaval and violence. During a debate over whether to initiate a lectureship in United States history, literature, and institutions at Cambridge University in Britain, those opposed to the idea successfully argued that "infecting undergraduates with republican principles" would result in the spread of "discontent and dangerous ideas." In the 1850s, when Laboulaye realized that he needed to suspend his lectures on the United States, he turned to the legal institutions of ancient Rome, a subject with which he was thoroughly familiar. Ancient Rome, even the Roman republic, was adequately distant in time to be an acceptable, nonthreatening topic for discussion. Notwithstanding this change in subject matter, Laboulaye's enthusiasm for individual liberty continued to pervade his lectures. His reputation as a speaker and a proponent of liberty spread in and beyond Paris.

By the early 1860s this mild-mannered scholar, now in his fifties, standing five feet seven and habitually attired in a black frock-coat fully buttoned to the neck, had gained a following and assumed a place in the center of French intellectual life. At the same time, a

Engraving of Édouard Laboulaye, from an article in *Harper's Weekly* in 1866. Library of Congress, Prints and Photographs Division, LC-USZ62-99551.

loosening of censorship that began in 1860 allowed Laboulaye to return to his series of lectures on the United States. Published as the three-volume *History of the United States* (*Histoire des États-Unis*), these lectures earned him respect on both sides of the Atlantic, along with a steady stream of visitors seeking to attend his talks or visit with him. He was known as "one of the most distinguished men in France," in the words of the U.S. minister in Paris. The American architect Richard Morris Hunt, the future designer of the pedestal for the Statue of Liberty, felt a similar regard for the French scholar. There was no limit to Hunt's admiration for Laboulaye, Hunt's wife later recalled.

Promoting a way of life founded on respect for individual liberty, Laboulaye translated American articles and books for publication in France, including Benjamin Franklin's autobiography. This 1866 translation was credited with "keep[ing] alive in France that friendship for the United States which Franklin . . . had the merit of inspiring." Laboulaye's text was also appreciated for its insightful introduction, from which the subsequent English edition quoted. Laboulaye's reputation as a friend of America grew in the United States and he became known as one of the "two illustrious chiefs" —the other being Tocqueville—"of the American school in France."

Having successfully tried his hand at fiction with children's stories that exemplified morality, Laboulaye ventured to write a novel to further his cause. Perhaps he was encouraged by Lafayette's interest in such a work. The result was a witty political tale, *Paris in America* (*Paris en Amérique*), which astonished both French and American readers. This is "one of the most original and entertaining books of the day," the *New York Tribune* raved. Here, "in the shape of a magnetic dream," enthused the publisher of the Philadelphia *Press*, "is one of the closest and most philosophical inner views of American life, habits, opinions, and peculiarities, ever read or written." U.S. secretary of state William Seward, who received a copy of the book from consul-general John Bigelow, wrote to Bigelow: "I have had leisure to look into Dr. Lefebvre's dream and am infinitely pleased with its humor as well as its spirit." Writing under the name of Dr. René Lefebvre, which made little attempt to conceal his identity, Laboulaye picked up on the nineteenth-century fascination with illusion and mediums of the spirit-world to set the stage for his story. Finding himself magically transported to a city in New England, "Paris, Massachusetts," the narrator launches his story with a scene of heroism by volunteer firefighters, which was inspired by an incident during Lafayette's visit to New York in 1824. Americans, the narrator tells his readers, are "a people intoxicated with hope," a trait that intrigues and impresses him. Laboulaye's tale avoided censorship, yet its message was clear. "By its grace of style, by its moving narrative, by its growing interest," *Harper's New Monthly Magazine* wrote about *Paris in America*, "the book of Laboulaye is a living lessen given to the people in the difficult and necessary art of self-government."

The popularity of Laboulaye's courses and public lectures throughout the 1860s was depicted in an article in *Appletons' Journal of Popular Literature* in 1869: "So great was the demand for seats that many would wait through the hour of the lecturer before him, that they might thus make sure of a place. . . . Young and eager faces were seen beside those who wore the shrewder expression of years. Rough, uncultured men mingled their hearty applause with the more cultivated and high-bred." Laboulaye was especially satisfied by the scope of the audience for his lectures. An essential foundation for government reform and lasting democracy, he believed, was an intellectual vibrancy in the life of the people. Education, exchange of ideas, and expression of the public conscience through a free press were necessary components of this vitality. "An ignorant democracy is a doomed democracy," he cautioned.

Laboulaye emphasized in his courses that America's founders "gave liberty not only to America but to the world." He constantly linked America's future with that of other nations, in particular France. He was glad, too, to learn that Montesquieu's writings had a place in the personal library of several of the founders, including Washington, Adams, Jefferson, and Franklin, and that the colonists' rebellion had been informed by European, in particular French and British, political thought. The founders had followed the example of British constitutional government, adapting it as they saw fit, while paying close attention to Montesquieu's ideas for balancing government branches.

Skillfully blending modern European philosophies with ancient political thought, the American founders had identified examples to emulate along with explanations for their unprecedented actions. Infused with principles of the eighteenth-century Age of Enlightenment, which looked to advance civilization through the guiding light of reason and knowledge, they based their commitment to a principled government on the traditions of ancient Greek democracy and Roman republicanism. From ancient Greece they admired ethical principles, an emphasis on individual responsibility, and a faith in popular government. These values they merged with the Roman republican sense of community and dutiful participation in the community's political life. They associated an ancient concept of virtue with the practice of placing primary consideration not on one's personal interests but on the common good, a quality they highly regarded. "Only a virtuous people are capable of freedom," commented Benjamin Franklin. The potentially conflicting perspectives on social life of individual liberty and public spirit were melded, at times, in the classical world and as such were argued about, contrasted, and interwoven in eighteenth-century Western culture. As part of this balancing act, the founders reined in the passions of the American revolutionaries, which had been necessary in gaining independence, to establish a cohesive political order and the assurance of personal security. In the words of an ancient Roman expression that had particular meaning for Laboulaye, they perceived that there is liberty under the law (*sub lege libertas*).

The two Americans who most vividly and enduringly captivated the Europeans imagination, George Washington and Benjamin Franklin, possessed the qualities their generation admired most. French soldiers who met Washington during the War for Independence brought home glowing accounts that shaped his international image. François-Jean, chevalier de Chastellux, a major-general and chief of staff in Comte de Rochambeau's army in America, and whose writings on philosophy earned him membership in the French Academy, published his impressions of Washington in *Travels in North America:* "I soon felt myself at my ease near the greatest and the best of men. The goodness and benevolence which characterize him are evident in all that surrounds him . . . the sentiment he inspires has the same origin in every individual, a profound esteem for his virtues and a high opinion of his talents." There was no one comparable to George Washington in terms of moral character. He displayed considered judgment, aimed to be fair and calm in the midst of crisis, and thought always of what was best for the nation. He not only conducted himself with dignity but also was a man of honor.

"Washington," Laboulaye wrote in a preface to his *History of the United States,* "resembles the heroes of Greece and Rome." In fact Washington earned the title Cincinnatus during his lifetime, in reference to the ancient Roman gentleman farmer turned military leader and political leader. Cincinnatus was never smitten by the power he commanded but instead resigned from each position once his task was complete. Cognizant of the fine line between leadership and power, Washington astounded the nation and the world by surrendering his position as commander-in-chief in 1783. Similarly, at the conclusion of two terms in office as the country's first president, he stepped down rather than retain the position for life. Revered for the important examples of leadership and character that he set, he earned respect and an exceptional level of trust at home and abroad. At a time when authority depended on respect—the new authorities in the United States had little ability to compel compliance—the integrity of the government was essential. Washington's truly patriotic spirit, moreover, symbolized the nation's proud identity.

Franklin displayed other qualities at which Laboulaye, among his many European admirers, marveled. Not a leader in the manner of Washington, Franklin expounded a rustic philosophy based on daily virtues such as frugality, diligence, honesty, and humility. He was also opposed to the institution of slavery. His simple attire, philosophically inspired practical advice, and scientific learning captivated the French people. Affable and witty, Franklin nurtured an extraordinary bond of goodwill during his eight years in Paris, from 1776 to 1785, as a representative of the U.S. Congress; this was time spent, Franklin wrote, as a laborer "in the best of all works, the work of peace." While modestly describing himself as "an old man with gray hair appearing under a martin fur cap, among the powdered heads of Paris," he admitted with some pleasure that "perhaps few strangers in France have had the good fortune to be so universally popular." This popularity, he explained in a letter to his daughter, extended beyond social engagements to include the distribution of his likeness for decoration on snuff boxes and rings, or larger as prints "of which copies upon copies are spread everywhere." Your father, he continued, "may be truly said . . . to be *i-doll-ized* in this country."

At the same time, Franklin was treated with the "respect and esteem of all ranks, from the highest to the lowest." Even Louis

XVI's minister of foreign affairs, the Comte de Vergennes, who was motivated by the power struggle between Great Britain and France rather than concern for personal liberties of the colonists, acknowledged the influence of the high regard in which Franklin was held. The esteem and "the confidence we put in the veracity of Dr. Franklin," Vergennes informed the minister of France at Philadelphia, was the reason the government agreed to provide funds on several occasions. These funds were necessary to "relieve the pecuniary embarrassments in which [Franklin] has been placed by Congress"—Congress having expected its ministers in France to procure war materiel for shipment to the United States. The spirit of the American founders was frequently associated with an image of light, and in an address to the French National Assembly the Comte de Mirabeau, a leader in the early years of the French Revolution, described Franklin as having "poured a flood of light over Europe." On Franklin's death in 1790, the National Assembly wore mourning for three days; public officials of France, individual departments, and districts of France all joined with private citizens for a large memorial ceremony held for Franklin in Paris.

A democratic government such as the American founders established depended on each citizen sharing in the nation's mission; and liberty, Laboulaye admonished, requires that "each citizen [be] master of and responsible for his actions and his life." Personal responsibility was a fundamental element of the system. The founders had been well aware of the risk inherent in this form of government and that the liberties they had fought for might seep away through inattention to the unique quality of the United States. A lasting government and a lasting liberty, John Adams worried, depended on "a positive passion for the public good." Special interests, party politics, and usurpation of power were constant threats. James Madison, who drafted the Bill of Rights as the first ten amendments to the Constitution and served as president from 1809 to 1817, was so wary of infringing on individual liberties that he failed to adequately prepare as the War of 1812 approached. "Of all the enemies to public liberty, war is, perhaps, the most to be dreaded," he explained. Although Madison's aversion to war, compounded by his party's insistence on limited government, was criticized as contributing to the initial weakness of the United States in the war, his administration was respected for not sacrificing liberties under the pretext of national struggle.

Since its founding the country faced daunting challenges and threats to its survival. Already during the Union's first decade the inability of the states to function as a nation based on their agreement of confederation had become evident. When Congress resolved to address the problem in 1787, twelve of the thirteen states sent delegates to a special convention in Philadelphia to amend the Articles of Confederation under which the nation was governed.

Many of the delegates initially wondered whether a government comprised of thirteen independent-minded, self-interested states could in fact survive. During the months of the convention they debated a variety of proposals and, in the end, abandoned the Articles of Confederation altogether. In their place the delegates drafted a Constitution, which both strengthened ties between the states and created a structure "to form a more perfect Union." Even then, opinion remained divided and only thirty-nine of the

Howard Chandler Christy, *Signing of the Constitution*, 1940. George Washington presided over the Constitutional Convention of 1787, which was held in Independence Hall in Philadelphia; Benjamin Franklin is seated in the center of the painting. Architect of the Capitol.

Detail of *Signing of the Constitution*. Howard Chandler Christy depicted the ornate rising sun on Washington's chair with a line drawing of seven rays. Architect of the Capitol.

fifty-five delegates signed the Constitution that was proposed to the states for ratification. An oft quoted remark by Benjamin Franklin expressed the uncertainty that underlay the Convention's agreement on a framework and guiding principles for the union of states. When asked at the close of the Convention what the delegates had established for the future life of the country, Franklin replied, "A republic, if you can keep it."

It was, however, another one of Franklin's remarks regarding a rising sun that made a particularly strong impression on Laboulaye. In 1774 the delegates of the First Continental Congress met in a room in Carpenters' Hall, built by the Carpenters' Company of the City and County of Philadelphia four years before. The coat of arms of the Carpenters' Company, which includes an image of a seven-rayed sun on the horizon, could be seen here. Carpenters' Hall had also been the setting for Benjamin Franklin and John

Jay's secret meeting in 1775 with an unofficial emissary of France, which opened the way to French involvement in the War for Independence. Twelve years later, in 1787, Franklin recognized a sun design on the chair used by George Washington during the Constitutional Convention.

He became convinced that this sun prophesied the future of the new government. Pondering the image through the "vicissitudes of [his] hopes and fears" he was uncertain how to interpret it. Was the sun setting on their work, or was the sun rising? Already quite frail at the time of the Convention, Franklin would have only a few years remaining to observe the nation's development. But as the Convention came to an end in September 1787, he felt confident that the image validated their efforts. The decoration, he decided, was indeed that of the rising sun.

Laboulaye frequently repeated this story. He liked the image of the sun enlightening the founders' creation, and in turn, the world. In the 1860s, the meaning of Franklin's sun assumed special relevance once more, as the United States experienced "a new birth of freedom," in the words of President Lincoln, words which Laboulaye certainly knew and took to heart.

3

BONDS OF
FRIENDSHIP

The one aspect of the American republic that Laboulaye could not explain was its justification of the institution of slavery. The framers of the Constitution had left unresolved the contradiction between the assertion in the Declaration of Independence that "all men are created equal" and endowed with unalienable rights of "life, liberty, and the pursuit of happiness" and the oppression of close to one-fifth of the population. In a concession made by the states with few or no slaves to those states dependent on slavery, the Constitution protected the institution for the country's first twenty years. It obligated states to return fugitives rather than provide them refuge and counted slaves in each state's population, in accordance with the 3/5 clause, to increase the representation of the southern states in Congress. An unfortunate result of this compromise for the South was that its economy became more dependent on large plantations and slave labor during the first half of the nineteenth century. For enslaved African Americans, it instituted generations of suffering and bondage.

For the nation, it set in place a divided loyalty. Debates in the House of Representatives on the institution of slavery reflected the passionate sectionalism resulting from the controversy, and as early as the 1840s debates degenerated into verbal and physical abuse. "Vulgarity and violence, so common of late," one politician confided in his journal in 1841, "have rendered the American Congress little better than the National Assembly of France during the reign of terror." The severity of the strife over slavery in the United States became palpable to Laboulaye in the late 1850s when he learned about the attack that Senator Charles Sumner suffered for his antislavery convictions.

Until the 1850s compromises, such as the Missouri Compromise of 1820, which permitted slavery south of a line drawn east to west across the middle portion of the country but precluded its spread into areas north of the line, had served to subdue tensions and forestall the threat of disunion. In 1854, however, Senator Stephen A. Douglas of Illinois pushed through the Kansas-Nebraska Act, which initiated a popular sovereignty approach to determining the constitutions of new states. By permitting the people within a territory, including territories above the previously designated east-west line, to decide for themselves whether to join the Union as a free state or a slave state, the bill outraged Americans who favored emancipation or at least confinement of the institution of slavery.

In the Nebraska territory, which was organized to become two states, Nebraska and Kansas, the offer of popular sovereignty incited violent confrontations in what became known as "bleeding Kansas." A clash of settlers aiming to decide the future of the territory would have caused trouble enough. But proslavery residents from western Missouri, referred to as Border Ruffians, crossed into Kansas to cast fraudulent votes and terrorize residents of Kansas who sought the admission of the territory into the Union as a free state. When Sumner railed in the Senate against the unprecedented "crime against Kansas," committed with the complicity of the administration of President Franklin Pierce, he did not mince words. "In vain do we condemn the cruelties of another age—the refinements of torture to which men have been doomed—the rack and thumb-screw of the Inquisition . . . for kindred outrages have disgraced these borders. Murder has stalked—assassination has skulked in the tall grass of the prairie, and the vindictiveness of man has assumed unwonted forms." Sumner's outspokenness, too, met with vindictiveness, when a few days after his speech he was subjected to a cane beating while seated at his desk in the Senate chamber.

Sumner's speech had focused on the "rape of a virgin Territory" by the Slave Power and had mentioned two senators responsible for the Kansas-Nebraska Act, Douglas of Illinois and Andrew Butler of South Carolina. Butler and Sumner had carried on pointed debate for many years. Butler, Sumner said, has made his vows to "the harlot, Slavery," and she is always lovely to his eyes. Butler may not have taken particular offense at this depiction of his position on slavery but a young relative of his, the representative of South Carolina Preston Brooks, did. A few days after Sumner made his comments, Brooks entered the Senate chamber during a quiet period, approached Sumner as he sat working at his desk, and abruptly attacked him with a gold-tipped cane. Beating Sumner repeatedly on the head until the cane was broken in pieces, Brooks drew blood and knocked the senator unconscious. Sumner suffered damage to his spinal cord and never fully recovered, physically or psychologically, from this assault by a fellow congressman. Rather than bring about a rapprochement, the incident widened the sectional divide of the nation. Brooks resigned from his seat in the House, but his constituents found his actions justified. Not only did the voters reelect Brooks as their representative, Laboulaye later recounted in disbelief, but his friends gave him a new cane "gold-mounted, bearing the inscription, 'Hit him again.'"

Shortly thereafter, *Dred Scott v. Sandford,* argued before the Supreme Court in 1856–57, intimated weakening of another branch of government on account of the conflict. Hearing a case for freedom brought by a slave, Dred Scott, the court ruled in favor of a master's property rights, finding that only white persons could be United States citizens and possess individual rights protected under the Constitution and the Bill of Rights. The nation's highest court suffered a notable loss of standing, as the majority decision was widely seen as politically and regionally motivated. "No wonder that the Chief Justice should have sunk his voice to a whisper" upon delivering the opinion, the *New York Daily Tribune* sneered; the Chief Justice knew perfectly well that the majority opinion was based on "false statements and shallow sophistries, got together to sustain a forgone conclusion." The court's decision highlighted as well the country's laggard position in protecting human rights. Already in 1772 the King's Bench in England had ruled in favor of freedom when petitioned by a slave brought by his owner to England from America. Liberty was a human right, the British court ruled, and a man on English soil could not be held as another man's property. Within the British Empire, slavery was abolished by 1838.

In France, slavery was abolished in 1794 during the French Revolution, was reintroduced under Napoleon in 1802, and was permanently abolished in 1848.

The majority opinion in *Dred Scott v. Sandford* further inflamed the national argument over slavery by not only ruling against Scott but also asserting that Congress did not have the authority to preclude slavery from a territory. This decision, many Americans believed—Abraham Lincoln among them—was made in error. Lincoln, then an Illinois attorney involved in politics, was committed to adhering to the law of the land, even when it was not to his liking. But he could not accept the reasoning behind this decision from the nation's highest court. The justices, he contended, erred when they stated that "the right of property in a slave is distinctly and expressly affirmed in the Constitution."

Those who supported the extension of slavery were misinterpreting the spirit and meaning of the Constitution and the Declaration of Independence to suit their purpose, Lincoln argued. Speaking in Springfield, Illinois, in 1857, Lincoln declared that in the days of our nation's founding, "our Declaration of Independence was held sacred by all, and thought to include all." The founders had dealt with slavery as "an evil not to be extended" and anticipated its eventual demise. But now, he continued in Springfield, the Declaration of Independence and the principles it embodies are "assailed, and sneered at, and construed, and hawked at, and torn, till, if its framers could rise from their graves, they could not at all recognize" the document they authored. "It is now no child's play," Lincoln wrote to a group in Boston that had invited him to a celebration of Jefferson's birthday, "to save the principles of Jefferson from total overthrow in this nation." Some people "insidiously argue that [Jefferson's principles] apply to 'superior races'. . . . [But] he who would be no slave must consent to have no slave. Those who deny freedom to others deserve it not for themselves."

As a fellow Illinoisan, Lincoln offered political speeches throughout the state to reply to Senator Douglas and the Kansas-Nebraska Act. In 1858, when Douglas ran for reelection to the U.S. Senate, Lincoln ran against him. It was a tight race and, although Douglas retained his seat in Congress, the contest won Lincoln the notice of antislavery politicians and journalists across the country. Lincoln's responses to Douglas in a series of debates in seven towns in northern, central, and southern Illinois were printed in news-papers; several of his speeches were reprinted on the east coast in papers such as the *New York Times* and the *Evening Post*. Lincoln exhibited a moderate tone that appealed to many Northerners who opposed the spread of slavery but were scared by the unknown consequences of radical change, which abolition implied. Lincoln also demonstrated an ability to respond to accusations concerning his motives without vindictiveness, including Douglas's appraisal of the motives behind suggesting that the Declaration of Inde-pendence applied to all people. It is "counterfeit logic," Lincoln countered, "which concludes that, because I do not want a black woman for a *slave* I must necessarily want her for a *wife*." In the 1850s, accusing one's opponents of envisioning this level of equal-ity between the races was a serious affront.

In June 1860 Sumner had recovered his strength adequately to participate in debate in the Senate for the first time since he was assaulted four years before. "Pronounced the most ultra violent and offensive speech ever delivered in either branch of Con-gress," according to the *New York Times,* Sumner railed once again against the "madness for slavery." Sumner responded to the declarations, made by numerous members of both houses of Con-gress, characterizing slavery as a blessing for slave and master alike. The same perspective was promulgated by James Buchanan, the president of the United States, who assured the American peo-ple in his State of the Union address in December 1859 that the slave "is treated with kindness and humanity. He is well fed, well clothed, and not overworked." Now Sumner emphasized the ap-pearance of "the barbarism of Slavery . . . in the character of the slave masters" and the inevitable, degrading influence of the in-stitution. "How can that man respect his own dignity, his own rights," Sumner asked, "who has learned not to respect either the rights or the dignity of his fellow man?" He accused proponents of slavery, insensible to the true nature of slavery, of evincing "an equal insensibility to the true character of the Constitution." They foist "into this blameless text the barbarous idea that man can hold property in man." It is time to lift the debate from details, such as the crime against Kansas, "to principles. Grander debate has not occurred in our history; rarely in any history; nor can this debate close or subside except with the triumph of Freedom."

The liberal opposition in France, which aimed to replace Napoleon III's authoritarian government with that of a republic, anxiously watched as this grand debate evolved. The increasing threat to the stability of the American republic in the years leading up to the Civil War was greatly disheartening. Britain had attempted a republic with the Commonwealth of 1649, which lasted a mere four years; France's two attempts had been similarly short-lived. It was essential to democratic republicanism that the United States remain the exemplar of a democratic representative government.

The French people's sense of kinship with the people of the "great, and free and enlightened American Republic" was strained by the persistence of slavery. Those who wished for its end were disappointed by the assertion by both houses of Congress and the Lincoln administration at the start of the war that secession, and not the institution of slavery, was at issue—that "this war is not prosecuted . . . [for the] purpose of overthrowing or interfering with the rights or established institutions of those states . . . but to preserve the Union." The *New York Times* Paris correspondent assessed the impact of these claims with similar frustration: "In the European view of the question, self-government has proven itself a failure. . . . The great and immortal Constitution which was to be a model and a beacon-light for the political regeneration of the world, turns out to be a sham."

The dramatic change in policy of the North demonstrated in September 1862 by Lincoln's publication of the Proclamation of Emancipation helped to restore the French people's confidence in the exemplary character of the American republic. They had hoped for a more comprehensive commitment to emancipation; as one Paris journal, *La Presse,* stated, "half-measures satisfy nobody." But the portion of the press that already supported the North accepted this move as a preliminary step, including the *Courrier du Bas-Rhin* of Colmar, Auguste Bartholdi's family home, in Alsace. "In simple truth," Laboulaye and three other prominent "friends of justice and human liberty" wrote in defense of the Lincoln administration in October 1863, "Mr. Lincoln should be accused neither of timidity nor indifference." While it is essential that slavery be abolished, they argued, the president must not disregard the Constitution and the limits of his authority. If liberty is "strong enough to survive civil war" and if slavery alone—not the Constitution—fall in such a conflict, then the United States "will have won the most glorious of victories."

Another factor, however, now complicated relations between France and the United States: the protracted war was affecting the French economy. A Northern blockade of exports from the Southern states had disrupted trade and led to a shortage of cotton in Europe, resulting in the closing of factories, unemployment, and higher prices for cotton clothing. The market for luxuries, such as silk, china, and wine, in the United States had also fallen off in 1861. Napoleon III was "besieged with complaints" from the manufacturing districts and with petitions "entreating the Emperor to endeavor to bring the American war to a close." Doubtful that a reunion of the North and the South was feasible at this point, many people felt that the Lincoln administration was senselessly prolonging the war. Much to Laboulaye's chagrin, Napoleon III considered recognizing the Confederacy and recommending a truce. Laboulaye urged the French people to recall France's role in the founding of the United States and to assist in the preservation of the Union. Speaking at the funeral of the U.S. minister to France, William L. Dayton, in 1864, Laboulaye stressed that although there "have at times been clouds between the two governments, there have been none between the two peoples."

Despite these difficulties, the years of the Civil War strengthened Laboulaye's case for friendship with the American people in several respects. First, the nation's progressive abandonment of the institution of slavery eliminated a primary criticism of the United States. Second, the preponderance of articles about the Civil War in newspapers over the course of four years brought the government of the United States to the attention of the French public. An 1865 Fourth of July celebration in the Bois de Boulogne featuring band music, speeches, food, and fireworks was well attended, not only by Americans but also government officials, diplomats, and the public. The American "democratic-republican government is no longer an experiment," John Bigelow exclaimed in his opening speech to the crowd; and the Declaration of Independence "has now acquired an importance in the eyes of mankind which it never possessed before."

In addition, the actions of the government of the North in the later years of the war had created a following in France for the American president. Upon Lincoln's death, the newspapers "appear[ed] never to tire of dwelling on the noble characteristics of the deceased President." Lincoln's reputation for honesty and personal integrity was widely known; in the words of one letter of condolence to Mary Todd Lincoln signed by thirty-three people in France, he was "the greatest and most honest citizen in the universe." Over the next decade, references to Lincoln drew hearty applause, especially reference to his role as the Great Emancipator. People were eager to see photographs or paintings of this leader of the United States; and this interest continued after his death. In 1867, a portrait of Lincoln by the painter William Morris Hunt—brother of the architect Richard Morris Hunt—was displayed in the American section of the Universal Exposition, which had opened in Paris that summer. The painting's portrayal of the late president, sympathetic yet without either personal embellishment or supporting emblems of liberty, received mixed reviews. But for the public in France it offered an opportunity to view the man. "I noticed how many persons stood before" the painting of Lincoln, the newspaper publisher and secretary of the U.S. senate John W. Forney remarked, "and how universally his fame was diffused among the working classes of the Old World."

Laboulaye kept Lincoln's following energized with his writings, lectures, and speeches at conferences, an effort that he easily combined with his support of the abolitionist movement, which the recent conflict had reinvigorated. In 1865 Laboulaye became president of the French Emancipation Committee, an organization that sought to aid newly freed, impoverished slaves in the United States and work for broader emancipation with a global view. His wife, Micheline, also became involved, joining the women's division of the committee, which raised funds and made clothing for freed slaves.

When an international antislavery conference was held in Paris in 1867, Laboulaye's opening speech transformed the meeting into "one of those feasts of liberty which move the souls of men to their deepest depths, and give one new hopes of humanity," recounted the *New York Times* Paris correspondent. "What now will result from this meeting?" Laboulaye prodded his audience. "Good, most assuredly! . . . We are only a small number, but our voices will be multiplied by innumerable echoes. They will be heard in America; they will carry the assurance of hope where it does not exist, and will force those to decide who are now hesitating which side they shall take." Concluding his prepared speech at the conference the following day, Laboulaye assured attendees that "we serve his [God's] interests and the interests of all mankind when we defend, with firm hand, justice, liberty and humanity." His message, strengthened by his intimate knowledge of American history and "that wonderful command of language for which he is celebrated," roused notable enthusiasm. Laboulaye "avoided the [censorship] law so adroitly," the *New York Times* reported, "as to excite the hilarity as well as the enthusiasm of the audience. Every mention of the Republic, of Washington, of Lincoln, of Mrs. Beecher Stowe, threw the audience into an excitement we have never before seen."

Animating Laboulaye's deep respect for the leaders and institutions of the United States was his perception of the kinship between the American and French people. For Laboulaye, who had immersed himself in the history of America's founding, the bond between the two peoples established during the American War for Independence remained as strong as ever. He had never visited the United States, yet he felt certain that Americans remembered the role France played in its history. To a certain extent this was true. Although the experience of the War for Independence belonged to a past generation, Americans did acknowledge the considerable assistance France provided and the personal sacrifices of Frenchmen. The commitment of the Marquis de Lafayette, the army under the Comte de Rochambeau, and the navy under Comte de Grasse to the American cause had initiated a tradition of friendship and gift exchange. Most important to maintaining this sense of shared history were personal memories of Lafayette. In the 1860s, Lafayette's spectacular visit to the United States in 1824–25 was still fresh in the minds of many Americans as well as French.

Lafayette had become a symbol of the alliance between France and the newly proclaimed United States within a year of his arrival on the coast of South Carolina in 1777. Inspired with a "romantic devotion . . . to the cause of freedom on these shores," in the words of the New York *Independent,* Lafayette "revealed to [Americans] in the heart of the French people a common ground of sympathy." Born into a prominent family of long military tradition, Lafayette was raised on anecdotes of glorious deeds and grew up quickly. He lost his father to the Seven Years' War when he was not yet two and then lost his mother when he was thirteen. At fifteen he became an officer in the Mousquetaires du Roi, a body guard of the king, and at sixteen he married into a powerful fam-

ily of nobility. Although still young and nurturing a mildly rebel-
lious frame of mind, he mingled with prominent figures in France
and was invited one evening to a dinner held for the Duke of
Gloucester, the brother of Britain's King George III. Hearing about
the events unfolding in America in 1775, he was gripped by the notion of a people fighting for freedom and independence. "Never,"
Lafayette later recorded, "had so noble a purpose offered itself to
the judgment of men! This was the last struggle of liberty; its defeat would have left it without a refuge and without hope."

A youth of nineteen, Lafayette parted from his young wife and
child and, having outfitted a ship at his own expense, set sail for
the colonies in April 1777. Offering his services to the struggling
Continental Army, Lafayette quickly proved "his zeal, courage,
and attachment" to the American cause. The special friendship
that developed between Lafayette and the commander-in-chief,
General George Washington, is well known; in fact, the young
man's enthusiasm and sincere goodwill seem to have captured the
hearts of all he met. It is telling that a number of generals took a
fatherly interest in guiding this "most sweet tempered young gentleman," as General Nathanael Greene described Lafayette to
Greene's wife, in his ambition to serve as a wise commander.
Lafayette proved a quick thinker in the heat of combat and possessed a knack for strategy and judgment.

Equally significant was Lafayette's unofficial activity as an American ambassador to France. He frequently wrote home about the
courage and discipline of the troops; and for General Washington
he could not find enough praise. "Our General," he wrote to his
father-in-law, a man of influence at the French court, "is a man
truly made for this revolution, which could not have been accomplished without him. . . . I admire more fully each day the beauty
of his character and spirit." Later, when French regiments arrived
to join the American forces, Lafayette introduced Washington to
friends who similarly recorded their favorable impressions of the
commander-in-chief. Deep admiration for Washington shaped the
European image of America; and once France involved herself in
the war, this common assessment of Washington's worth smoothed
the cooperation between the allied forces. Lafayette's service in the
Continental Army also earned him high regard at the French court.
As the "connecting link" between the two peoples, he facilitated
greater French commitment and the decisive deployment of the

The Marquis de Lafayette, a hero of the American War for Independence. Library of Congress, Prints and Photographs Division, LC-USZ62-56176.

Comte de Rochambeau, with his detachment of 5,500 troops, and the Comte de Grasse, with his fleet of 28 ships of the line (large sailing ships equipped to engage in battle).

A coincidence of good fortune and sound judgment allowed Lafayette to cap his contributions to the war by setting the stage for victory at Yorktown. After maneuvering a relatively small force in Virginia over several long summer months in 1781, he caused the British troops under the command of General Charles Cornwallis, second in command of the British army in North America, to pull back to the coast near Yorktown that fall. The timing of these movements was propitious, as de Grasse's fleet was near at hand and Washington and Rochambeau were prepared to rapidly move their troops from the north. After six years of struggling to hold the army together through unfavorable odds, Washington was elated by the situation his young protégé had created. As his troops approached Chesapeake Bay and he learned of the French fleet's safe arrival, Washington waved his hat in the air in an unusual show of emotion. "I have never seen a man more overcome with great and sincere joy," the Duc de Lauzun recalled afterward, "than was General Washington."

The surrender of British forces at Yorktown on October 19, 1781, is considered the most influential event in the conclusion of the Revolutionary War. Although the peace treaty concluding the war was not signed, in Paris, until September 1783, negotiations rather than action in the field dominated the final years of the struggle for independence. The victory at Yorktown also effected a shift in attitude; no longer was America's cause felt to be the "last struggle of liberty." Now the American union of states was seen as the founding of a new, enlightened political order. A medal made in France to commemorate the victory at Yorktown portrayed a liberty goddess with hair blowing in the wind. Representing the advancement of liberty, this image was repeated on the first coins minted by the United States in 1793.

Lafayette's words to a special committee of Congress that bid him farewell as he prepared to return home after a five-month visit in 1784 made clear that the ideals of liberty, which first brought him to America in 1777, remained as compelling as ever. "May this immense temple of freedom," he proclaimed, "ever stand a lesson to oppressors, an example to the oppressed, a sanctuary for the rights of mankind!"

Lafayette did not return until forty years later, this time as a guest of the nation at the invitation of Congress and the U.S. president. Assured that the whole nation wished to see him, Lafayette made plans for a visit and, to his astonishment, discovered that he had become a military legend throughout the country. His tour took him to every one of the twenty-four states, and everywhere he went he was greeted with great ceremony. From the moment he set foot in New York in August 1824 to the day of his much-delayed departure from Washington, D.C., thirteen months later, Lafayette was overwhelmed by enthusiastic crowds and an abundance of invitations to towns (with their parades, speeches, receiving lines, dinners, and balls), university commencements, military reviews, and anniversary celebrations of revolutionary events. Noting the "delirium into which our citizens are thrown by a visit from General La Fayette," Thomas Jefferson cautioned his sixty-seven-year-old friend to take care of his health, which was surely threatened by the discomforts of travel and the strenuousness of the schedule demanded of him. "Indeed I fear they will kill you with their kindness, so fatiguing and exhausting must be the ceremonies they force upon you. Be on your guard, against this," Jefferson wrote to Lafayette, conceding, a few sentences subsequent, that he had been compelled to arrange for ceremonies in his hometown of Charlottesville as well.

Lafayette was reported to recognize and embrace a man in Virginia whose freedom from slavery he had helped win in the 1780s. On the recommendation of both his master and Lafayette, who wrote a testimonial of the man's valuable contributions during the War for Independence, James Armistead Lafayette (the name he adopted) received his freedom from the Virginia General Assembly in 1787.

Over the holiday season in December 1824, Lafayette had the pleasure of spending time in Washington, D.C., with comrades from his war days, including presidents (current and future) James Monroe, John Quincy Adams, and Andrew Jackson. The Senate invited him to its chamber one day, and the House of Representatives the next, whereupon the Senate joined in attendance for Lafayette to address a joint session of Congress. Also during this holiday season, Congress resolved to add to the gifts Lafayette had received from the people he visited, such as relics from the war, along with a dog and farm animals, thereby strengthening a tradition of gift exchange. In January 1825 it voted to grant Lafayette two hundred thousand dollars—justified, when criticized by some Americans, by the amounts he had personally contributed on America's behalf—in addition to a township in Florida. During the same holiday season, Lafayette's friend, the painter and sculptor Ary Scheffer, offered one of his portraits of Lafayette to the U.S. Congress. The House of Representatives accepted the gift for its chamber and commissioned a portrait of George Washington from the American painter John Vanderlyn to accompany it.

Lafayette was deeply impressed by the sincerity of Americans' gratitude and their love for him, not only in the thirteen states of the revolutionary period but in all of the twenty-four states that made up the Union in 1824. He could not help but be tremendously moved by the hospitality shown during his visit and by the fact that organizations and places were named in his honor, either as Fayette, Lafayette, or La Grange, the name of his home in the countryside east of Paris. In people's minds Lafayette stood alongside George Washington, the man Lafayette called his adopted father. The American people honored Lafayette for his leadership during the war, his courage and clear-headedness in battle, his generosity of disposition under conditions that were often trying, and his "winning kindness," which induced "the aged man to submit himself to the command of a youth [and] the hardy native of the soil to receive and submit to the command of a foreigner." Any man of ordinary mold, they mused in admiration, would have remained at home to enjoy the life of ease his prospects offered, whereas Lafayette chose to suffer the fatigues of travel and war, even risking his life, to support their ideals. As his later life confirmed, it was not a short-lived interest in military adventure that had fostered his attachment to the American cause but rather a lifelong commitment to individual rights and liberty.

Lafayette's son, George Washington Lafayette, joined him on his tour of the twenty-four states in 1824–25, as did his secretary Auguste Levasseur, who kept a daily record of their travels and sent regular reports to the newspapers in France. On their return home, the amazing story of the American people's show of friendship spread, retold and reread by the following generation. These stories made a lasting impression, especially on those who found meaning in the ideals Lafayette fought for in America. For Édouard Laboulaye, this remarkable thirteen-month-long tour reflected a fundamental bond between the two peoples, one with roots deeper than any passing political dispute. He had read the story of Lafayette's visit and he had heard Lafayette's expressions of sympathy with America and her people. It served each nation well, Laboulaye believed, to foster the unusual bond that had been established during the American Revolution and to focus on the shared ideals of the people on either side of the Atlantic.

4

THE FRENCH
SCULPTOR

When Édouard Laboulaye first proposed a monument to liberty and the independence of the United States during a dinner party at his home in 1865, the sculptor Auguste Bartholdi was among the evening's guests. Bartholdi was by this time already gaining a reputation as a sculptor with "a goodly array of excellent works." As a youth he had received his training from highly respected artists in Paris. As a recognized sculptor, he mingled with other artists in the capital and was regularly invited to the salon of Émilien de Nieuwerkerke, the superintendent of fine arts at the Louvre. Bartholdi's work, which included private and public statuary, had been accepted for the government-sponsored Paris Salon, an annual show and competition of paintings and sculpture, and an important venue for artists to display their work.

Notwithstanding his qualifications as a sculptor, it is unlikely that in 1865 Bartholdi was prepared to make the personal commitment that the liberty project required. As he would discover once he began work in earnest, the project Laboulaye initiated differed immeasurably from that of a typical commission for a work of art. It would demand of Bartholdi not only the offering of his time and expenses, but also a dedication lasting two decades. The artist's "generous impulses," an article in 1885 observed, acknowledging Bartholdi's years of devotion to the project, "must be on a scale commensurate with this noble work." In the time between the conception of the idea for a statue and its unveiling in 1886 Bartholdi would make several visits to the United States, tirelessly promote the idea, assist with fundraising efforts in France and the United States, complete a design balancing familiar, traditional methods with the expression of contemporary meaning, and arrange for the construction of the sculptural form and supporting structure. To realize this statue, it became clear, required the attention of someone who believed strongly in its meaning and purpose. In 1865 Bartholdi was not yet motivated by this strength of feeling. The experience of the Franco-Prussian War of 1870–71, however, effected a change in him and kindled the passion that would distinguish his later work and sustain his commitment to the Statue of Liberty.

Born in 1834 in Colmar, a city located close to the German border in the Alsace region of France, Bartholdi lived in Paris from the age of nine. At the urging of his father's uncle who resided in the capital, his mother had moved the family to Paris following the death of her husband, all the while retaining her family home in Colmar. Bartholdi was enrolled in the prestigious school Louis-le-Grand in the Latin Quarter, but, with the exception of history in his high school years, his studies there did not pique his curiosity. The subject that interested him most, and for which he appeared to possess some ability, was art, and he filled his class notebooks with drawings. Recognizing her son's inclination, Madame Bartholdi nurtured his artistic talents and obtained instruction for him in drawing, painting, and sculpture. The Dutch painter and sculptor Ary Scheffer, one of the artists who had gathered around Lafayette in the 1820s, became Bartholdi's principal teacher as well as a family friend. By the time Bartholdi completed his examinations for the baccalaureate it was evident that he was headed not for the Collège de France—where Laboulaye was making his name —but for a career in art.

Bartholdi likely studied with the accomplished sculptor Antoine Étex in the 1850s. Étex had been responsible for the design of two bas-reliefs for one of the most prominent projects in Paris, the Arc de Triomphe de l'Étoile, located at the western summit of the Champs-Élysées. This triumphal arch, the largest in history, was started under Napoleon Bonaparte in 1806 and finally completed with sculptural decoration under Louis-Philippe in the 1830s. The

Auguste Bartholdi, c. 1882. Musée Bartholdi, Colmar. Reproduction by C. Kempf.

Arc de Triomphe's four large reliefs, designed by three different artists, attracted considerable attention due both to their important setting and to the controversial subject of one relief in particular, "The Departure of the Volunteers of 1792" (also known as "The Marseillaise") by François Rude. Rude's mythic assortment of volunteers rallied by a ferocious, sword-wielding liberty figure depicts the people's resolution to defend their country from threatened invasion during the French Revolution and to support the spread of liberty across Europe.

In 1854, Étex completed an influential funerary structure for the Père Lachaise Cemetery. The wife of François Raspail, an activist for human rights and the welfare of the common people, had died while languishing in prison. Departing from standard practice for funerary sculpture, Étex imbued his figure with deep emotion, portraying grief in the person of Henriette-Adélaïde Raspail. Veiled and leaning upon the wall of her husband's prison cell (in reality, the wall of the family tomb) the figure extends an arm to grasp the grated window opening. When Bartholdi designed a commemorative gravestone following the Franco-Prussian War of 1870–71, he similarly endowed an outstretched arm with uncommon pathos.

Another accomplished sculptor who may have provided Bartholdi with images that pertained to his future work was Jean-François Soitoux. In response to the announcement in 1848 of an official competition for a symbolic figure to personify the Second Republic, Soitoux designed a classically draped woman holding, among other emblems, a scroll depicting the constitution of the Republic. Soitoux constructed his statue of *La République,* but by the time of its completion the character of the government had changed, transformed in 1852 into the Second Empire by proclamation of Napoleon III. As a consequence, the statue was relegated to a warehouse, where it remained until the Third Republic, when it was retrieved for display in 1880.

In addition to the work of his instructors, sources of inspiration were plentiful in Paris, especially for a student intrigued by abstract or timeless themes, appreciative of the historical past, and attracted to large-scale sculpture. During his years as emperor, Napoleon I had initiated an impressive building program modeled on the grandeur of the ancient construction he saw as his armies moved through Italy and Egypt. Besides monumental arches, many public buildings in Paris were constructed in the manner of ancient temples, enveloped by a colonnade; hence, the temple of finance, the temple of the laws, and so forth. Even an enormous elephant fountain at the Place de la Bastille, completed only as a lath-and-plaster mock-up, was ingrained in the French consciousness on account of the street urchin Gavroche, who took shelter inside the elephant in Victor Hugo's *Les Misérables.*

When he was twenty-one, Bartholdi embarked on a seven-month-long tour of Egypt and remote parts of Yemen. The grand tour was a common element in gentlemen's education, often commencing with sites of antiquities in Italy and covering a number of countries along the Mediterranean. Arriving in Egypt in November 1855, Bartholdi was initially uncomfortable with the unfamiliar culture and landscape. But after two months he reported that he had "perfectly recovered" and was feeling right at home in the marvelous port city of Alexandria. He journeyed in Egypt with a small group of artists, including Jean-Léon Gérôme, whose work as a history and genre painter would reflect his interest in ancient Greece and Rome. Bartholdi then left his travel companions in Egypt and ventured south to Yemen with an explorer of Arabia he met on the ship from Marseilles. The stark landscapes and ancient ruins Bartholdi saw throughout his seven-month adventure made a strong impression on him, as did the scale of monuments. The sense of "infinity," or timelessness, that many of the ancient statues expressed greatly appealed to him. Years later, Bartholdi would credit this type of personal and professional discovery with releasing him from formulaic design. "If I have had some success, it is to this that I owe it," he reflected; it was during his travels that he gathered "genuine treasures" of experience. In the spring of 1865 Bartholdi complemented his earlier travel experience with a month-long stay in Italy, where he explored ancient ruins in Rome and Pompeii.

Around the time that he first traveled to Egypt, Bartholdi began his career as a sculptor of public statuary. He quickly discovered his comfort with larger-than-life-size, "heroic," sculpture and was encouraged by the recognition received by his statue of a local hero of Colmar, General Rapp. The statue of Jean Comte de Rapp, a valorous general who served as a personal aide-de-campe to Napoleon I, was displayed at the Paris International Exhibition of 1855 and praised by at least one Paris newspaper. Over the next decade Bartholdi demonstrated an ability to work at a variety of sizes and with a breadth of composition ranging from busts and figures of individuals to complex compositions for architectural monuments. By 1865 he was eager for the challenge of a significant project.

The dinner party at the home of Laboulaye in the months after the end of the American Civil War pointed to such a project. Bartholdi would have been ready to pursue this immediately, but the completion of a large project promoting liberty and a republican form of government was not possible in France in the mid-1860s. Although government censorship had become less restrictive since

1860, even the Lincoln medal faced substantial resistance. In the meantime, Bartholdi prepared by gathering some of Laboulaye's writings. He hoped to better understand what Laboulaye had in mind when he talked about liberty, as Laboulaye would be the primary patron for this artwork. Over the next few years, Bartholdi reported to Laboulaye, he read and reread Laboulaye's works on the subject.

As Bartholdi contemplated the potential commission for a liberty statue, he recognized some of the difficulties involved. Liberty figures were common in Europe and certain elements were widely understood as emblems of liberty. Foremost among these was the liberty cap, which derived from the *pileus* in ancient Rome, a soft round pointed cap worn by liberated slaves. The cap had been adopted as the basis for the Phrygian bonnet (*bonnet phrygien*), an article of revolutionary dress during the French Revolution. During the nineteenth century the liberty cap was routinely employed in painting and sculpture to symbolize political liberty.

The pursuit of liberty, however, was claimed on all sides in the nineteenth century, from revolutionaries to Emperor Napoleon III, and was represented in a variety of ways. Undoubtedly the most striking depiction of liberty with which Bartholdi was familiar was the painting by Eugène Delacroix, completed shortly after the revolution of 1830. In *28 July, Liberty Guiding the People* (*Le 28 juillet, La Liberté guidant le peuple*) Liberty is portrayed wearing a Phrygian bonnet as she leads the people across fallen bodies. With one hand she raises the tricolored flag and in the other she carries a bayoneted rifle. This interpretation of liberty made impassioned struggle part and parcel of the process of throwing off the bondages of the past, acknowledging the tumultuous aspect of change.

A liberty sculpture of quite different meaning had been built in Paris in the late 1830s. Erected at the Place de la Bastille, a 154-foot-tall (47 m) *July Column* commemorated the defense of liberties during the revolution of 1830 and the beginning of the reign of Louis-Philippe, the so-called July Monarchy, for which many people had high hopes. With one foot lightly perched on a globe that sits at the top of the column, a liberty figure by the sculptor Auguste Dumont raises a torch in its right hand and a broken chain of oppression in its left. Unlike Delacroix's Liberty, who is grounded in the reality of revolution, this winged *Genius of Lib-*

erty (*Le Génie de la Liberté*) floats above worldly practice, in the realm of the spirits.

The official seal adopted for the Second Republic in 1848 (and again for the Third Republic), designed by Jean-Jacques Barre, features a seated liberty figure in ancient drapery, wearing not a liberty cap but a crown of seven rays. A similar design for an 1848 medal of the Republic depicts Liberty standing, crowned by nine rays and supporting the Constitution with her right hand. The Roman head ornament of rays gained favor during the nineteenth century as a result of the archeological discoveries of ancient sculpture. Symbolizing light or divine inspiration, the rayed crown "seems to have been reserved for ideal heads, and is only found in Art," London's *Art-Journal* reported.

During the next several years Bartholdi continued to formulate design concepts appropriate to liberty while focusing his efforts on other projects. For Auvergne, a province in central France, he designed a dramatic monument commemorating the region's Gaullist leader Vercingétorix (the statue was not built until 1902, in Clermont-Ferrand). Bartholdi's depiction of Vercingétorix shows him charging forward, rousing his compatriots to defeat the advancing Roman army. The sculpture portrays his courage and leadership rather than success, for he eventually surrendered to Caesar to save the lives of his countrymen. Bartholdi's model for this monument was accepted in 1870 for the Paris Salon.

While the liberty statue for the United States was on hold, Bartholdi eyed an opportunity to contribute to the monumental statuary of Egypt, which he so much admired. The potential commission had the additional benefit of allowing him to explore ideas for a symbolic figure. The Suez Canal, nearing completion in the late 1860s, was widely acclaimed for its technical achievement and was seen to exemplify the progress of the modern era. Bartholdi expected that a structure would be required to mark the entrance to this massive canal and developed a scheme for a sculptural lighthouse. His design, which he called "Egypt (or Progress) Bringing Light to Asia" or "Egypt Enlightening the Orient," consisted of a large female figure lifting a lantern. He imagined this lantern as a beacon, both practical and metaphorical. The statue would recall a long tradition of monumental statuary and shoreline markers while serving as a testament to the technological achievement and social significance of the Suez Canal.

Bartholdi traveled to Egypt in 1869 with drawings and a clay model to present to the viceroy of Egypt, Ismail Pasha. He met with the Frenchman responsible for the canal, Ferdinand de Lesseps, who welcomed Bartholdi as a visitor to Egypt, though he did not favor Bartholdi's idea for a lighthouse. The viceroy showed interest in the design and its melding of historical and modern aspirations. However he declined to commission this work, perhaps in part because of the budgetary strain caused by the many costly projects Egypt had recently undertaken. Bartholdi may have continued to entertain hopes of obtaining a lighthouse commission during the spring of 1870, but his personal and professional pursuits were soon superseded by national events. In July 1870 Napoleon III declared war on Prussia, and Bartholdi prepared to participate in the French military effort.

France and Prussia had been teetering on the threshold of war since the conclusion of the Austro-Prussian War in 1866. Prussia's quick victory emboldened the Prussian rulers, who sought to expand the North German Confederation through the unification of German principalities. The confederation was able to annex a number of German states following Austria's defeat; however, it continued to face resistance from the southern German states, which preferred to retain their autonomy. Nothing, predicted Count Otto von Bismarck (the Prussian prime minister and, after the establishment of a German Empire in 1871, the German chancellor), could better arouse German sentiments and provide a convincing pretext for pressuring these states into the North German Confederation than war with a Napoleon. For his part, France's Napoleon III viewed the outcome of the Austro-Prussian war with indignation, as Prussia's pretensions to becoming a great power were evident. "Weak Governments," he emphasized in a speech in 1867, "often seek to divert public attention from domestic troubles, by fomenting foreign quarrels." Yet the German confederation's increasing strength and activity were veritable causes for anxiety in France. As Empress Eugénie prophetically complained to the Prussian ambassador in Paris: "The energy and rapidity of your movements . . . [have made it clear] that with a nation like yours as a neighbor, we are in danger of seeing you in Paris one day unannounced. I will go to sleep French and wake up Prussian."

At the same time, domestic tensions in France were peaking in the late 1860s. Aware that his support was precipitously eroding, most alarmingly among his own military, and under pressure to act, Napoleon III declared war on Prussia on July 19, 1870. The best way to distract the French army from its restlessness, Prussia's military attaché in Paris noted, was for Napoleon III to occupy it in a war.

Handicapped by France's relative lack of preparedness and smaller army, soldiers' weakening loyalty to the empire, and the abysmal leadership of Napoleon III as well as some of his chosen commanders, the French army nevertheless fought adamantly. But a series of battles and defeats led to the capture of the French emperor at Sedan by September 2, 1870. Assuming that the French army and nation would accept defeat, Bismarck dictated terms of an armistice. He soon discovered, however, that forming a treaty with an unpopular emperor served little purpose, as the national legislative body in Paris simply dethroned Napoleon III. On September 4, 1870, speaking from a window of the Hôtel de Ville, a young member of the legislative body, Léon Gambetta, proclaimed a new Republic of France and announced a provisional Government of the National Defense. The Government of the National Defense, as its name implies, had no intention of surrendering and accepting Bismarck's terms of peace.

Once the war was underway, Bartholdi requested permission from the National Guard to go to Colmar, where his mother was living, to assist in this city close to the German border. His request was readily granted, and he was in Colmar by early September 1870 when the Republic was declared. Prussian troops passed through Colmar on their way south with little disturbance, as the residents of the small city had no illusions about their ability to halt the movement of Prussian troops. Bartholdi could have remained in Colmar, following their departure, but the brief contact with potential occupiers of his homeland had a profound effect on him and he felt compelled to actively support the war effort. Deciding to offer his services where French and Prussian forces were engaged, he made his way south to Belfort, a garrison town of Alsace, approximately 45 miles (72 km) from Colmar. Rather than retain him in Belfort, however, the National Guard sent him across the country to Tours, approximately 370 miles (600 km) to the west. A government delegation was establishing itself there, correctly anticipating the siege of Paris as the Prussian army pressed into the interior of France. Indeed, Léon Gambetta, the acting minister of the interior, having failed to leave Paris for Tours before routes out of the capital were blocked, was forced to rely on prevailing westerly winds and a hot-air balloon to transport him beyond Prussian lines.

From the south another fighting force entered France, this one in defense of the republic declared by the provisional government. Giuseppe Garibaldi, the Italian champion of independence, felt compelled to aid the fragile new republic in France. He probably also thought that his very presence would kindle a passion of enthusiasm for this national struggle, as it had in Italy. Notwithstanding Garibaldi's intentions, the response to his presence in France was mixed. Many people disliked the idea of the legendary Italian revolutionary assuming a position of leadership in the war. Bartholdi let it be known that he felt otherwise. Shortly after his arrival in Tours, he was assigned communications with Garibaldi on behalf of the government. He subsequently remained with Garibaldi as an intermediary for communication and requisition of provisions for his army of volunteers.

By the end of January 1871, the delegation at Tours determined that it was in the interest of France to conclude the war. It agreed to terms of a preliminary peace between France and the German Empire, which had been proclaimed at Versailles earlier that month. This time around, however, Bismarck insisted that national elections be held to install a credible provisional government for the purpose of accepting the terms of peace. Accordingly, a National Assembly was elected, a president, Adolphe Thiers, was chosen, and the provisional treaty of peace was concluded. In May of that year the Treaty of Frankfurt formalized the terms. It was said by those who negotiated with Bismarck that he sought to revenge grievances of the past two centuries. Bismarck recalled the aggression and annexations of Richelieu and Louis XIV in the seventeenth century, along with those of Napoleon in the early nineteenth century, and insisted on at least some territorial gains. In the end, the German Empire gained control of a large part of Lorraine and the entire region of Alsace, in addition to a hefty monetary obligation from France. The indemnity of five billion francs (on top of war costs of twelve billion francs) was seen by many in Europe as a crippling weight from which it would take the country decades to recover.

Most people in France desired an end to the war and the restoration of order, and the National Assembly reflected this perspective. But not all of the representatives elected to accept the peace supported the terms. Notable among those opposed were Gambetta, Garibaldi, who to the dismay of many of the other delegates had been elected, and Victor Hugo, representing Paris. Many people in France, in Paris especially, were angry about the conduct of the war and believed that the provisional government had surrendered too much too easily. The Parisians had suffered tremendously during the siege, now seemingly for no purpose, and they felt betrayed both by the provinces, which had not come to their aid, and by the government.

Included in the armistice was a partial occupation of Paris, beginning on March 1, 1871, in the event the terms of peace were not ratified. German troops were present in the city for only a couple of days; nevertheless, the additional offence of their march into the capital sharpened the antagonism between Parisians and the provisional French government. Further widening the gulf between the two, the Assembly passed measures affecting the capital that set the stage for violent confrontation and the imposition of national authority. One measure, certain to provoke rioting of the lower middle classes, declared unpaid wartime rents in Paris payable immediately. At the same time—probably sensing the volatile state of the city—all government authorities departed. "How great was my surprise," recalled the American minister Elihu Washburne, to find that "there was not a shadow of a legal and responsible city or national government" remaining in Paris by March 21.

Left to their own governance, the leaders of the insurrectionary movement assumed power and quickly held an election to establish a municipal government known as "la Commune," which espoused social transformation, communal governments, and a redistribution of wealth. Dominated by radical factions, eager to refute the policies of Napoleon III's Empire, and at odds with the national government—"We must wipe out the past and make the world over again," one leader pronounced—the Commune was bound to be unstable and characterized by paranoia. Moreover, the bombardment of Paris began again, this time by French troops rather than Prussian. After two months of this postwar turmoil, people in the city were weary and demoralized. When troops sent by the French government finally entered Paris on May 21 and began to seize control, the anguish and frustration of the past year fueled a brutal confrontation between the two sides. The Communards hastened their shootings of prisoners and set fire to buildings, concentrating on those associated with the Empire, such as the imperial residence at the Tuileries, thereby starting the conflagration of the city. The more powerful forces sent by the French government, meanwhile, began rounding up thousands of Communards and other suspected enemies of the government. By the end of a week, the fighting had ended; by the time a semblance of normalcy returned, an estimated twenty thousand people had died in Paris.

Apparently by chance, Bartholdi returned to Paris from Colmar, where he had gone at the end of the war to see his mother, on May 30. It is not clear that he recognized how dangerous the environment in Paris had been only a few days before or realized the enormity of the events that had occurred. What he noticed first was the physical destruction of the city, including the street where his home and studio were located. "Rue Vavin—what a surprise!" he noted in his journal, "houses in ruins, facades torn to pieces." He found that his house had been occupied by troops and suffered some damage. There were large holes in the courtyard walls, and all the window panes of the building had been broken. "But," he added, perhaps recognizing that the condition of his house was better than others, "no rubbish inside."

In the years following the war Bartholdi received several commissions for war memorials, for which he designed fiercely patriotic sculptures. For the grave of two National Guardsmen at a cemetery in Colmar, he sculpted a monument to portray both Alsace's suffering and its determination to rise from defeat. In a highly effective yet surprisingly simple monument, two bare stone slabs covering a gravesite separate slightly as one slab is pushed up from below by an arm stretched out toward a sword that lies nearby. In another design, he portrayed Alsatian gratitude for the principled career of Léon Gambetta, who continued to seek liberty for the provinces taken by the German Empire. Bartholdi's statue depicts Gambetta fallen yet unwilling to surrender the flag of the French Republic. Decorating the pedestal are the coat of arms of eleven Alsatian towns, among them Colmar.

Most well-known of Bartholdi's war memorials is the Lion of Belfort. The fortress city of Belfort had successfully hampered

Prussian supply lines to the interior of France, despite being besieged by Prussian forces for more than three months. Bartholdi's enormous lion sculpture, at once serene and furious, overlooks the city from the rock surface of the Vosges Mountains directly below the citadel of Belfort. Depicted in a subdued sphinx-like position that acknowledges the region's suffering during the war, the lion's boldly lifted head and visible roar commemorate, in Bartholdi's words, the "proud struggle, the tradition of which should be remembered and handed down." When the city launched a national fundraising campaign, it publicized the Lion of Belfort as representative of not only the Alsace-Lorraine region but all of France. As donations were received, the local paper *Le Journal de Belfort et du Haut-Rhin* published the names of contributors in a method of public recognition that would be repeated during the Statue of Liberty subscription campaign.

This monument illustrates the nature of Bartholdi's gift for design, which was not centered on artistic originality; the image of a lion had been used in earlier works to honor a people's virtue, loyalty, or strength. Rather, his talent lay in the ability to draw on precedent and endow familiar images with fresh meaning and expression. He wanted to express ideas and aimed to bestow his sculpture with moral authority. Although his works for Alsace held specific meaning for the people of the region, they were also well received in Paris and accepted for the Salon. In a review of the Gambetta monument, which was displayed in the 1872 Salon, the *Encyclopédie d'Architecture* complimented the design, concluding that "this work of art does great honor to Bartholdi." Upon viewing his design for the Lion of Belfort, the town council of Paris requested a replica for the city, which had likewise endured a siege. In 1880 a copper lion was placed on a pedestal in the 14th arrondissement, in a square that was named for Colonel Denfert-Rochereau, commander of Belfort during the Franco-Prussian War.

Before Bartholdi was able to settle back in Paris in June 1871 and consider new projects such as these memorials, his thoughts turned to the liberty statue for the United States. He had contemplated a trip to America already the previous year. Now, impassioned by a completely new sense of longing for liberty, Bartholdi contacted Laboulaye and suggested that he make an exploratory visit to the United States. He would talk with Americans about the idea of a liberty monument and gauge the level of their support.

Laboulaye knew that it was not possible to propose a costly project of this nature to the French public when the country was burdened by the costs and suffering of the war. Nor was the political climate suitable in 1871—not until 1875 did the country as a whole accept the concept of a republic. Laboulaye's spirits, moreover, were unusually low. During the last years of Napoleon III's reign he had tried to encourage the liberalization of the government rather than work for its removal, an approach that had drawn sharp criticism within his own party. And despite liberalization of the government, his attempts to obtain a seat in the National Assembly in the late 1860s had been unsuccessful. The declaration of a provisional Government of National Defense in 1870, the extremism of the Commune in 1871, and the ruthless reaction of the French army in May 1871—an unpromising beginning for the new government—appeared to reinforce the cycle of revolution and reaction, anarchy and imposed order, from which he longed to free France. The brutality of war that he witnessed when the Prussian army encircled Paris added to his gloom. After spending several months in Normandy, where he helped to organize ambulances and aid the wounded, Laboulaye returned to his home near Versailles to find that it had been occupied by Prussian officers; only *"moderately* pillaged" compared to his neighbors' homes, he acknowledged. Especially demoralizing for a man intent on peace was his sense that this war was not the last, but instead pointed toward a future, larger, conflict.

Nevertheless, when Bartholdi told Laboulaye about his idea for an exploratory visit to the United States, Laboulaye offered his support and letters of introduction. He must have understood that the experience of the war and the uncertainties associated with the future government caused Bartholdi to embrace the project with increased determination. Indeed, Bartholdi's extraordinary devotion to the liberty project over the next fifteen years can be explained only by his personal, emotional, attachment to the vision of life that the statue portrays. The heartfelt longing for independence and self-governance that the loss of Alsace instilled transformed Bartholdi's interest in the commission for a statue into an unshakable commitment to a powerful statement of both national and individual meaning.

5

BARTHOLDI'S TOUR
OF AMERICA AND
THE AMERICAN
ARCHITECT

Only nine days after his return to Paris at the end of the Franco-Prussian War, Bartholdi boarded a steamship in Brest for a twelve-day voyage across the Atlantic. Although Laboulaye and his colleagues had not offered him a firm commission for an American liberty monument, Bartholdi felt certain of Laboulaye's personal commitment to the project. Through Laboulaye's connections Bartholdi was also assured access to numerous people of influence. Laboulaye had formed many friendships in America. He was a dedicated correspondent and a gracious host; those who wrote to him received a response, and those who visited France were won over by his perceptive and sympathetic view of the United States. Laboulaye had also established a friendship with the translator of several of his writings, Mary L. Booth. Booth welcomed Bartholdi when he arrived in New York and immediately introduced him to others.

Beginning on the East Coast, in New York, Washington, D.C., Philadelphia, and Boston, Bartholdi met with many prominent people in the United States, among them the nation's president, Ulysses S. Grant. Laboulaye had supported Grant during the presidential campaign of 1868. Grant represented a different outlook from that of Lincoln's successor, Andrew Johnson, whose actions set back much of the progress abolitionists had made, and impeded more that had been anticipated. "I have confidence in the good sense of the American people," Laboulaye wrote in a letter intended for publication in a U.S. newspaper, "and do not doubt the election of Gen. Grant."

Bartholdi was not an observer of society as Tocqueville had been, yet he wanted to gain an understanding of the American way of life. Cultural differences between the United States and France highlighted some aspects of the American character. Bartholdi found the people he met on the East Coast to be at once welcoming and stiff. Invited to a lovely resort on the beach in Long Branch, New Jersey, he was surprised by the careful propriety of people's dress and was particularly embarrassed by his bathing suit—"too scanty!!" On the contrary, with the president "there [was] no formality. . . . One is received as by the simplest bourgeois," Bartholdi wrote his mother, having visited Grant at his summer cottage. "I met his children, and his gouty father-in-law seated by a spittoon. I spent an interesting half hour with the Grants."

In Washington, D.C., Bartholdi spent much of his time with Senator Charles Sumner of Massachusetts, who "loves the arts" and "loves France," Bartholdi noted with unusual exuberance. Sumner and Laboulaye had met in France when Sumner was recovering from the attack he suffered in the Senate Chamber. He welcomed Bartholdi to Washington, D.C., in June 1871 and was enthusiastic about the idea for a statue. One of Sumner's primary objectives following the Civil War, fellow senator Carl Schurz later recounted, was that "from its new birth the republic should . . . be a shining example and beacon light to all the nations of the earth." Sumner may have shared his thoughts about the need for a statue of national meaning with Bartholdi, as he had with an American sculptor seven years earlier. "The fate of Slavery is settled," Sumner wrote to William Wetmore Story in 1864, anticipating the conclusion of the Civil War. "This will be a free country. . . . Give us, give mankind, a work which will typify or commemorate a redeemed nation." Although Story had not taken up his suggestion, Sumner likely saw the possibility that his wish for a commemorative statue might be realized in Bartholdi's ideas.

A one-day expedition from the capital, traveling by steamboat along the Potomac, took Bartholdi to Mount Vernon. The home of George Washington, preserved and open to the public, recalled Washington and Lafayette's friendship. Bartholdi noted that one room was designated as belonging to Lafayette. Also on exhibit was the key to the Bastille in Paris, "the token of victory gained by Liberty over Despotism," which Lafayette had sent to Washington after the fall of the Bastille on July 14, 1789.

While Bartholdi was in Washington, D.C., he met the newspaper publisher John W. Forney, probably through the introduction of Sumner. Sumner had introduced Forney and Laboulaye in Paris in 1867. Forney invited Bartholdi to Philadelphia and took an immediate liking to him. He hoped to convince the artist, Forney later told his readers, to "make Philadelphia his chosen residence." As John Forney's guest, Bartholdi frequented the Union League of Philadelphia, a club that had been established during the Civil War to support Lincoln and the Union. The Union League possessed a painting that may have been familiar to Bartholdi. Completed by Edward Dalton Marchant in 1863, the canvas depicts Lincoln seated at a table, having just signed the Proclamation of Emancipation. Seen in a niche behind the president is the lower part of a heroic liberty figure whose foot tramples on a broken chain. To eliminate any uncertainty, "Liberty" is written on the thin base of the statue. "In this I have sought," explained the artist about his painting, "to symbolize, on canvas, the great, crowning, act of our distinguished President. The act, which more than all others, must signalize the grand epoch in which we are privileged to live." Lincoln was pleased with the result, as was Marchant, who arranged for an engraving of the painting to be made by John Sartain. Completed in time for distribution during the 1864 presidential campaign, Sartain's lithograph helped to popularize the image of Lincoln as the Great Emancipator. It is reasonable to assume that Laboulaye, who supported Lincoln's reelection in 1864, owned a copy of Sartain's print. If so, Laboulaye surely displayed it in his home and showed it to interested visitors, among them Bartholdi.

Bartholdi also visited Independence Hall, originally the Pennsylvania State House, where the Second Continental Congress adopted the Declaration of Independence in 1776. Bartholdi seems to have imagined the excitement of this period, taking note of "the window from which Independence was proclaimed." In 1787, the Constitution of the United States was drafted in the same room at Independence Hall. This was the occasion for Benjamin Franklin's memorable remark about the sun. As delegates added their signatures to the Constitution, Franklin pointed to the decoration on

Abraham Lincoln by Edward Dalton Marchant. Oil on canvas,
55" × 45". The Abraham Lincoln Foundation of the Union League
of Philadelphia, commissioned by members and friends of the Union
League, 1863.

the back of Washington's chair. "Painters," Franklin remarked,
"had found it difficult to distinguish in their art a rising from a setting sun." He had been pondering the design on Washington's
chair for months, he explained, wondering what it meant for them.
Finally, with the successful conclusion of the Convention, he felt
renewed with optimism and convinced that the sun was rising on
the nation. Laboulaye was fond of this story and Bartholdi was
certainly familiar with it. Bartholdi may have visited Carpenters'
Hall as well, only two blocks from Independence Hall, where the

Carpenters' Company of the City and County of Philadelphia coat of arms includes another sun design, this one with seven rays.

Later that summer, when working on a study model for his liberty figure, Bartholdi incorporated the image of the sun, in the form of a crown of rays. His visit to Philadelphia may have reminded him of the close association of the sun with the founding of the nation. Similarly, a broken chain trampled underfoot found a place in Bartholdi's design, and the portrait of Lincoln as the Great Emancipator, as painted by Marchant and engraved by Sartain, may have been a source for this element of design.

In addition to Philadelphia's association with central moments in the history of the nation, the city anticipated hosting a world's fair in 1876, to commemorate the signing of the Declaration of Independence. In March 1871, the U.S. president signed an act providing for "celebrating the one hundredth anniversary of American independence by holding an international exhibition of arts, manufactures, and products of the soil and mine." Philadelphia was designated by Congress as the site for the Centennial Exhibition, and Philadelphia's Fairmount Park was selected as the setting. Forney showed Bartholdi the enormous park and acquainted him with park commissioners, hoping to obtain work for Bartholdi. Forney, who would soon be named the Centennial's commissioner to Great Britain and the continent of Europe, also may have begun to encourage Bartholdi to think about how he might participate in the world's fair.

Bartholdi traveled north from Philadelphia and New York to Boston, where he visited the poet Henry Wadsworth Longfellow, a longtime friend of Sumner, and to Newport, Rhode Island, where he stayed at the family home of the artist John La Farge, with whom he had developed a friendship. La Farge was a painter working in oil and watercolor who extended his perspective to large-scale murals in the 1870s and later to stained glass. His ties to France were strong, and he could sympathize with Bartholdi's grief over *l'année terrible,* as the French termed the period of the Franco-Prussian War. Stories of the experiences of his father, Jean-Frédéric de la Farge, during the Revolutionary and Napoleonic years lived in his imagination. Jean-Frédéric had departed France as part of an expedition sent by Napoleon in 1802 to reassert France's rule in Santo Domingo, the West Indian island where Admiral de Grasse first brought his large fleet from France in 1781 before sailing on to

Chesapeake Bay to participate in the siege at Yorktown. The French were not successful in subduing the uprising, and by the end of the following year they conceded defeat. (The colony declared its independence as the Republic of Haiti in 1804.) Jean-Frédéric de la Farge escaped imprisonment on the island and made his way to the United States, settling in New York. John La Farge's maternal grandfather likewise arrived in the United States via Santo Domingo. This grandfather, however, had resided comfortably there for many years before the uprising, owning a large plantation and once receiving Lieutenant General Rochambeau as his guest. During the rebellion in the early 1800s he left his possessions and, together with his family, took refuge in the United States.

La Farge, who was thirty-six in 1871—one year younger than Bartholdi—remained linked to his ancestral home of France as well as to the historical past. He greatly enjoyed classical Greek and Roman literature, took an interest in the life of the ancients, and could knowledgably entertain Bartholdi's musings over the recent discoveries from classical antiquity. American friends of La Farge remarked on his tolerance for shades of meaning and even contradictory ideas. Bartholdi probably discussed with La Farge the ideas he was forming in his mind for the liberty statue and was encouraged by his friend to present more than a single idea. Although a large monument required simplicity and visual clarity, it did not have to confine itself to one aspect of liberty.

While John La Farge exuded European sensibilities, his wife, Margaret Mason Perry, represented an alternative facet of the American experience. Her ancestors in America included leading figures such as Thomas Sergeant, a chief justice of the Pennsylvania Supreme Court, and, according to her son John La Farge Jr., Benjamin Franklin. She was a grand-niece of Commodore Matthew Calbraith Perry, whose distinguished naval career included negotiations for the conclusion of an important peace treaty with Japan in 1854. Margaret Mason Perry was also a granddaughter of Commodore Oliver Hazard Perry, who at the age of twenty-eight challenged British control of the Great Lakes during the War of 1812 by leading the Lake Erie fleet to an astonishing victory. A painting in the United States Capitol commemorates Perry's naval victory, which became widely known by the dispatch he sent to his commander at the conclusion of the battle: "We have met the enemy and they are ours."

It was in the La Farge home in Newport, during Bartholdi's second visit to the United States in 1876, that he was married. According to the account Bartholdi gave his mother, Jeanne-Émilie Baheux de Puysieux was a relative of La Farge's whom he met for the first time in 1871. When Bartholdi met her again during his visit in 1876, again through the La Farge family, he decided on marriage. The story passed down in the La Farge family was rather different: Bartholdi brought Jeanne with him to Newport in 1876 and, as the La Farge children understood it, was promptly advised by John and Margaret La Farge to marry.

The La Farge home was also the setting for Bartholdi's introduction to the architect Richard Morris Hunt. Hunt and La Farge were part of a circle of painters, architects, and writers—among them, Henry James, Henry Hobson Richardson, and Henry Adams —that formed in the 1850s and 1860s. These young men shared European, in particular French, sensibilities at a time when many of their compatriots had not traveled abroad. They were Americans, yet because of their training in French culture and art, they did not fit seamlessly into the American tradition. These men occasionally found the opportunity to work together; Richardson, for instance, involved La Farge in some of his residential projects, for which La Farge created stained glass windows. It was also Richardson's idea that La Farge paint murals in Boston's Trinity Church—exquisite murals that drew public attention to his work. In June 1871, La Farge suggested that Bartholdi work on a project of Richardson's. By the time Bartholdi returned to France that fall, he had obtained a commission to design the four sculptural friezes for the tower of Boston's Brattle Square Church (now First Baptist Church), for which Richardson was the architect.

Hunt, like numerous New Yorkers of the period, spent time during the summer in Newport. When he and Bartholdi met in 1871, they did not foresee Hunt's future involvement in the liberty project as the designer of the pedestal. Their personalities and backgrounds were quite different, and their acquaintance did not blossom into friendship. Hunt was six years older than Bartholdi and a man "of substance and social position." From Bartholdi's perspective, Hunt seemed too "pleased with himself." Nonetheless, the two men shared an appreciation for the ideals that inspired the liberty monument and a fondness for ancient tradition and technique. Hunt's own work was strongly influenced by French neoclassical architecture and reflected a thoughtful reverence for the accomplishments of the past. Like Bartholdi, he was not inclined to pursue the new direction of design that was emerging in the 1870s, which emphasized the expression of a personal style.

Hunt had lived in Europe from the time he was fifteen until he was twenty-seven. His father had died in 1832, when Hunt was not yet five years old, and in 1843 his mother had taken her five children to Europe, intending to stay for one year. They began with an expedition to Italy, exploring the ancient ruins in Rome and Pompeii, after which Richard Morris Hunt was enrolled in a boys' school in Geneva. By the end of the first year in Europe, the family's plans for the future had changed. Hunt decided on a career in architecture and settled, along with other family members, in Paris. He entered the atelier of architect Hector Martin Lefuel to commence his architectural training. The next year, in 1846, Hunt was admitted to the École des Beaux Arts, becoming the first American architect to study at this prestigious school.

Hunt was residing in Paris at the time of both the Revolution of 1848 and the coup d'état of 1851, which preceded the declaration of Napoleon III's Second Empire. He took an interest in these events; however, it appears from his notes and those of friends that he did not feel personally affected by them. Shortly after King Louis-Philippe abdicated the throne in February 1848, Hunt left France for a long holiday in the United States. This was his first trip home since leaving in 1843. He spent the summer months traveling with his mother, sister, and one brother. They explored parts of the country that would be central to the national conflict the following decade, as well as cities that Bartholdi would visit in 1871, the year he and Hunt met. The Hunt family traveled south from Philadelphia into Virginia, where they lingered for two months, and west through Kentucky and Tennessee to St. Louis. Turning back east toward the family base in Vermont, they stopped in Chicago and Detroit before crossing Lake Erie to Buffalo and Niagara Falls. In December of that year, Hunt returned to Paris and his architectural studies.

In 1852 Hunt completed his course work at the École and embarked on a longer expedition, a yearlong grand tour. He was joined by his brother, the painter William Morris Hunt, for the beginning part of his trip in northern Europe and in Italy, which, he observed with irritation, was occupied by Austrian troops. Hunt

Portrait of Richard Morris Hunt by John Singer Sargent, completed in 1895.
Used with permission from The Biltmore Company, Asheville, North Carolina.

sailed to Malta, where he visited the old capital of the Knights of Malta, and to Alexandria, the port city where travelers to Egypt typically disembarked. Following a well-trodden route—traversed by Bartholdi during his shorter grand tour a few years later—Hunt and his companions traveled up the Nile to Cairo. From Egypt, Hunt journeyed to Gaza, explored Palestine on horseback, and was baptized in the Jordan River. He visited Beirut and then traveled in a steamer to Rhodes, where he admired the capital city with its towers and minarets. He continued along the coast of modern-day Turkey and on to Greece.

This year-long exposure to antiquities and the countries of their origin was complemented by regular discussion of the ancient world among his travel companions and with other travelers they met. Nearing the end of the trip Hunt acquired a small souvenir from the grounds of the Acropolis that connected him with antiquity. While sketching the ruins, a small sparkle had caught his eye. Gathering a piece of metalwork in his handkerchief, he asked archeologists about his find and discovered it was a piece of inlaid gold repoussé from the colossal ivory-and-gold-embellished statue that once stood inside the Parthenon. This jeweled figure had been one of the several depictions of Athena at the Acropolis built by the revered fifth century B.C. sculptor Phidias. It is believed that the gold was subsequently removed, and the statue, having suffered from neglect and possibly also earthquakes, was eventually lost.

Returning to France at the end of his grand tour, Hunt extended his exploration, this time accompanied by his mother and sister, with the study of Roman ruins in the south of France and a visit to Rome. The Maison Carrée at Nimes offered a fine example of ancient Roman temple construction, as it remained in good condition and was relatively accessible. With the renewal of interest in classical architecture the temple had drawn many disciples in the eighteenth and nineteenth centuries, among them Thomas Jefferson, who based his ideas for the Virginia State Capitol Building on its design.

Following this period of adventure, Hunt entered Lefuel's office in 1854, now as a practicing architect. Lefuel had recently been appointed Architect for the Louvre by Napoleon III for the purpose of completing the wings connecting the Louvre and the Tuileries Palace, and he invited his former student to work on this important project. Hunt served as an inspector for the construction of one of the new pavilions, preparing drawings and learning about practical construction. (In May 1871 the Tuileries Palace fell victim to the destruction that engulfed the last weeks of the Paris Commune.) Despite the valuable experience the project offered it did not hold his attention for long, and by late 1855, after twelve years abroad, Hunt was ready to return home. He felt confident in the training he had received and expected that his contacts in the United States would assist him as he started his career. During his stay in Rome he had also met with the sculptor Thomas Crawford, who was working on designs for the decoration of the U.S. Capitol expansion. Crawford's work may have suggested to Hunt a possible transition from Paris.

Soon after his return to the United States in 1855, Hunt obtained employment with the Architect for the Capitol, Thomas Ustick Walter. He remained in Washington, D.C., however, for only a few months. He was eager to establish his own firm in New York and even considered opening a school of art and architecture with his brother William. There were no architecture schools in the United States at the time and no professional organizations to bring architects together. Settling in New York at the age of twenty-eight, Hunt became involved in efforts to elevate the architecture profession. He was one of the founding members of the American Institute of Architects (AIA) in 1857. The AIA held its first annual dinner the following year on Washington's birthday, February 22, a day Hunt always commemorated in some fashion. Over the next few years, his thoughts of opening a school of architecture led him to model his office on the type of instructive studio he had been trained in, the atelier. Hunt's studio would be the first of its kind in the United States. Among his students were Henry Van Brunt, Frank Furness, Charles D. Gambrill, George Brown Post, and William R. Ware. Appreciative of this experience of architectural instruction, Ware subsequently established and directed the first school of architecture in the United States, at the Massachusetts Institute of Technology, which opened in 1868.

It was rumored that Hunt shipped several thousand architecture books from France on his return. Certainly no one in America had a library to rival his, nor his formal schooling; and as respect for Hunt grew, he earned a reputation as the learned "dean of the profession." Hunt respected the standards established by the profession's ancient Roman and Greek ancestors and advocated learning, and employing, fundamental architectural principles to achieve design excellence. In his view, the logical clarity and proportions of the classical tradition endowed architecture with the harmony of parts "so essential to good work."

Hunt's arrival in the United States in late 1855 coincided with the heightening of sectional conflict that preceded the secession of southern states and the outbreak of civil war in April 1861. Throughout these years the issue of slavery dominated American political discussion, secession by southern states was threatened (as it had been for decades), and differing points of view seemed more and more irreconcilable. Americans argued over whether the institution of slavery should be abolished completely, tolerated in the states where it already existed, allowed to expand into new territories, or protected by the federal government in all territories and even all states.

It is likely that Hunt read the newspapers and that he took some interest in politics, if only because his father had been a representative of Vermont in the U.S. Congress. Although Hunt's efforts were focused on establishing his architecture practice, he socialized with people in New York who were deeply concerned about the future of the Union and the abolition of slavery. One such acquaintance was William Cullen Bryant, a poet and an outspoken advocate of emancipation. Bryant edited and owned the *Evening Post,* together with John Bigelow, who was appointed a consul-general to France in 1861.

If Hunt did not hear about John Brown, one of the participants in the contest taking place in Kansas, in 1856, he undoubtedly learned of Brown in 1859. John Brown had moved to Kansas with the intention of supporting the territory's establishment as a free state. The loss of a son to the violence in the territory had only strengthened his resolve to oppose slavery and deepened his dislike of "the do-nothing policy of the abolitionists." With the goal of arming slaves so as to give them the opportunity to defend themselves and seize their freedom, Brown organized a raid on the federal arsenal at Harpers Ferry in Virginia. During the planning, one of Brown's coconspirators had discovered that a local resident, a great-grandnephew of George Washington, owned a dress sword and a pistol that belonged to Washington. The pistol was a gift to Washington from Lafayette, from the period of the American War for Independence; the sword was said to be a gift from either Lafayette or Frederick the Great. Lafayette had strongly favored emancipation and Washington had also wished "to see a plan adopted for the abolition" of slavery. It would be appropriate to free slaves in the presence of these relics of the heroes who had fought for liberty.

On October 16, 1859, Brown's group of twenty-two men took possession of the armory at Harpers Ferry, holding a watchman and a few nearby residents prisoner. The men did not attempt to rob the paymaster's office or take other funds, news reports noted; however they demanded Washington's sword and pistol from Washington's great-grandnephew. Brown wore the sword and a companion carried the pistol. Notwithstanding the meaningful influence of these relics, Brown and his group were defeated in less than two days' time. Brown, one of the few survivors, was quickly tried in Virginia and on October 31, 1859, was convicted of "treason, advising and conspiring with slaves and others to rebel, and for murder in the first degree." In the South, Brown's plan for the rebellion of slaves supported the argument of secessionists, who feared that northerners would settle for no less than changing their way of life. In the North, politicians strenuously disassociated themselves from Brown, a "madman" who had taken the law into his own hands.

Brown complained that he had only fired in response to violent attack and that his son had been killed "whilst bearing a flag of truce." Brown had also treated his prisoners with "consideration and kindness." But while Brown's altruistic ambition to release slaves in the "cause of human freedom" had not softened the jury's verdict, his explanations and behavior during the trial fostered a feeling of sympathy in likeminded observers. In the six and a half weeks between his arrest and execution, Brown became for many a martyr and a sign of the rapidly approaching "settlement of that question" of slavery. In Massachusetts, Henry Wadsworth Longfellow wrote in his diary, "they are leading old John Brown to execution in Virginia, for attempting to rescue slaves! This is sowing the wind to reap the whirlwind, which will come soon." Henry David Thoreau presented a lecture on Brown in Concord and Boston, "to plead his cause," in the belief that "when you plant, or bury, a hero in his field, a crop of heroes is sure to spring up." In Guernsey, where Victor Hugo lived in exile during Napoleon

III's reign, Hugo wrote: "I kneel with tears before the grand starred flag of the New World, and I implore . . . this illustrious American republic . . . to save John Brown . . . and not permit . . . the first fratricide to be surpassed."

In Brooklyn, on the Sunday preceding Brown's conviction, the Reverend Henry Ward Beecher devoted his sermon to Brown, the Kansas-Nebraska Act, and the strangely disproportionate response to Brown's raid. Suppose this small group of men had seized the armory at Springfield, Massachusetts, he observed. "Do you suppose that the Government would be alarmed, and that the President would have to deliberate with the Secretary of War" and that the militia of neighboring states and federal troops would have to be called out? "Not at all," he concluded. "There is a dread hanging over the Southern States."

Abraham Lincoln was invited to speak at Beecher's Plymouth Church in Brooklyn as part of a lecture series in 1859–60. At the last moment the venue was changed and he spoke instead at the Cooper Institute in New York. This speech, which a Lincoln scholar refers to as "the speech that made Abraham Lincoln president," was enthusiastically reported, in particular by the *Evening Post,* printed in full by four of the largest newspapers in the New York area, and reprinted by other papers around the country. William Cullen Bryant, who introduced Lincoln that evening, reminded the audience that Lincoln had proven himself "the great champion" of freedom during his many debates with Douglas in 1858. Lincoln's speech to the large "assemblage of the intellect and mental culture" of New York predictably addressed the pressing issues of the period: the future of slavery, the intentions of the framers of the Constitution, and the threat of secession. He had devoted considerable effort to researching the views and voting records of the signers of the Constitution and could confidently report that the majority of the framers considered there to be nothing in the Constitution forbidding Congress from restricting the spread of slavery to the territories. Lincoln then concluded by pointing to the crucial moral issue, "the precise fact upon which depends the whole controversy." Proponents of slavery believe that "slavery is morally right, and socially elevating." We, to the contrary, believe that slavery is wrong. Let us not "be slandered from our duty . . . nor frightened from it. . . . Let us have faith that right makes might, and . . . dare to do our duty as we understand it." Enthusiasm about Lincoln and his speech spread rapidly and before he was able to board a train to return home to Illinois, he was pressed into speaking in eleven New England cities and towns in the next eleven days.

In November of that year Lincoln won the election for president of the United States. By his inauguration in March 1861 seven states had seceded from the Union. A standoff at Fort Sumter in South Carolina provoked a confrontation between the state and the government of the United States and on April 15, 1861, Lincoln announced a state of insurrection, marking the beginning of the Civil War. Hunt, who supported the preservation of the Union, apparently approached fellow members of a social club to which he belonged, the Century Association, with the idea of organizing a regiment. As a youth—before the move of his family took him to Europe for twelve years—Hunt had considered a military career, and he might have felt excited about the possibility of joining the war effort; also, several friends and acquaintances had enlisted. He soon put aside the idea of enlisting, however, and settled for aiming to raise a flag, the biggest in New York, on the club building. His doctor had dissuaded him from personal involvement in the war and his wife, Catherine, undoubtedly opposed the prospect of his departure as well. Having met in Newport the previous year, Richard and Catherine Hunt had married only two weeks before the start of the war, and they had probably already made plans for their eighteen-month sojourn in Europe. At the end of April 1861, just as the war began, the newlyweds boarded a steamship for France.

William L. Dayton, the new U.S. minister to France, happened to be traveling on the same ship. Hunt and Dayton became friendly and later met with each other on occasion in Paris. It may be that Dayton introduced Hunt to Édouard Laboulaye. Laboulaye was attracting broad attention in the early 1860s, and, according to Catherine Hunt, Hunt became one of Laboulaye's many admirers. Laboulaye's political and humanitarian concerns may also have impressed Hunt and his wife.

After their return to the United States in November 1862, the Hunts spent a large part of their time in Newport and thus remained removed from much of the tension surrounding the Civil War, including the draft riots in New York. Nevertheless, Hunt found ways to contribute to the war effort and the Union cause.

In 1863 he helped establish the Union League Club in New York, and in 1864 he and Catherine volunteered to assist the U.S. Sanitary Commission with an extensive fundraising fair. When the assassination of the president in April 1865 stunned the nation and the Union League Club hurriedly made plans for a funeral service in New York, Hunt assumed a central role. With his supervision, the club decorated Union Square and erected a temporary monument to Lincoln. Included in the service was the reading of Bryant's verse "The Death of Lincoln," written for the occasion. Bryant acknowledged Lincoln's moderate political leaning and personal inclinations— "slow to smite and swift to spare"—which had been at times the source of frustration to him and others. But Bryant sorrowfully praised this "gentle and merciful and just" man who had attained his goals for the nation in his own way; "whose proudest monument shall be," Bryant said of Lincoln, "the broken fetters of the slave."

The preparations for the ceremony at Union Square commenced Hunt's association with patriotic, public monuments. Over the next two decades Hunt collaborated with sculptors on a series of monuments; primary among these artists was fellow Union League Club member John Quincy Adams Ward. Hunt worked especially well with Ward and joined him on at least thirteen projects. For Central Park they designed the Seventh Regiment Memorial, honoring the fifty-eight men from the regiment who died in the Civil War, and the Pilgrim monument, commissioned by the New England Society. For Newport, they designed a monument honoring the naval hero Commodore Matthew Calbraith Perry.

In 1875 centennial celebrations of events of the American Revolution began. Two of the commissions Hunt and Ward received in this period were for monuments that paid tribute to the participation of France in the War for Independence. One was a statue of Lafayette, always central to people's memories of the war. The statue was a gift to the University of Vermont, in memory of Lafayette's visit in 1824 during his thirteen-month tour of the country, when he laid the cornerstone to mark the rebuilding of the university after a fire. The other was for a monument to the alliance between the American and French forces and their victory at Yorktown in 1781. This commission was unusual in that it was from the United States Congress and concerned a significant national victory made possible by the participation of French forces.

The project had actually been authorized a century before, by the Continental Congress. Immediately following the victory at Yorktown in October 1781, the Continental Congress had passed a resolution calling for the erection of a "marble column, adorned with emblems of the alliance." Nearly one hundred years later, in the late 1870s, Congress decided to proceed. In 1881, as part of the Yorktown centennial celebrations, the cornerstone for the Yorktown Monument was laid. Hunt's former student Henry Van Brunt worked with him and Ward on the classical design, which included thirteen maidens around the base of the tall column and a marble liberty figure at its top. The approximately 150-foot-tall (46 m) monument, which, with the exception of these marble figures, was predominantly an architectural design, was considered an important project in the architecture profession.

For the centennial of Evacuation Day, the day in 1783 when the British departed Manhattan Island and Washington entered in triumph, Hunt and Ward designed another monument of particular notice. This one, a statue of George Washington, honored the commander-in-chief and the nation's first president at a site that itself held special significance. On this spot, at the corner of Wall Street and Nassau, had stood a building from which the Declaration of Independence was read to the people of New York in 1776. In the late 1780s, the building was remodeled by Pierre Charles L'Enfant to serve as Federal Hall, the seat of the newly created government; and on its second-story front porch George Washington took the oath of office as the nation's first president in 1789. "The very air about this hallowed spot is the air of American patriotism," George William Curtis, the orator for the unveiling opined. "To breath it, charged with such memories, is to be inspired with the loftiest human purpose, to be strengthened for the noblest endeavor." After the federal government relocated in 1790, first to Philadelphia and then to Washington, D.C., the building was returned to its former use, and in the early nineteenth century the structure was replaced twice by new construction.

At the time of the design of Ward and Hunt's statue, the "hallowed spot" was occupied by the broad steps leading into the New York Subtreasury Building, and a vote of Congress was required to place the statue in this location. Ward and Hunt were among the invited guests at the unveiling ceremony, joined by New York governor Stephen Grover Cleveland and U.S. president Chester A.

Arthur. Arthur accepted the statue from the New York Chamber of Commerce, which had been its sponsor, on behalf of the federal government. For Hunt and others who were familiar with this site, the original Federal Hall, while no longer standing in the 1880s, held an important place in the history of the birth of the nation.

When the time came to select an architect experienced with public monuments to design the pedestal for the Statue of Liberty, a patriotic statue designed in France and inspired by antiquity, Hunt would clearly be an ideal choice. But in 1871, when Hunt and Bartholdi met for the first time, they little anticipated their future association. Bartholdi was still formulating his ideas for a statue, and he could not be certain that it would even materialize. He was focused on "getting [his] bearings among the Americans" and determining "just what to do" to gain support for the concept. Following their initial meeting at a social event in 1871, therefore, Bartholdi and Hunt probably had no contact with each other until after Hunt began his work on the pedestal a decade later.

After two months of traveling between Washington, D.C., and Boston and meeting with people, Bartholdi took the opportunity to try out the recently completed cross-country rail connection. Traveling primarily by train and occasionally by stagecoach, he headed west. It was a long, tiring trip and the conditions of the places he visited were sometimes quite uncomfortable. But the sights he saw and the exposure to America he gained were, he felt, well worth the effort. He started with a journey north to Niagara Falls, which were as thrilling as he had imagined. Next he headed to Chicago, a city that appeared "more American than all the others—streets full of life, straight, wide, full of telegraph poles and wires, and manure." He visited the Chicago Historical Society and viewed an original signed copy of the Emancipation Proclamation. Lincoln had donated this signed copy for the auction held by the Sanitary Commission during one of its fundraising fairs in Chicago, but in October 1871, only two months after Bartholdi's visit, the document was lost in the Great Chicago Fire.

As Bartholdi entered the prairie west of Chicago, the scale and nature of America impressed him tremendously. He began to paint the scenes he saw and describe them in detail. Until this point his journal had served as a travel log, in which he noted the names of places and people together with little, if any, commentary. Now, his journal entries and letters suddenly filled with description, lyrical on occasion. From the train Bartholdi viewed prairie dogs, antelope, wolves, and buffalo, as many as a thousand in one herd, he estimated. He saw fires in the distance "where Indians are encamped" and an Indian woman carrying a child on her back. "Here," he wrote, James Fenimore Cooper's "novels and all other such tales come alive." As the train approached California, Bartholdi became painfully aware of the destruction caused by gold mining, likening it to that of a battlefield. California's fertile land and "magnificent fruits" presented an equally dramatic scene. In two paintings of California he depicted these contrasting aspects of the west, referring to the miners' "furious search for gold" as Old California and the farmers' "enormously productive" cultivation of the land as New California.

In addition to its fertile land, Bartholdi admired California's famed redwood trees. "These colossi are superb. . . . I have seen nearly a hundred," he recorded in his journal. He also made a sketch of the redwood forest for Laboulaye. The fact that he described the trees in this manner and wrote to Laboulaye about them suggests that Bartholdi had not only decided on a colossal scale for his liberty figure by this time but was also trying to convince Laboulaye that this scale was appropriate for America.

Bartholdi made a few stops along the way on his return to the East Coast, notably in St. Louis. In addition to meeting people through contacts in the east and by way of letters of introduction, he seems to have befriended people easily. On the train he met the superintendent of schools and training in St. Louis and was invited to his office on their arrival in the city. "When you observe the attention given here to training and education," Bartholdi afterwards emphasized to his mother, "you understand the great achievements of Americans. . . . It is one of the finest things about America —and the noblest." Bartholdi likely recognized that he was repeating an observation that other Europeans, in particular Laboulaye, had made about the United States.

Bartholdi toured St. Louis and found a park named for Lafayette. He also met with one of the state senators, Carl Schurz, a naturalized citizen of German birth. Schurz had been a leader in the failed revolution of 1848 in Germany and had been compelled to flee the country. He stayed first in France and then, when the character of the Second French Republic changed as Napoleon III prepared to declare the Second Empire, emigrated to the United

States. Schurz remained a reformer throughout his life. He was an outspoken critic of slavery, of nativist laws (having prejudicial effect on foreign-born Americans), and of government corruption. Schurz campaigned for Lincoln in 1858, 1860, and 1864, represented the United States as minister to Spain in 1861, and served in the army during the Civil War. In 1867 he became an editor and co-owner of a St. Louis newspaper, the *Westliche Post,* and in 1869 he was elected to the U.S. Senate. When Bartholdi met Schurz in 1871, Schurz was in open conflict with President Grant, in part because of his efforts at civil service reform. The next year, while arguing in the U.S. Senate for the investigation of alleged corruption in government offices, Schurz's patriotism was called into question, drawing forth his memorable reply: "'My country, right or wrong.' . . . I say so too. . . . If right, to be kept right; and if wrong, to be set right."

Bartholdi may have been sent to call on Schurz by Sumner, who was a close colleague in the U.S. Senate, or by Forney and other members of the Union League of Philadelphia. Schurz was likely to support Bartholdi's suggestion of a monument to liberty. "Ideals are like stars," Schurz had told an audience in 1859 while in Boston for the celebration of Jefferson's birthday. "You choose them as your guides, and following them you will reach your destiny." Talking with Bartholdi in 1871 about a monument to liberty, Schurz encouraged Bartholdi to pursue the idea. He may also have told Joseph Pulitzer, who was employed as a reporter at the *Westliche Post,* about Bartholdi and his plan. In 1883, Schurz and Pulitzer both offered their support for the liberty monument by serving on the executive committee that organized the Pedestal Fund Art Exhibition, a large fundraising event. Two years later, Pulitzer led his own, exceptionally successful, fundraising campaign.

Bartholdi arrived back in New York by the middle of September and spent the next three weeks visiting Philadelphia, Washington, D.C., and Newport one last time before his departure for France. He felt pleased with his visit to America. He was glad to have seen the "vast country" and had learned a great deal about the American character. At the same time, though his hosts were supportive, he had experienced considerable frustration. Many of the people he met with showed only slight, if any, interest in a statue. The impression he formed shortly after his arrival—that the idea for a statue would not "take root immediately"—had been confirmed during his visit. Executing this project, he predicted in a letter to his mother, "is sure to be a long and laborious process." Bartholdi felt confident, however, about pursuing the endeavor, and he was motivated by a sense that this work of sculpture might achieve a depth of meaning and importance to make the effort worthwhile. He would have given up on the project several times during his exploratory visit to the United States, he admitted, if it were not for this conviction. This liberty figure, he eagerly wrote to Laboulaye, "may end up not just a monument but a work of greater moral value."

6

WASHINGTON, D.C., AS A NATIONAL SYMBOL

Many reasons explained the conflicting responses Bartholdi received to his proposal for a liberty statue. Although gift exchange was part of the friendship between the people of France and the United States, demonstrating and strengthening the ties between the sister republics, the suggestion of building a large monument in collaboration with the French made some people uncomfortable. Would this create an obligation on the part of the United States, and would it be costly to erect and maintain? The country was still recovering from the Civil War and the government already had ample obligations. During his visits to Washington, D.C., Bartholdi had heard about the government's work to establish national cemeteries for the fallen soldiers. He also learned about a program, proposed by Lincoln's secretary of war Edwin M. Stanton, to provide wooden legs and arms for wounded soldiers. His notes do not make mention of war memorials; but in the early 1870s a fervor for monuments to national heroes was building momentum. The government had accepted a role in their construction, often providing federal property for sites and funding for pedestals. Development projects in the capital were another priority. With the Capitol Building expansion complete in 1865, the government had begun work on new federal buildings and the improvement of street conditions. For decades, roads of mud and an increasingly smelly canal had contradicted the intentions of the early planners who hoped this federal city would represent the nation's ideals. Three years of steady construction, starting in 1871, included the placement of water and sewer lines below streets and the encasement of the open canal in a trunk sewer. Streets were graded, paved, or graveled; sidewalks were built, and curbs installed.

The enforcement of laws initiated during Reconstruction incurred another expense for the federal government. By 1868 it had become clear that free elections were not occurring in many places in the South; office holders had been assassinated and voters intimidated. The violence and interference with elections, suggested Senator James Warren Nye of Nevada, was reminiscent of former "operations in Kansas"—though on a larger scale. In 1866 and 1869 Congress passed the Fourteenth and Fifteenth Amendments to the Constitution (ratified in 1868 and 1870, respectively). The Fourteenth Amendment established citizenship for all persons born or naturalized in the United States and aimed to assure all Americans of "equal protection of the laws" and to encourage universal male suffrage. The Fifteenth Amendment prohibited the denial of a citizen's right to vote on account of race or "previous condition of servitude."

As resistance to Reconstruction strengthened, however, instances of violence and intimidation escalated, in spite of the intentions of Congress. Of particular concern was the emergence of the Ku Klux Klan, which had gained considerable influence since the organization's founding in 1866. State governments and local police were either unable or unwilling to provide protection for targeted individuals and groups. A majority in the U.S. Congress became convinced that the federal government would need to assume a central role in law enforcement in the states. In 1870 and 1871, Congress passed three enforcement acts. The third, referred to as the Ku Klux Klan Act, provided for federal intervention when two or more persons conspired to prevent "by force, intimidation, or threat" any person from holding office and discharging the duties thereof, testifying in court, serving on juries, voting, and, generally, enjoying equal protection of the laws. The presence of federal marshals and courts impeded the activities of the Ku Klux Klan; nevertheless, the federal program was severely hampered by its inability to adequately protect witnesses, by lack of funds and of courts, and by local authorities that failed to cooperate.

"We are re-laying the very corner-stone of our temple of liberty," Willard Warner of Alabama, one of the U.S. senators to vote for the Fifteenth Amendment, had said at the time. "Enlightened by the experience of eighty years" since the drafting of the Constitution, let us "follow our principles to their logical conclusion and found this nation on the rock of universal equal human rights, thus settling forever the questions which, never settled aright, have risen again and again to disturb, and finally to desolate our beautiful land." Two years later, when Bartholdi visited the United States in 1871, the process of reconstructing the temple of liberty was proving to be extremely complex.

At the same time that the nation was struggling with issues of state governance and civil rights, it was also adjusting to rapid industrialization coupled with an expanding population. Large cites were growing and smaller communities were settling the frontier. Territorial expansion placed economic and social strains on the country. As homesteaders pressed westward, inevitably claiming (together with miners and other adventurers) land from beleaguered Indian tribes, the violence of confrontations intensified. Americans' thoughts revolved around securing their livelihood and safety. They were not thinking about a statue in New York Harbor.

Nor was a lackluster response unique to Bartholdi's proposal. Even the Centennial Exhibition, planned to celebrate both the nation's progress and its one hundredth anniversary of independence, initially suffered from want of enthusiasm. In early 1871 Congress passed an act that provided for the exhibition but specifically withheld funds. "The government had refused aid," Daniel J. Morell, chairman of the Centennial's executive committee, recalled five years later. "Local jealousies were powerful. The newspapers of the country, with few exceptions, were lukewarm or openly hostile, and the mass of the people could not be interested in a thing which some feared for in the future. During the first year of the life of the [Centennial] Commission, doubt everywhere prevailed." The Commission proceeded in its work, all the same, and organized a highly successful world's fair. But in June 1871 the national frame of mind, Bartholdi concluded, was "hardly open to things of the imagination."

At first Bartholdi was "pained" by the muted and noncommittal responses to his idea. But a sufficient number of people had reacted with enthusiasm, and this convinced him not to give up on the project. What became clear to him, however, was that France would have to take the initiative. Skepticism of a mere proposal was a natural response, he concluded, one that showed a preference for tangible realities. Americans could not be expected to prepare for a monument that had not yet been constructed or even funded in France.

Bartholdi gained important insight into the spirit and practical nature of America during his summer-long visit. On the one hand, he was astonished by the emotion he witnessed one Sunday in an African American church in Philadelphia. "It commanded respect," he wrote in a letter to his mother, "this demonstration by people, slaves only yesterday, who turned their minds to the ideal, who have faith, and who interest themselves so violently in moral questions." The parables recalled in the sermon, he added, were ones they heard in their local church in Colmar. On the other hand, he realized that abstract or philosophical notions of universal rights did not hold the attention of the people with whom he talked about a statue. Discussing his ideas with members of the French community in New York Bartholdi realized that his statue needed a clearer definition. They suggested that the monument be associated with the centennial of independence that was approaching in 1876. A statue described in terms of American independence, Bartholdi found, appealed to people's imaginations. His design would similarly need to articulate its connection with America's history and qualities.

Bartholdi's notes do not indicate whether he attempted to identify appropriate design features for the statue while he was in America. He had formulated a preliminary design concept for an allegorical figure already the year before and, according to La Farge's son, Bartholdi worked on his "first plans" for the statue in La Farge's studio in Newport. The result of this work was likely a clay model that Bartholdi left in New York in 1871 when he returned to France. As he toured cities in the United States and met with people over the summer, he looked at works of art and undoubtedly made a mental record of how Americans chose to represent themselves and their country. The artwork he saw must have put him at ease, while challenging him to grasp the American character. The architecture and statuary in the United States derived from the same Greco-Roman models and design principles he was familiar with in France. Yet, their interpretation was particularly American.

In Washington, D.C., expressions of liberty, enlightenment, and American achievement were readily apparent, in the works of art and the design of the city itself. Established for the purpose of creating a federal city, the Territory of Columbia and its development symbolize the nation in a special way. President Lincoln referred to this symbolic link when he ordered work on the Capitol to continue during the Civil War. A major expansion project had commenced in the 1850s to accommodate the growth of the Union. With the start of the war, construction activity was halted, in part because the building's corridors and the Rotunda were filled with hospital beds for wounded soldiers. Notwithstanding the difficulties involved and the expenditure associated with the work, Lincoln decided that the expansion project should continue and thus dispel any sense of uncertainty regarding the future of the *United* States. "If people see the Capitol going on," Lincoln explained, "it is a sign we intend the Union shall go on." With the completion of a spectacular 287-foot-high (88.3 m) outer dome, the enlarged Capitol became a primary symbol of national identity.

Considerable contemplation and effort in the years following independence went into the formation of the federal city. The names and designs selected for the Capitol (first referred to as the Congress House), the city, and the territory itself recalled treasured historical images. The name City of Washington memorializes the proud image of the first general and commander-in-chief, and the city's street layout is replete with historical meaning. The very geography of Washington, D.C., is infused with democratic republican ideals.

Pierre Charles L'Enfant, the initial designer of the city, had been among the volunteers from France drawn to the revolutionary cause. Arriving in America in 1777 at the age of twenty-three, L'Enfant's contribution to the war effort had quickly been recognized by Washington and the Continental Congress. He was commissioned captain of engineers in February 1778 and over the course of the war rose to the rank of major of the engineer corps. At the same time, L'Enfant became known for his portraits—he at least once drew General Washington—and assisted Baron von Steuben with illustrations for his *Regulations, Order, and Discipline for the Troops of the United States* (1779). In the years following the war, L'Enfant made his home in America and earned a reputation for architectural design. When the drafting of the Constitution in 1787 established a form of government with two houses of congress and a president, L'Enfant was selected to remodel New York's city hall to house the national government in its first year. The second-story porch, which he added between the two projecting ends of the building, may have been designed with Washington's inauguration in mind, for it was here that the first president took the oath of office in 1789. Federal Hall, as the remodeled building was named, apparently fulfilled its purpose because when plans progressed for the making of a completely new federal city, Washington hired L'Enfant for the project. Unfortunately, L'Enfant's enthusiasm and determination to create a plan worthy of the capital's important place in history led him to neglect the delicate negotiations necessary. He became entangled in disagreements with influential local residents as well as the commissioners assigned to oversee the project. He may also have offended Secretary of State Thomas Jefferson with his rejection of a grid pattern, initially favored by Jefferson, for the city. Such a tiresome plan, L'Enfant wrote to the first president, lacked "a sense of the really grand and truly beautiful."

Despite his difficulties and consequent shortened commission, L'Enfant set the tone for the city, blending a system of diagonal avenues and broad streets responsive to topography with a grid of smaller streets. "The immense lay-out of very wide avenues," Bartholdi noted on touring the city in 1871, reminded him of Versailles. L'Enfant also linked the two focal points for the city, the Congress House and the President's House, with Pennsylvania Avenue, in honor of the state where the Union's first congresses met. This revolutionary war veteran then named the rest of the avenues for other states, arranging them according to their geographical location. In addition, he adjusted the street lengths and sizes to reflect both the size of the states and their relative contribution to securing national independence and the establishment of a new system of government.

L'Enfant's plan designated large intersections for public squares and parks. These spaces have been developed slowly over the years and honor significant people and events in the nation's history. President's Square bordering the White House grounds was the setting of a grand reception for Lafayette when he visited in 1824, at

George Washington's inauguration on the porch of Federal Hall in New York. In the nation's first inaugural address, Washington spoke of the "sacred fire of liberty . . . entrusted to the hands of the American people." (*The Papers of George Washington*, Presidential Series, vol. 2, ed. Dorothy Twohig [Charlottesville, 1987], 175.) Engraving by Amos Doolittle, after Peter Lacour, 1790. I. N. Phelps Stokes Collection, Miriam and Ira D. Wallach Division of Art, Prints and Photographs, The New York Public Library, Astor, Lenox and Tilden Foundations.

which time it was renamed Lafayette Park. In 1853 the first statue in Lafayette Park, a memorial to Andrew Jackson, was inscribed with words from a toast Jackson made on Thomas Jefferson's birthday in 1830, in response to threats of secession by southern states: "The Federal Union, It Must Be Preserved." A statue of Lafayette in the park includes a large pedestal depicting Rochambeau along with three other French compatriots; Rochambeau has his own statue as well. Two more Revolutionary War monuments were installed in the park in 1910: one of Baron von Steuben, who made his mark by bringing organization and discipline to a notably disorderly force of untrained soldiers; and Thaddeus Kosciuszko, a Polish volunteer who was recruited while in Paris and served the Continental Army in the capacity of civil engineer.

Although the act of Congress that designated funds for the Congress House and the President's House authorized George Washington, as the nation's first president, to determine the layout for the new city and the design for the two focal buildings, Washington left the details of the project to his secretary of state, Thomas Jefferson. Jefferson immersed himself in planning the city, getting involved in the intricacies of the budget, the planting of trees along Pennsylvania Avenue, and the design of the buildings, in particular, the Congress House. Seeking to substantiate and illustrate the founders' grand visions for the nation through historical association, Jefferson borrowed from the Roman Republic's political center to name the congress building the Capitol. By selecting architectural models of antiquity having "the approbation of thousands of years," Jefferson wrote to L'Enfant, they could secure a historical footing for the new republic. While Jefferson, along with many Americans, was pleased to blaze a new trail, he was not tempted to throw off the past but rather looked to it as a guide to the future. Historical precedent was important to the fledgling republic, not only for legitimizing a political organization unique among empires and kingdoms, but also for enlightening its people as they determined how to put into practice this new mode of government.

Veneration of the classical world was deeply ingrained in the consciousness of Europeans and Americans in the eighteenth century and into the nineteenth century. Students learned Latin, and to a lesser extent Greek, absorbed ancient legends, knew Roman maxims, studied Livy's *Early History of Rome,* and were well versed in Virgil, Cicero, and Horace. "For every eventuality I had a Greek proverb, a classical allusion or a line from Virgil," Victor Hugo recalled about his youth in the early nineteenth century. The classical writings held the imagination with charming tales of Wisdom and Virtue in conflict with, in the words of John Adams, Vice and Folly "painted in all their Deformity and Horror." The stories told in classical writings seemed remarkably contemporary to many people and their lessons offered an important form of moral education, fostering knowledge and wisdom. From Cicero the revolutionary generation absorbed ideas about natural law and natural rights: "Natural law," the Roman statesman and philosopher asserted, "is stamped in invisible characters upon our very frame." The Roman founding myth told by Livy provided its own parallels to the founding fathers and the New World's asylum for liberty. According to Livy, Romulus, who together with his brother Remus founded Rome, decided to increase the population of the city by establishing a sanctuary for refugees "wanting nothing but a fresh start" on the slopes of the Capitoline Hill. Seeking to establish a governing body and political stability, Romulus appointed a senate of one hundred "Fathers."

As visitors flocked to Rome the images they brought with them, culled from years of schooling in classical literature, came to life. Stepping through the halls of the Senatorial Palace at the Capitol or strolling among ancient ruins that mingled in the life of the city, they were moved by an appreciation for this past civilization. The stones themselves seemed to carry moral weight, and, as one traveler enthused, the "greatness of antiquity overshadows the pettiness of the present." Visiting for the first time in 1886, Emma Lazarus was similarly moved. She felt herself absorbing the spirit of the classical world, she told friends in her letters home, as she read the classics in Rome.

Archeological discoveries in the eighteenth and nineteenth centuries encouraged interest in ancient art, culture, and political institutions. One astonishing find was the Roman city of Pompeii, along with that of Herculaneum, which had been completely buried by the eruption of Mt. Vesuvius in A.D. 79. Stories of the two cities and their burial had been passed down through the centuries, but it was not until 1763 that their locations were confirmed. As excavation of these sites progressed entire buildings were revealed. The extent to which the ancient world had been perfectly preserved under the debris of the volcano was bewildering. Even as the many descriptions of Pompeii became familiar in the nineteenth century, the richness of the findings, ranging from food on kitchen tables to entire streets, amphitheatres, and temples, continued to fascinate visitors. It is remarkably moving to find oneself "so close to Antiquity," Bartholdi remarked during his visit to Pompeii. The ancient world appeared to come to life.

When Napoleon Bonaparte led French troops into Egypt in 1798, he took with him a traveling academy of scientists, artists, architects, engineers, and poets. Although some of the artifacts they gathered were lost on account of the war between the European powers, many made their way to France or to Britain. The success of larger-scale archeological expeditions later in the nineteenth century infused these artifacts with life, prompting casual attention to blossom into widespread fascination. By the 1850s organizations and individuals eagerly joined in the search for ruins. Expectations were high as wondrous legends of sculpture and jewels were authenticated. Along with ancient ruins, people sought to uncover fine artwork and precious stones. Dashiell Hammett's tale of the Maltese falcon depicts the anticipation with which Europeans entered this exotic past. The ambition to locate the "glorious golden falcon encrusted from head to foot with the finest jewels," crafted by the Knights of Malta in the sixteenth century, obsessed the lives of several of Hammett's characters.

Artists' imaginations were inflamed by the new archeological finds as well. Greek and Roman texts had recorded some details of the ancient artists and their work; now, as examples of their skill were discovered, admiration for the artists increased. When Lord Elgin brought the famous Elgin marbles (portions of the frieze that decorated the exterior walls of the Parthenon in Athens) to Britain in the early 1800s, the reputation of the Athenian sculptor Phidias soared. People claimed Phidias a man of genius and created a personality for this artist of ancient Greece, recounting spurious tales of his life. Based on literary texts, Phidias was known to have designed the 39-foot-high (12 m) sculpture of Athena inside the Parthenon, along with the extensive sculptural decoration on the exterior. He was also responsible for the statue of Zeus at Olympia, one of the Seven Wonders of the Ancient World.

Visual artists seized on Greek and Roman mythology as one component of this revival. Architects, meanwhile, looked to ex-

amples and instructions presented in books dating back as far as
the first century B.C., namely *The Ten Books of Architecture* (*De
Architectura*). Written during the reign of Augustus by Marcus
Vitruvius Pollio, the books provide a record of Hellenist methods
of construction and rules of proportion. Vitruvius described the
different orders of temple colonnade construction, naming these
orders after the people or places he associated them with. Believ-
ing that architecture could not be understood in isolation, he included generous insight into ancient scientific and philosophical
considerations. Vitruvius's record had practically been forgotten
for over a thousand years, but in the fifteenth century it was re-
discovered and in 1521 it was translated into Italian. Carrying this
as their guide, Italian Renaissance architects studied the ancient
buildings around them and identified a total of five orders from
classical Rome. Each order was represented by a type of column
and capital, together with a supported horizontal element, of certain character and proportions. The appeal of this rejuvenated
classical tradition stemmed from the historical continuity of ancient wisdom that it signified and the aesthetic harmony that it
provided. In the late eighteenth and early nineteenth centuries, observations in Greece complemented lessons from the early Renaissance and strengthened the regard architects had for antiquity.

Architecture, Eugène-Emmanuel Viollet-le-Duc asserted in 1872,
"is the visible sign of the morals of a nation, of its taste, its inclinations." With a similar conviction, the designers of America's federal city set out to express the sovereignty of the people and the
character and principles of American social and political institutions as they constructed buildings of national significance. Captivated by ancient Greece and Rome, the designers of the Capitol
crafted a modern neoclassical style weaving the universal past into
the national past. Employing an eclectic combination of symbols
for decorative paintings and sculpture, artists represented the
many attributes associated with the new nation while recounting
scenes and heroes from American history.

When architect Benjamin Henry Latrobe worked on the Capitol and the President's House from 1803 to 1817, he demonstrated
his mastery of the classical tradition by skillfully incorporating
variations into the classical models. Among his notable inventions
for the Capitol are two designs for column capitals based on the
American crops corn and tobacco. He created these designs for

specific areas where space was not available to adhere to the prescribed proportions of the order previously established for the setting. By designing new botanical motifs, these columns melded in spirit with the classical framework governing the building while deceiving the eye into accepting the imposition of unconventional proportions into the spaces. These "Americanized capitals," wrote George C. Hazelton, who served in Congress from 1877 to 1883, in his history of the Capitol, "might command attention on the score of a 'Columbian order'"—that is, an American order. "Why should not these designs made by Latrobe from the natural products of the country be as stimulating in artistic beauty and suggestion as the acanthus of Greece or the lotus of the Nile?" Bartholdi may have seen these column capitals during his tour, for he incorporated corncobs into the torch balustrade of the Statue of Liberty.

On July 4, 1851, the cornerstone was placed for the major expansion of the Capitol necessitated by the growth of the Union from fourteen states in 1791 to thirty-one in September 1850, when California became a state. As decades passed between the day George Washington laid the building's first cornerstone in 1793 and the completion of the Capital dome in the 1860s, the character of the symbolism shifted slightly. Artwork decorating the building focused less on the struggle for independence and embraced the concept of Manifest Destiny that justified the nation's territorial and cultural expansion across the breadth of the Continent.

The lasting symbolism in Washington, D.C., is most dramatic; but in the nineteenth century patriotic images were by no means limited to government architecture. Whether in formal settings or more rural ones, one rested on seat cushions, viewed inlay in furniture, and drank from engraved glassware, all decorated with representations of national pride, primary among them the figure of liberty. Bartholdi was attentive to the decorative and industrial arts and compiled his observations in a report on the arts in America during his second visit, in 1876, in his role as a member of the international jury for the Centennial Exhibition.

With the exception of portraits of national heroes, figural art was dominated by female imagery. In American as in European art, abstract principles such as liberty, along with geographical and political entities, were primarily personified in female form. During the first two centuries of settlement in America, the western hemisphere was represented by an Indian Princess. America was considered to be the fourth of the continents, and the four continents (America, Europe, Asia, and Africa) were often portrayed together as female figures. The Indian Princess (sometimes referred to as an Indian Queen) typically wore a feathered headdress, skirt, and cape, and remained bare footed as well as bare breasted.

About a decade before the American Revolution, a slightly different image began to identify the thirteen British colonies. Intended to be a relative of Britannia, this personification of the colonies assumed a British likeness yet conveyed the colonists' strengthening desire for freedom from British authority. After independence was attained, a new figure emerged. Columbia (whose name derives from Columbus) represented the new political entity and was frequently accompanied by either the Declaration of Independence or the Constitution. Columbia expressed a moral strength and purpose for the United States and initially had multiple associations—peace, justice, the plenty of America. But it was liberty, the idea specially linked to the founding of the nation, that rose to prominence among these. In the early nineteenth century, this American liberty figure reached back to the ancient Roman republic for inspiration and assumed an eclectic neoclassical style. While oftentimes wearing a feathered headdress, her profile and hairstyle were classical, Roman garments enveloped her figure, and sandals fitted her feet.

By the time the Capitol in Washington, D.C., was built and decorated, the turn toward classical representation was evident. If Bartholdi had any doubt about the appropriateness of a classically conceived liberty figure for the United States, the artwork at the Capitol set his mind at ease. One of the earliest works of sculpture, planned as part of the building's original construction, was a liberty figure presiding over the Hall of Representatives. Placed above and behind the speaker's chair, *Liberty,* by Giuseppe Franzoni, reflected the pride of a nation that cultivated liberty, while reminding the people's representatives of their responsibilities as protectors. The statue held a traditional liberty cap in one hand; in the other a scroll representing the Constitution. The fire that devastated the Hall of Representatives during the War of 1812 claimed the sculpture, but another was made for the space. The design for the new figure clad her in a timeless classical toga and placed a feathered Indian headdress decorated with stars on her head. It was in this chamber that Lafayette addressed a joint session of Congress in

1824 and where Ary Scheffer's portrait of Lafayette was hung. When the Representatives moved to their current chamber in 1857, they left behind *Liberty and the Eagle* for display in what became the National Statuary Hall. They did, however, relocate Scheffer's portrait of Lafayette and the accompanying portrait of Washington to the new House Chamber.

At the time of Bartholdi's visit in 1871, shortly after the completion of the expansion of the Capitol, an extensive art program was underway. Responsible for much of the interior painting was an Italian American artist, Constantino Brumidi. Brumidi had

Liberty and the Eagle, plaster sculpture by Enrico Causici, 1817–19, is located in National Statuary Hall at the Capitol. The scroll in Liberty's right hand represents the Constitution of the United States. Architect of the Capitol.

studied painting and sculpture in Rome and had launched a successful career as a painter. The tumultuous revolutionary period of the late 1840s had interrupted his path, however. According to Brumidi's son, he was serving in the Papal Guards in 1848 and refused to shoot at the revolutionaries; another account describes him as participating in the revolution. In either case, he was arrested and held in prison as turmoil engulfed Rome. When Pope Pius IX returned to power in 1850, the pope intervened on behalf of the painter, whose painting in the Vatican he admired, securing Brumidi's release on the condition that he leave Italy. Brumidi settled in Washington, D.C., in 1854 and obtained a commission at the Capitol for a painting in the specialized method of fresco. A tentative start evolved into an intimate association with the building, and Brumidi continued to decorate the Capitol's interior for the next twenty-six years, until a fall from the scaffolding in the Rotunda led to his death in 1880. Brumidi's paintings include liberty portraits and historical scenes relevant to the nation's founding, combining abundant classical symbolism with specific American motifs. His grand apotheosis of George Washington for the ceiling of the Rotunda portrays the commander-in-chief in military dress with the addition of a lavender blanket across his lap, intended to recall a classical robe. Washington points to a book held by the Goddess of Liberty seated next to him, who wears a soft liberty cap. Thirteen maidens represent the original states and a figure of *Armed Freedom* holds an upraised sword in one hand and a shield in the other as she defeats tyranny.

The dome that encloses the Rotunda is supported by thirty-six columns coinciding with the number of states for the period from 1864 to 1867. Atop the dome stands a 19.5-foot-tall (6 m) cast-bronze liberty statue, titled *Statue of Freedom,* which its sculptor, Thomas Crawford, described as "armed Liberty." Crawford initially considered a simple liberty cap decorated with a circlet of stars for the figure's head. But this was in the period immediately preceding the outbreak of the Civil War and Secretary of War Jefferson Davis, who was in charge of Capitol decoration from 1853 to 1857, disapproved of the liberty cap on account of its potential reference to slavery. Crawford complied with his request to replace the cap with a helmet, embellishing it with an eagle's head and arrangement of feathers. In one hand, he placed a wreath and shield; in the other, a sword. This combination of emblems reflects an attitude common in liberty figures: Freedom (or America) celebrating triumph yet remaining alert to threats to independence and the people's liberties.

In an earlier sculpture by Luigi Persico, adorning the pediment above the central steps of the east front of the Capitol and titled *Genius of America,* the themes of Liberty, Justice, and Hope are personified together. In this sculpture, the figure of Liberty, also referred to as America, wears a liberty cap and rests a shield on a pedestal carved with the date of independence, July 4, 1776; behind her stands a spear. To her right, Justice holds a scroll on which is visible "Constitution, 17 September 1787." To her left stands Hope, ebullient as ever. Charles Bulfinch explained the particular meaning of this composition in 1825 when he was Architect of the Capitol: "The whole [is] intended to convey that while we cultivate *Justice* we may *hope* for *success.*" Bartholdi likely observed the use of the Constitution as a symbol of justice in the Capitol's decoration, along with the date of the Declaration of Independence as a sign of American liberty.

Facing the east front of the Capitol when Bartholdi visited in 1871 was a statue of George Washington by Horatio Greenough. The manner in which Greenough depicted Washington in this statue refers to one of the Seven Wonders of the Ancient World, the statue of Zeus, father of the gods, designed for the temple at Olympia by the sculptor Phidias. Images such as this had been retrieved from antiquity during the eighteenth century; one of the pioneers of neoclassicism, Anton Raphael Mengs, emulated Phidias's Zeus for a portrait of the Apostle Peter, considered a pillar of the church. Greenough's Washington, however, caused considerable distress when it was completed in 1841, due in part to the figure's bared chest. "Washington was too prudent and careful of his health," Philip Hone complained, expressing a common sentiment, "to expose himself thus in a climate so uncertain as ours, to say nothing of the indecency of such an exposure." A more traditional covering such as the Roman toga, "that grand resort for artists in search of the picturesque," would have been more suitable. The reaction of the public to this statue, intended to honor the father of our country, made it clear that Americans' sense of propriety was not to be disregarded. It also reflected a growing preference in nineteenth-century America for statuary that related to contemporary experience, as opposed to representations depicting a purely ancient heritage.

Bartholdi was no more impressed with this portrayal of Washington than were Americans. But he may have been pleased by Greenough's reference to Phidias and the Seven Wonders of the Ancient World. Bartholdi was at this time already envisioning his liberty statue at an unusually large scale. In 1875, when the statue was announced to the public, it was referred to as "a colossal statue" and compared to the Colossus of Rhodes, one of the Seven Wonders. If Bartholdi had not fully formulated the connection between his liberty statue and the wonders of the ancient world prior to June 1871, Greenough's statue of George Washington may have convinced him to think in these terms.

7

BARTHOLDI'S
DESIGN

"Everyone," Philo of Byzantium avowed as early as the third century B.C., "has heard of each of the Seven Wonders of the World." Over the following centuries the list of Seven Wonders occasionally varied (some lists included the Capitol in Rome, among other variations) but during the Renaissance the canon of seven was definitively established.

The oldest of the wonders is the Great Pyramid at Giza. Built around 2560 B.C. to a height of 481 feet (146.6 m), it claimed the title of world's tallest structure for over four thousand years. Egypt was also home to the Pharos at Alexandria, a widely acclaimed lighthouse at the harbor to this city founded by Alexander the Great. From here the trail of Seven Wonders leads to Mesopotamia in modern-day Iraq, where an elaborate system of canals and aqueducts supplied water to the Hanging Gardens of "Babylon"; then to modern-day Turkey, to the Temple of Artemis at Ephesus and the Mausoleum at Halicarnassus, the latter a monumental tomb erected for King Mausolus from which the term "mausoleum" derives. Next, in southern Greece, one finds the site of the temple of Zeus at Olympia, which drew pilgrims from all around the Greek world. The pilgrimage rituals at Olympia included athletic contests held in Zeus's honor, as the classical Greek concept of manhood melded excellence in intellectual, ethical, spiritual, and physical abilities. Abandoned in the fourth century, these Olympic Games were reintroduced in 1896, reflecting an enduring enthusiasm for antiquity. The last of the Seven Wonders was the Colossus of Rhodes, an immense bronze statue completed around 280 B.C. This "very remarkable piece of work" stood apart, in the eyes of Bartholdi, as the "most celebrated colossal statue of antiquity."

With the exception of the pyramids, the ancient wonders were either destroyed by earthquakes or disassembled by later generations that valued them primarily as a resource for building materials. Interest in the ancient monuments started to grow in the West in the fifteenth century, and over the next two centuries publications attempted to illustrate and explain them, often by mere conjecture. In the late eighteenth century, archeological and other expeditions further drew the attention of the Europeans to antiquity and instilled a sense of wonder. "Soldiers!" a commemorative medallion records Napoleon exclaiming in Egypt in 1798. "From the height of these pyramids forty centuries are watching us."

The Seven Wonders of the Ancient World were noted for their size and for the power they exerted on people's imagination. Part of their fascination was, and remains, the inconceivable precision with which these colossal monuments were constructed. The first century B.C. architect-engineer Vitruvius characterized the Seven Wonders as works of extraordinary skill, mentioning them in his *Ten Books of Architecture*. These marvels, the largest and finest of constructions, displayed obvious determination on the part of their builders along with impressive collective effort. In their scale and majestic beauty the works inspired a sense of mystical delight. While celebrating human achievement, these monuments proclaimed the harmony in which people lived with their gods; their power in the world was rooted in the power of the spirit.

In the years following Laboulaye's suggestion of a statue of liberty and independence, Bartholdi may have discussed the wonders of the ancient world with one of Laboulaye's friends, Henri Wallon, a scholar of Hellenist culture. In any case, by the early 1870s Bartholdi linked the character and significance of the proposed monument with the Seven Wonders, in particular the Colossus of Rhodes. The Colossus of Rhodes had been built in the third century B.C. to commemorate the conclusion of a yearlong siege of the island's capital city, which shared the name of the island, Rhodes. Demetrius "the Besieger" abandoned the siege by negotiation in 304 B.C. and left behind his siege equipment, which the Rhodians sold to finance the construction of the statue. In raising "high to heaven this colossus" as an offer of thanks to the city's patron god, Helios, according to an ancient Greek verse, the people of Rhodes "establish[ed] the lovely light of unfettered freedom."

Although traces of the 110-foot-tall (33 m) bronze figure no longer existed in the sixteenth century, imaginative artists generated interest in the statue. Europeans assumed that it was built to light the shoreline at Rhodes. Moreover, so immensely tall was it, stories went, that ships could easily pass between the legs of the colossus as it bridged the harbor. This popular image, depicted by the French artist Jean Cousin the Younger in a sixteenth-century publication *Cosmographie de Levant* by André Thevet, held sway over Western imagination for the next four centuries. In the nineteenth century some people, Bartholdi among them, began to question the "fantastic legend" of ships passing through the statue's legs, suspecting that it more reasonably stood on one shore or on a hilltop overlooking the city. Notwithstanding such doubts about the story's practicality, the legend of the Colossus of Rhodes was known to such an extent in the eighteenth and nineteenth centuries that people could allude to it, confident that it would bring forth associations of liberation and heroic qualities inherited from the ancient world. Speaking to a group of businessmen in 1797, Congressman Edward Livingston linked commerce and freedom with the toast, "The Colossus of American freedom—may it bestride the commerce of the world."

Another sixteenth-century illustrator of the Seven Wonders, the Dutch artist Maerten van Heemskerck, suggested that a statue representing the sun god Helios must have been adorned with a sunburst, that is, a crown of rays. His illustration added this detail and included as well scenes from the construction. Van Heemskerck depicted the sculptor Chares of Lindos standing by the statue and contemplating his drawings while workers busily polished the statue's bronze face and one foot. This composition likely appealed to Bartholdi because he arranged for similar workshop scenes to be photographed when his "colossus" was rising in Paris.

The image of this impressive ancient wonder, brilliant in the sun and reaching to the sky, understandably held an allure for a sculptor fascinated with large statuary and motivated by the ideal of liberty. The attitude of the Colossus of Rhodes, honoring the struggle to gain freedom while triumphantly holding forth freedom's bright light, might also have suggested a corresponding attitude for the American liberty statue. Similar to the ancient statue, Bartholdi's modern colossus would proclaim accomplishment while acknowledging the effort and dedication involved in attaining liberty.

Life size and heroic sculptures were common in Europe in the nineteenth century. The new liberty statue for America, portraying not a single person but a vital idea and a country's achievements, called for a distinct scale, one that recalled the colossal wonders of the ancient world. It is likely that Bartholdi contemplated this scale quite early in the process of design, even before he sailed for the United States in 1871.

The day after his arrival in New York in June 1871 Bartholdi identified "the best site" for his liberty statue. An island in New York Harbor presented a "site favorable by its own nature," one that would be unique to the statue and suitable to its meanings. The island setting was, besides, fitting for a colossal monument. Over the next several weeks Bartholdi continued to study Bedloe's Island (today named Liberty Island) and became convinced that this "site is superb!"

Set apart from the mainland yet surrounded by activity—commerce in the harbor was brisk—Bedloe's Island belonged to the New World while reaching out to the continents beyond its borders. The island bore the name of its seventeenth-century owner, but by the time Bartholdi discovered it, it belonged to the United States government and was occupied only by a scattering of army buildings and an eleven-point star-shaped fort wall. A liberty monument on Bedloe's Island could properly represent the people of the entire nation. At the same time, located at a principal gateway to the country, a statue here would serve as a marker for those seeking the shore and, possibly, as a lighthouse. Standing high above the water, the statue would speak equally to people at a distance, whether on shore or onboard a ship, and to people visiting the island. Bartholdi envisioned a colossal liberty statue reaching as high as 80 feet (24.6 m). With time, this figure gradually increased to a height of 151 feet (46 m).

When Bartholdi visited President Grant in the summer of 1871, he told Grant about the idea for a statue and asked about the prospect of locating it at Bedloe's Island. Grant assured Bartholdi that securing "the site will not be difficult." Six years later, Grant made certain that an island site was provided for the statue. On his recommendation, Congress passed a joint resolution authorizing the president of the United States to accept a statue from the people of France, when presented in the future, and to designate a suitable site on either Governor's Island or Bedloe's Island for the statue. Grant signed the resolution on his last day in office in March 1877. During a visit to France later that year, Grant toured the workshop in Paris where construction of the statue had commenced.

Bartholdi's enthusiasm regarding the island location undoubtedly helped sustain his determination to pursue the project. The island site also confirmed a connection he had previously made between the American liberty statue and his ideas for a Suez Canal lighthouse. The figures were both conceived in relation to the spread of enlightenment or progress, and this similarity had recommended the earlier design as a starting point for the new work. Now the basis for this connection was strengthened. (In later years, he attempted to downplay the association of the two sculptures, when he realized that some Americans shared the opinion of "an evilly disposed newspaper" article, which accused him of simply reusing an old design.)

The preliminary studies for the American liberty figure, which Bartholdi completed in his studio in Paris prior to his visit to the United States, assumed the gentle female form of the Suez Canal project. Bartholdi formed a clay model that showed the figure swinging one arm back and twisting her torso. As he started to outfit her with emblems of liberty, he appears to have looked for both familiar symbols, common to nineteenth-century European art, and signs particular to America. He strove to fashion a figure with broadly understood meaning; and yet he set aside a number of conventional methods for more specifically meaningful ones.

Statues celebrating liberty and patriotism often grasped a shield in one hand and a raised sword in the other. In America this imagery appears in statues and paintings decorating the Capitol, often balanced by symbols of peace and triumph such as the laurel wreath. It had earlier served the revolutionary cause; the baked pudding displayed on the head table during the congressional delegates' Fourth of July celebration in 1778 supported a figure with

Study model of the sculptural lighthouse
proposed by Bartholdi for the Suez Canal.
Musée Bartholdi, Colmar. Reproduction
by C. Kempf.

raised sword in hand. In its other hand, however, the delegates replaced the shield motif with the Declaration of Independence.
Bartholdi's figure went a step further, relinquishing shield and
sword for symbols of peace. In her raised hand he placed a torch,

which, as he and Laboulaye later emphasized, burned not with an inflammatory flame but with the passion of enlightenment. He had included a raised source of light, either a lantern or a torch, in his Suez Canal lighthouse design, and a torch fit with his early ideas for a liberty figure. The enlightening torch was a favored symbol in the nineteenth century, commonly associated with justice and liberty. It also represented the victory of light over darkness, which related to the special role of the United States as an exemplary republic, enlightening the world.

An additional aspect of the symbolic flame, especially relevant for those who recognized the fragility of liberty in the years surrounding the American Civil War, is its dependence on the attention of those already on shore. As demonstrated in the ancient tradition, whether in figures from the Old Testament or the maidens tending the sacred flame at the temple of Vesta in ancient Rome, those who have received the gift of light are tasked with keeping it shining for eternity. Referring to the ancient tradition of an eternal flame, Congressman John Quincy Adams, during a memorial address on the occasion of Lafayette's death in 1834, reminded the American people that the "vestal fire of Freedom is in your custody. May the souls of [the nation's] departed founders never be called to witness its extinction by neglect." Americans, Adams emphasized, have inherited from the founders the privilege and the responsibility of keeping the light imperishable, burning bright.

The second design element Bartholdi included in the first known model for the statue, dated 1870, was a broken chain, trampled underfoot. This feature has been interpreted as a sign of America's independence from British authority and a symbol of resolution. For an artist of the nineteenth century, however, the liberty cap would have been a more natural choice to convey this meaning. A chain, if used, was traditionally placed in the hand of Liberty. The image of a trampled chain had, moreover, been employed by the abolitionist movement and had raised considerable controversy when suggested by an American sculptor, Hiram Powers, for a statue for Washington, D.C., in the 1850s.

Bartholdi's use of the trampled chain in his earliest clay model suggests that he borrowed this feature from a particular source. If he was indeed familiar with Sartain's engraving of Lincoln as the Great Emancipator, this is the most likely one. Bartholdi could have adopted the trampled chain motif from the portrait of Lincoln for a number of reasons. First, this was probably the one contemporary American liberty figure (or portion thereof) with which he was most familiar, prior to his visit to Washington, D.C. In addition, a broken chain in the manner of the Lincoln portrait commemorated the end of the institution of slavery in the United States, an important aspect of the American republic in the eyes of the French. This subtle reference to the portrait also provided a means of honoring Lincoln and his role in having "saved the Republic" established by the founders, "without veiling the statue of liberty." At the same time, Bartholdi was cautious not to stress the presence of the chain, partially concealing it under the figure's flowing robe.

Bartholdi evidently distinguished between the trampled chain and the traditional broken chain symbol. As he continued to shape his liberty figure, in New York in 1871 and subsequently in France, he considered placing a broken chain or a broken jug, both accepted symbols of liberation, in her left hand.

Another important decision concerned the head-covering for the statue. The Roman *pileus,* the cap given to enfranchised slaves in antiquity, was a standard symbol used to represent liberty. Bartholdi initially tried fitting a simple cap on his figure, shaping it so as to provide openings for beacon lights. But when he modeled the figure again, during the summer of 1871, he changed the character of the cap by attaching to it rays of the sun. There was abundant precedent for a crown of rays in sculptural art. In ancient art the rayed crown represented divine inspiration. The Colossus of Rhodes, built as an offering of thanks to the sun god Helios, may have been adorned with a sunburst. More recently in France, the rayed crown had been used in images depicting liberty, truth, faith, and the republic, notably the Republic of 1848.

For a French sculptor of the nineteenth century, therefore, a crown of rays was a reasonable choice for the head-covering of a statue. However, the model Bartholdi left in New York suggests that he made the decision to change from a cap to a rayed crown while he was in the United States. In later years, Bartholdi told Americans that Bedloe's Island "was the inspiration of the statue." It may have been the sunburst that he was referring to in that statement. Bartholdi took pleasure in the sight of the New York bay in the morning sun, which could have brought to mind Benjamin

Franklin's story of the sun rising on the nation, giving it fresh pertinence. If Franklin's sun inspired the addition of the crown of rays, Bartholdi not only gave his figure a strong presence by way of this design element but also linked her to the story of the birth of the nation.

The sun had risen on the experiment of the American founders, the statue affirms. The inclusion of the sun also points to the exemplary republic's role as the sun of the political community, providing inspiration to others. Given the precedent for and relevance of the sun motif, it seems inevitable that Bartholdi took advantage of this meaningful symbol. Nevertheless, he might have anticipated a certain amount of criticism from people who preferred the traditional liberty cap. The liberty cap, one displeased critic pronounced in a review of the statue's design, "is as unavoidable an attribute of a statue of Liberty as grammar is necessary to language."

To Bartholdi, the importance of the traditional soft liberty cap may have been diminished by the inclusion of the trampled chain. This sign, as employed in the portrait of Lincoln, referred to slavery in the United States. Yet *slavery* also assumed a broader meaning for people living under authoritarian rule. The American revolutionaries had emphasized the threat of slavery to British authority; and the French people responded intuitively to the rhetorical use of slavery as it applied to their own lives under Napoleon III. At a time in the nineteenth century when artists were beginning to look for contemporary symbols to replace ancient ones, the broken chain must have seemed an excellent alternative to the traditional cap, representing both the event of emancipation and the ideal of individual freedom.

The sun headdress could have any number of rays; Bartholdi selected seven. It has often been suggested that, because the statue symbolizes liberty's enlightenment of the world, the seven rays represent light shining across the seven seas to the seven continents. Another direct association with the statue can be made as well, in that there are seven wonders of the ancient world, and it is this ancestry on which the liberty statue is founded. Seven, moreover, is a sacred number of long history. Nature followed an ordering system based on seven, such as the cycles of lean and fruitful years in the Books of Moses. In Greek literature there were seven sages, distinguished by the life they led and the advice they gave. Ancient

Rome was built on seven hills. An early Christian legend of the seven sleepers of Ephesus confirmed the presence of God in our world, and the Koran revealed the creation of seven heavens, or stages of blessed afterlife. Throughout the history of Christianity, the number seven has been significant; while there are seven capital vices, visualized by Dante in the *Inferno*, there are also seven gifts of the Holy Spirit and seven virtues. Having been raised in a household governed by a lively Christian faith, the prominence of this number and its special meaning in spiritual life would not have escaped Bartholdi. He could also feel confident that nineteenth-century Americans, known for their familiarity with the Bible and their adherence to its strictures, would understand the number seven to connote fullness and completeness. Alternatively, the seven-rayed sunburst of the Carpenters' Company coat of arms, which Bartholdi could have seen or heard about in Philadelphia, might have settled the matter for him.

Bartholdi's later models reflect one last major decision, that regarding the emblem to be placed in the hand of the statue. Reiterating the chain motif by prominently displaying it in her hand would have raised numerous concerns. Although respect for the United States in France was strengthened on account of the abolition of slavery, abolition remained a sensitive issue in the United States. Bartholdi may have observed that the nation was grappling with the changes and tensions associated with Reconstruction during his visit in 1871. He might also have learned from Sumner that the abundant historical imagery decorating the Capitol carefully avoided reference to slavery. Similar to the Capitol, the liberty statue was intended to represent the nation and had to respect, therefore, national standards of expression.

On another level, interpreting this symbol of liberation in the context of American independence, a broken chain in clear view would have highlighted the separation of the colonies from Great Britain. While this might have been suitable for a nationalist statue, it was less so for a statue celebrating a new vision of life. The distinction had been essential even during the revolutionary war. "Considered merely as a separation from England," Thomas Paine acknowledged, independence "would have been a matter but of little importance, had it not been accompanied by a revolution in the principles and practice of governments. [America] made a stand, not for herself only, but for the world, and looked beyond the advantages herself could receive." It was this broader sense of freedom that Laboulaye and those who hoped to change France's system of government focused on, as had the American colonists who fought to obtain liberty through self-government.

It was of utmost importance to Laboulaye and other supporters of the project, that the statue convey none of the political upheaval and social disorder of revolution and civil war. They did not want to encourage the association of chaotic rebellion with the concept of a republic, which Delacroix's painting *28 July, Liberty Guiding the People* had impressed on the minds of many. "This is not Liberty with a red bonnet on her head," Laboulaye emphasized, referring to the revolutionary version of the liberty cap, "and a pike in her hand who runs over fallen bodies." It was important to the statue's sponsors that the symbolism foster respect for a system of government based on the law of liberty. Calm steadiness would influence every element of the design.

Bartholdi agreed that the traditional, handheld broken chain should be replaced and found another liberty symbol that appealed to Laboulaye; perhaps Laboulaye even suggested it. This change at once transformed the design and affirmed the statue's association with the life of the United States. In the arm of the statue, to be grasped by her left hand, they placed a tablet, which Laboulaye described as "tablets of the law." The inclusion of a tablet of the law had precedent in nineteenth-century European art. The tablet referred to the law that Moses delivered to the Israelites in the desert; as a symbol of contemporary meaning, it was understood to represent a nation's constitution.

This dual meaning had a rational basis, in that reverence for law is essential to the endurance of a constitutional government. As told in the Book of Exodus, the people had been liberated from slavery and were beginning life anew when God provided them with the Commandments. These Commandments were not intended as burdensome restrictions on the liberties of individual members of the community. Rather, they were laws, or teachings, given in the spirit of truth to assist each member attain a full life within the community. So, too, in the United States, the Constitution was not intended as a constraint on liberties. Instead, it was offered by the delegates of the Constitutional Convention in 1787 as a structure for the life of the nation. The Articles of Confederation of 1779, developed during the War for Independence, had

Bartholdi's model for the Statue of Liberty. Modèle du Comité, c. 1876. Musée Bartholdi, Colmar. Reproduction by C. Kempf.

furnished the states with neither the cohesion necessary for a nation nor the order necessary for the enjoyment of liberty. Replacing the Articles of Confederation with the Constitution and its Bill of Rights, the delegates aimed to provide a framework for a vast populace to live as a community. The richly symbolic tablet the statue holds in her arm, complemented by her enlightening torch, demonstrates that the people of the nation embraced a different way of realizing freedom, not with sword and shield but with law and light. As the Roman republicans might have said, "Let weapons yield to the toga," an ancient slogan the American revolutionary Samuel Adams resurrected as one of his pennames: "Cedant Arma Togae."

The Constitution of the United States was a document that Laboulaye in fact revered. He believed that it had served the American people well over the course of their nation's first century, and he looked to it as a model for the French people, as they worked to define their own system of government. Laboulaye and Bartholdi, however, chose not to identify the tablet solely as the Constitution. Instead, they wrote the date of the Declaration of Independence on the tablet. As the design evolved, this was written in Roman numerals as "July IV, MDCCLXXVI," which matches the example set by the founders in the design for the Great Seal of the United States.

Engraving this date on the tablet strengthened the statue's connection with the achievement of American independence and with its centennial. It also manifested the close association of the events and documents that shaped the birth of the nation. The Constitution was the culmination of a historical development of political liberty in America, Laboulaye understood. As such, the Constitution must be read with the Declaration of Independence in mind. In the draft for his inaugural address in 1861, Lincoln referred to the Constitution's embodiment of "the principles promulgated in the Declaration of Independence," and in a note to himself Lincoln described the Constitution as the picture "framed around" the Declaration of Independence. Since its drafting, the Constitution had been celebrated along with the Declaration of Independence on July 4.

With the tablet motif agreed on, Laboulaye may have recalled the verse written for Lafayette's visit to Boston in 1824. These "lines once so familiar" were brought to mind again on the occa-

sion of the statue's unveiling, when stories of Lafayette and the
friendship he represented were repeated:

> The fathers in glory shall sleep
> That gathered with thee to the fight,
> But the sons shall eternally keep
> The tablet of gratitude bright.
> We bow not the neck,
> And we bend not the knee,
> But our hearts, Lafayette,
> We surrender to thee.

The image of a tablet of gratitude was certainly fitting for a colossus of liberty, associated by Bartholdi with the ancient offering of
thanks, the Colossus of Rhodes. It was one of many small instances
of delightful design integrity. How many of these were intended,
rather than perceived only in hindsight or never perceived at all by
the statue's creators, is unknown. Neither Bartholdi nor Laboulaye
left a record that explains their decisions; and when they spoke
about the statue, they tended to refer to the design in its entirety.
Drawings and models show the progression of design, but the main
account we have of the creative process was written after the statue
was constructed in Paris. In 1885 Bartholdi explained the purpose
and the artistic background of the design in a short book written
to assist the fundraising effort that was still underway in the United
States. The recollections he presents in this book have to be understood in light of its intended audience. They also do not address
design details. Our knowledge of the design process, therefore, is
incomplete. Instead, we can speculate—with firm basis—the reasons each emblem of liberty was selected.

A defining aspect of Bartholdi's design, one that we can reasonably conclude was intentional, is its association of American independence with the forward-looking perspective of liberation
expressed by the founders. Rather than dwell on the burden of past
oppression the statue points to the new life of the nation. This perspective substantiates its role as a marker of new beginnings and
opens the design to interpretation in a particularly meaningful
manner. Illustrated in the composition of the liberty statue, in
terms taken from an age-old tradition, is the story of the creation
of the United States. The story begins with the statue's uplifted
arm, revealing the promise of liberty in the light associated with

the spirit of the founders. The effort of bringing forth a new life of liberty follows, in the broken chain of oppression and the people's declaration of independence. The story continues with the institution of a national community and the binding ties of a Constitution embodying the spirit of liberty. Finally, the tremendous changes of the new existence are balanced under the sun's rays, seven in number. The creation reflected a purpose, as opposed to an accidental occurrence; similarly, the nation's founding was arranged with reason to begin a new way of life. With the encouragement of classical dress and a scriptural tablet of the law, the design drew on the two main sources of moral authority in the nineteenth century. The creation story was of course known to everyone, and its interpretation reached beyond that of literal truth to assume a place in the fabric of society, as part of its understanding about the life of the world.

Complementing this sense of purpose, Bartholdi gradually imbued the statue with the strength of spirit that characterized his war monuments. He extended the figure's right leg to the back in a manner known as *contrapposto,* which suggests both a solid footing and an attitude more relaxed than that conveyed by two feet set side by side. It also implies movement, physically and mentally, which introduces a balanced sense of tension between standing firm and moving forward. With this stance Bartholdi depicted assurance in the achievements already gained along with eager anticipation of continued advancement. This approach to incorporating movement, which greatly improved the design, may also have been recommended by structural concerns. The straightened form and outstretched leg help stabilize the statue. With this improvement in the statue's structural stability, the figure abandoned the earlier carefree twist of the torso and acquired a quality of inner strength of character.

The elaborate folding of the statue's outer robe corresponds to the attitude expressed on each side of the figure. On her right side, the lines of the drapery reach upward, strengthening the spirit signified by her raised arm and torch. At the rear, the diagonal lines and abundant folds suggest movement on the figure's right side. On her left side, on the contrary, the drapery reaches to the ground, reflecting the stable footing achieved by way of the tablet of the law held in her left arm. And at the front, the larger expanses of fabric impart a sense of constancy. Contemporary observers frequently praised this element. "The drapery is both massive and fine," a reviewer wrote at the time of the statue's completion in Paris. "Some parts, where the sleeve falls under the right arm for instance, are as delicate and silky in effect as if they had been wrought with a fine chisel on the smallest scale." The French art critic who regretted the lack of a liberty cap complimented the statue for the "simplicity of its pose, [and] the nobility of its draperies."

In his design of a face for the statue, Bartholdi would need to affirm the mood and spiritual statement established by the rest of the figure. The statue's expression required a melding of traits so as to encompass the diverse aspects of liberty, from rebellion (albeit mutedly expressed) to enlightenment and justice. Even as construction proceeded, Bartholdi continued to make small adjustments, apparently pondering her character. In his 1875 working model he allowed a hint of anxiousness into her eyes. But as his design was progressively enlarged and shaped in plaster at full size, he heightened the sense of serenity and assurance she conveyed. The soft shapes of the plaster model were then slightly sharpened again when the final form was made in copper. This sharpness, which in photographs tends to appear as sternness, was probably not intentional; in her physical presence one still feels the gentleness in her face.

From the moment the statue's face was displayed in France, stories began to circulate about whom Bartholdi might have used as his model. Rumors assumed that his design depicted a single person. One of the several stories that circulated embraced a notably romantic and revolutionary vision of liberty: as Bartholdi thought about the face of liberty for his statue, this tale recounted, a young woman he had seen at the barricades during Louis Napoleon's coup d'état in 1851 came to mind. In the excitement of the fray, protesting for liberty and preservation of the Second Republic, she had been struck by a bullet. Mortally wounded, she collapsed. The tragic sight of this determined young woman stayed with Bartholdi over the many years and, it was claimed, now shaped his statue. A second story pointed to Bartholdi's wife as his inspiration. Not satisfied with his explanation that he met Jeanne in America, this account cast Jeanne as a modest milliner whom Bartholdi met in France. Wanting to marry her but fearful that his mother would not approve of such a match, he took her away to the United States, "made her acquaintance" through his respectable friend John La Farge, and married her there.

Yet another story, which might have mollified Bartholdi's mother, asserted that she alone was her son's inspiration. According to Senator Jules François Jeannotte-Bozérian, a glimpse he caught of Madame Bartholdi at the opera convinced him of a revealing likeness between her face and that of the statue. Bartholdi, the senator reported, had thereupon confirmed his suspicion, agreeing that the face of the statue was his mother's. Madame Bartholdi's austere deportment, recorded in photographs, certainly appears to resemble the steadfast expression of the liberty statue. This expression, however, was common in portraits and photos of the period. Both men and women generally offered a respectable, sober, and seemingly inexpressive face to the camera lens or painter's eye. One was not asked to smile obligingly.

The calm and stable persona that resonates from the liberty figure is also suggestive of the seriousness of purpose that characterized Americans in the view of the French. It would have been natural for Bartholdi to look to the faces of people he observed as models of American character. Could a portrait of Abraham Lincoln, the man most closely associated with the efforts of preserving liberty and the Union, have influenced him? Or the face of his friend La Farge as a young man? The likeness of each was believed to be included in his design for the Brattle Square Church tower in Boston.

We will never know for certain which and how many sources shaped Bartholdi's design. What is clear, and of greater importance, is that he intended to portray endurance and stability through a universal image. The statue's eyes are not fixed solely on the concerns of a moment. Instead, they present the "kindly and impassable glance" that looks to an "unlimited future," the words Bartholdi used when admiring the ancient statuary he saw in Egypt. This eternal relevance similarly pertains to the full design of the statue. Drawing on a range of sources, Bartholdi positioned America's achievements within the course of history. He assembled the individual emblematic elements into a composition that aimed for appropriate meaning, not innovation, and purposefully refrained from passionate expression.

It is all the more astonishing, then, to discover the multiple facets of liberty and independence the statue communicates. She speaks at once to different people and to different experiences. For those wanting to celebrate the triumphal joy of liberty, she proudly holds forth her bright torch from her back right side. The dynamic of her enthusiasm is startling, when seen from this position. Those who appreciate her blend of stability and readiness for advancement are drawn to her front right side. From this angle, some hear her speak as well about the tablet of the law, which she carries with her. Not a mere lawyer's document, Woodrow Wilson said of the Constitution, "it is a vehicle of life, and its spirit is always the spirit of the age." Her left side, on the contrary, offers another view of the nation's guiding laws. From this position, her arm, holding secure the tablet of the law, communicates the assurance of a steady, principled way of life. To those facing her straight on, the fullness of her meaning speaks most strongly. She offers her light to guide the nation as it continues along the path of liberty and calls forth a sense of wonder and respect for the achievements that endowed the nation with stability and justice.

Staying comfortably within the context of nineteenth-century sculpture, Bartholdi selected a traditional female form, classical dress, and symbols familiar to an audience of the period. And yet the design he crafted reached far beyond traditional nineteenth-century practice. Putting aside ancient symbols, such as the broken jug and the liberty cap, the meanings of which would soon be known to only select observers, he combined idealism and realism in an original synthesis with broad appeal. Through close attention to the significance of this liberty figure, he found the means to refer directly to the American experience and the birth of a nation in a fashion that speaks clearly to Americans and to other peoples around the world with common aspirations. With this design, he established a new prototype for a statue of liberty.

8

THE STATUE
TAKES SHAPE

By early 1872 Bartholdi was close to completing his design for the statue. It would not be until September 1875, however, that Édouard Laboulaye was ready to launch the project with a public announcement of their plans. The primary reason for this three-year delay was political. Although a republic had been proclaimed at the beginning of the Franco-Prussian War of 1870–71, in practice the governance of France did not follow this abrupt shift. Certain steps were taken to move in this direction. Elections were held again in 1871 and, for the first time, Laboulaye was seated in the National Assembly. He chaired the committee for the reorganization of public instruction in France and began drafting ideas for constitutional laws for a representative government. Despite the efforts of Laboulaye and others to formulate a structure and a constitution for the new government, the strength of the reactionary members in the assembly in the years immediately after the war threatened the survival of the republic altogether. Residual distrust of Parisians prevented the government from moving back to the capital from Versailles (it finally returned in 1879) and, exemplifying the republic's difficult beginning, Marshal Patrice de MacMahon was selected president. MacMahon's government of "moral order," recorded the U.S. minister in Paris, Elihu Washburne, restricted liberty of speech and exercised powers that "had never been exercised during the worst times of [Napoleon III's] Empire."

Members of the assembly were divided regarding the preferred form of government for France, with some favoring a return to monarchy or empire. By 1873, however, most members agreed on the importance of securing a stable, permanent government to preclude another slide into revolution. A committee was established to draft constitutional legislation, to which Laboulaye devoted much effort. He advocated borrowing features of the American system, namely the bicameral legislature and a president in an executive branch. To his delight the constitutional laws were adopted in early 1875, together with an amendment confirming that the "government of the Republic is composed of two chambers and of a president." Although passing by only one vote, 353 to 352, the Wallon Amendment's reference to France as a republic signaled an end to the dispute of the past four years. Those who favored a change from autocratic government to one based on respect for individual liberty had succeeded in setting the direction of France's future governance.

During these years, as Laboulaye waited for the opportune moment to announce the liberty statue project, Bartholdi investigated means for its construction. He needed to determine how, and of what material, the sculptural form would be built, and how this form would be supported. For advice on the first issue, Bartholdi turned to a metalwork foundry located in the city, the firm of Gaget, Gauthier & Co. (formerly known as Monduit and Bechet). The foundry had considerable experience with statuary and decorative art, especially in copper. Its work included large-scale projects such as the domes for the new Paris opera house, statues for the spires of Notre Dame and Sainte-Chapelle in Paris, and a statue of Vercingétorix at Alise-Sainte-Reine sculpted by Aimé Millet. Copper offered advantages for construction of a colossal statue; the material was malleable and relatively lightweight, and sheets of copper could be sculpted to form the figure and be transported to the United States.

For advice on the second question—how to support a sculptural form made of copper sheets—Bartholdi turned to Eugène-Emmanuel Viollet-le-Duc. It is not certain how well Bartholdi knew Viollet-le-Duc before this time. As a youth he may have attended courses taught by Viollet-le-Duc at the École de Dessin, and as an artist living in Paris he probably crossed paths with the architect at official functions. He may also have met him at social gatherings, or through a mutual friend, such as the painter Jean-Léon Gérôme. Bartholdi would have heard much about Viollet-le-Duc, for he was a highly influential architectural theorist as well as a practicing architect, an architectural historian, an instructor, and a prolific writer. Viollet-le-Duc advocated the study of past architecture, such as the excavations at Pompeii, as a means of learning principles that could be applied in a modern context. At the same time, he strongly disagreed with orthodox academicism, which aimed to derive rigid rules for classical design from past examples. This approach, Viollet-le-Duc argued, overlooked the most interesting and profound aspect of ancient architecture: the human thought reflected in each work of construction. Through his studies of Greco-Roman and Gothic architecture Viollet-le-Duc had concluded that architectural innovations historically emerged as solutions to questions concerning construction and were founded on structural rationalism.

Notwithstanding the respect he enjoyed as an architect and historian, Viollet-le-Duc's outspokenness about the architecture profession in France made him unpopular with some of its members. He was critical of the École des Beaux Arts architecture department, calling its academicism impractical and its influence over the profession in France unhealthy. Even the ateliers, he railed, which had previously stimulated "a ferment of intellectual activity," were now subject to the leveling effect of the school's architecture program. Moreover, the abundance of design commissions occasioned by an expanding economy, he argued, had dimmed architects' creativity. It was not surprising, therefore, that his appointment as one of the new professors at the École, following an imperial decree instituting reforms in 1863, encountered numerable difficulties. Students complained about this outsider and scorned his interest in Gothic architecture, which they associated with a period of intellectual darkness, in contrast to the age of enlightenment. Unruly students made it impossible for Viollet-le-Duc to lecture and within a few months' time he resigned from his position at the school.

Nonetheless he made good use of the lectures and essays that he wrote throughout the 1850s and 1860s, publishing them as a two-volume work, *Lectures on Architecture (Entretiens sur l'architec-*

ture). He also completed his *Dictionary of French Architecture from the 11th to 16th Century (Dictionnaire raisonné de l'architecture française du XIème au XVIème siècle),* which filled ten volumes over the years 1854 to 1868. These publications received considerable notice in the design profession in France and became known worldwide.

During the Second Empire, Viollet-le-Duc was on good terms with Napoleon III and the Empress Eugénie and received numerous commissions from the imperial government. This association with the Empire became a problem in 1871, when the contested conclusion of the Franco-Prussian war gave rise to the passions of the Commune in Paris. According to some accounts, Viollet-le-Duc fled the capital when he learned his life was threatened.

Once the French government reestablished its authority in Paris in June 1871, Viollet-le-Duc returned, again in good standing. He had never considered himself an imperialist or royalist, he insisted, and in the following years he openly supported the republican, as opposed to a reactionary, party. He continued to write books about architecture, covering a range of topics, and he joined in founding a monthly journal for architects and engineers, the *Encyclopédie d'architecture.*

In the early to mid-1870s Viollet-le-Duc became involved in the liberty statue project. He may have been approached by Bartholdi on the recommendation of the foundry Gaget, Gauthier & Co. Viollet-le-Duc was known to the foundry on account of his work with the sculptor Aimé Millet on a copper repoussé statue of Vercingétorix. It is also possible that Richard Morris Hunt, who knew Viollet-le-Duc, mentioned the French architect to Bartholdi when they met in the summer of 1871. In any case, Viollet-le-Duc agreed to work on the project and to design a structure to support the statue. He contemplated an innovative system for this unusually large statue, in which a layer of sand would stiffen the exterior copper skin. The sand would be held in place, Viollet-le-Duc proposed, by a second, inner layer of copper, built to follow the shape of the exterior skin. To facilitate future repairs to the copper skin, dividers would separate the space between the two copper layers into sections: sand could be drained out of one internal compartment instead of the entire structure. To support and stabilize the overall sculptural form, Viollet-le-Duc planned to construct a traditional masonry pier.

By 1875, Laboulaye felt that the climate in France was suitable for announcing plans for a liberty statue. The turmoil of the early years of the republic was beginning to calm and France's identity as a republic had been officially acknowledged with the Wallon Amendment. The economic situation in France was set to improve as well. The French people had shouldered a heavy tax burden following the end of the war to pay the indemnity demanded by the German Empire in the Treaty of Frankfurt. Defying initial predictions of gloom and long-lasting financial hardship, the indemnity had been fully paid by the close of 1873.

Circumstances, moreover, favored a project founded on the tradition of friendship between the people of France and the United States. For one, news about the upcoming Centennial Exhibition in Philadelphia was stirring memories in France of their common history. "I find," John Forney, the Centennial's commissioner in Europe, happily observed in early 1875, "that the French are alive to the Centennial. They regard it as the event of the age, and they recall, with characteristic pride, the efficient aid of Louis XVI to the American Colonies, and the romantic story of young Lafayette. The names of the French who fought under the handsome Count are still fondly cherished. Franklin's sojourn in Paris is spoken of as worthy of historic revival, and also that of Jefferson." Supporting Forney's efforts to secure European participation in the Exhibition was Elihu Washburne, who also took "a lively interest in the work."

Washburne, a former Illinois congressman and personal friend of presidents Lincoln and Grant, had been the first representative of a foreign power to recognize the provisional Government of National Defense in 1870. This prompt recognition provided France with important moral support; at the same time, it reflected well on the United States and strengthened the sense of kinship felt in France. "You have founded your wise and powerful institutions upon independence and upon civic virtue," the minister of foreign affairs in the provisional government, Jules Favre, wrote to Washburne in reply to his letter of recognition. "And notwithstanding the terrible trials sustained by you," Favre continued, referring to the American Civil War still vivid in people's memories, "you have preserved with an unshaken firmness your faith in that grand principle of liberty, from which naturally spring dignity, morality, and prosperity." Groups of private citizens similarly demonstrated their appreciation and assured him of their friendship: "America and France are sisters," wrote one delegation of French citizens, "sisters as republics, that is to say, sisters in liberty. The ocean which separates us is less deep than the sentiments which unite us."

Washburne had also assisted with the transfer of aid between the people of the two nations; first, following the siege of Paris, and soon thereafter, following the Great Chicago Fire of 1871. More recently, he had affirmed the tradition of goodwill and gift exchange by presenting Oscar de Lafayette, eldest grandson of the Marquis de Lafayette and a fellow senator of Laboulaye in the National Assembly, with his grandfather's watch. This was no ordinary watch but rather the one that George Washington had given to Lafayette during the American War for Independence. It had great sentimental value to Lafayette and had remained with him for nearly four decades. It was during his visit to the United States in 1824–25 that a visibly distressed Lafayette realized that the watch had been lost. A half-century passed before it was sighted in a pawn shop in Kentucky. Learning of the watch's discovery, the U.S. Congress rushed to provide funds for its purchase; and Washburne subsequently had the pleasure of delivering this cherished watch to Oscar de Lafayette, who as a child had known his grandfather well. "In fulfilling today this agreeable task which has been confided to me," Washburne concluded his presentation, "I am certain that I am the interpreter of the sentiments of the government and the people of the United States, in presenting to you, and to all the descendants of General de La Fayette, our most ardent wishes that happiness and prosperity will always accompany those who bear your venerated name; and we associate with these wishes, France, which was the ally of the United States, and who is its traditional friend, and whose glory is so dear to us." The Paris newspapers all reported on Washburne's presentation of the watch, creating "a most favorable impression."

Laboulaye hoped to tap this favorable impression of the United States to gain support in France for the construction of the liberty statue. He established an organization, referred to as the Franco-American Union, to pursue the work in France, and became its founding president. In addition to assuming responsibility for the project in this way, Laboulaye's prominent role lent the Franco-American Union respectability. Many of his associates and friends, the men who regularly met at his home in Glatigny, also joined as members. Five honorary members were named, including two descendants of France's heroes from the American Revolution, the Marquis de Noailles and the Marquis de Rochambeau, and a distant cousin of Bartholdi, Amédée Bartholdi, who was serving as the French ambassador in Washington. The two American honorary members were John Forney and Elihu Washburne.

The Franco-American Union opened its fundraising campaign with the public announcement of the project in September 1875. Placing a notice in newspapers throughout the country, the Union announced its plans for a "colossal statue," which, it emphasized, would preserve memories of the French and American collaboration during the American War for Independence and of the honorable Frenchmen who had risked their lives for the American cause, which was, in essence, a universal cause. Laboulaye wooed his colleagues in the assembly with assurances that, while commemorating past events, the liberty statue would lend support to France's transition to a system of representative government, a process kindled during the French peoples' participation in the American Revolution.

Liberty Enlightening the World, the name selected for this statue of multiple meanings, brilliantly alluded to two portrayals of France: *France Enlightening the World* (also referred to as *La République*), a painting by Ange-Louis Janet-Lange to represent the Second Republic, and *Imperial France Enlightening the World,* statuary designed by Jean-Baptiste Carpeaux under Napoleon III for the facade of the Flora pavilion at the Louvre in 1865. Reference to global enlightenment in terms already familiar in France affirmed the statue's relevance to French and Americans alike.

At the same time that it announced the project in France, the Franco-American Union appealed to Americans to accept this offer of a gift and to join in the fellowship of collaboration by preparing a site and pedestal for the statue. Writing to President Grant on behalf of the Union, Laboulaye requested that Bedloe's Island —Bartholdi's choice—be designated for the monument. Laboulaye emphasized the history and spirit of friendship that shaped the statue. In addition, he wrote, the statue will speak to the present age, demonstrating "our enthusiasm in France for this noble liberty, which embodies the glory of the United States and which enlightens . . . by its example."

In France, public response to the idea of a statue was generally positive. Some legislators questioned the grounds for a gift, considering the United States' inconsistent show of support for France over the years. They regretted that the United States had not aided France in her war with Prussia in 1870–71, announcing instead strict neutrality. Worse yet, the U.S. minister had accepted funds from the Prussian government, with which to assist the German people trapped in Paris during the siege. Nor had the nascent United States government supported France in the years following the French Revolution, thereby failing to abide by the spirit of its 1778 treaty with France. These critics of the proposed statue also asserted that Americans no longer thought about Lafayette or appreciated France's participation in their struggle for independence.

In spite of opposition of this type, memories of the friendship "sealed by the blood of both people's forefathers," in the words of the subscription appeal, along with the vision of spreading enlightenment, which the statue was meant to portray, gained wide support for the project. Individuals and municipalities sent contributions, and a major metal manufacturer offered to donate copper for the statue's construction. Seeking to broaden interest, the Union emphasized that this was an endeavor that every person could take part in. Even "trifling" contributions would be gratefully received.

Several events catering to the elite and the influential were scheduled for the first year of the fundraising campaign. An inaugural banquet at the Grand Hôtel du Louvre was also the occasion for presenting the design. Invited to the banquet were politicians, including President MacMahon (who did not attend) and his immediate staff, French and American journalists, artists, and others whose support was sought by the Union. A strong sense of historical Franco-American friendship pervaded this and subsequent gatherings; "these precious memories" of friendship, Laboulaye stressed, "are the links between the two nations." Among the banquet hall's lavish decorations hung portraits of Washington, Lafayette, Franklin, Rochambeau, Lincoln, and Grant. "The events of the evening were a cable dispatch to President Grant," John Forney recorded, "then the news from the Centennial Commission at Philadelphia . . . and, finally, the two remarkable speeches of Mr. Washburne . . . and M. Laboulaye." Washburne spoke on behalf of President Grant, thus implying government support for the project, and assured the gathering of his nation's interest in the statue.

Laboulaye's special talent for oratory served him well that evening. He "struck the rock of the past till the finest memories flashed before us like living water," Forney remembered in awe. "No one who then heard Laboulaye for the first time could wonder that he is so ardently beloved and so obediently followed by the people. He spoke . . . rather like a philosopher than a statesman." Even political opponents of the republicans could not remain indifferent to the "wit and pathos" of Laboulaye's speech, Forney surmised. "His words excited a prodigious enthusiasm" and "gradually unlocked their hearts till he had the whole house on his side."

Another fundraising reception held the following spring, in April 1876, featured a performance at the new Paris Opera, which had only just opened the year before. Laboulaye introduced the benefit with a stirring speech about both the role of the French people in the history of the United States and the merit of Bartholdi's design for the statue. While comparing the liberty statue with the Colossus of Rhodes, Laboulaye cautiously disassociated it from historical images of bloody battles and rebellion. This liberty figure, he declared, will symbolize "American freedom, which bears peace and enlightenment everywhere." The performance that night included patriotic songs and a cantata specially composed for the occasion by Charles Gounod (acclaimed composer of the opera *Faust*), with a hymn written by playwright Émile Guiard. An assembly of eight hundred singers from the men's choral societies of the Seine region joined the orchestra for a spirited performance of three choruses.

Once the Franco-American Union began to receive contributions toward the construction of the statue, it was able to commence this phase of the work. The liberty statue, Laboulaye had assured his listeners during the inaugural banquet of the fundraising campaign, "will not resemble those bronze colossi boasted to have been cast from the metal of captured cannon." On the contrary, he exclaimed, our statue will be a work "done in virgin metal, the fruit of labor and peace."

The method of construction that Bartholdi chose for the sculptural form, with the advice of the copper foundry Gaget, Gauthier & Co., was in fact a notably labor-intensive technique. Termed *repoussé*, this technique involved the hammering of thin copper sheets against forms from the reverse side. Repoussé was a millennia-old technique in which craftsmen at the foundry were skilled.

The scene in the busy workshop as copper sheets are hammered into wood forms. © Musée des arts et métiers–Cnam, Paris. Photograph by S. Pelly.

Nonetheless, the 151-foot-high (46 m) statue presented a special challenge, as its construction involved an enormous assortment of forms and unusually large size. Gaget, Gauthier & Co. devised a means of accomplishing this work that, though quite tedious, proved successful. Bartholdi's terra-cotta study model, just under 4 feet (1.25 m) high, was carefully reproduced at successively larger scale in plaster. Each increase in size was accomplished by taking detailed measurements throughout the surface area and multiplying roughly, first, by a factor of two and, next, by a factor of four. Based on these scaled measurements, the plaster models supported by timber and lath forms replicated the desired shape of the statue's exterior surface. Once the plaster dried, Bartholdi, together with an assistant, retouched the model until he was satisfied with the shape of the figure at each larger scale. The second plaster model, measuring around 28 feet (8.5 m) to the top of the head, or 36 feet (11 m) with the arm and torch added, was marked into three hundred sections and used as the basis for another enlargement, again at roughly a factor of four, this time as sections rather than an entire figure.

Giving the finishing touches to each of the three hundred full-scale plaster sections was especially important to Bartholdi, as this was his last opportunity to make refinements to the figure's surface and the only opportunity to make refinements at full size. Once this stage was complete, forms for shaping the copper skin of the statue were made. A negative form was constructed for each section, to allow the hammering to take place on the reverse (or inside surface) of the copper sheets, so as to avoid creating unsightly hammering marks on the exposed surface of the copper. Two types of negative form were made for each section, one of wood for the

Bartholdi's assistant Marie Simon has climbed onto the wood form for the statue's left hand to make an adjustment; Bartholdi is standing next to the arm with a visitor. Musée Bartholdi, Colmar. Reproduction by C. Kempf.

strongest hammering and one of malleable lead sheets for finish hammering. After the negative form in wood was built to fit snugly against the plaster on its outer surface, the inner wood mold that supported the plaster and the plaster itself were stripped away from the underside of the outer wood form. In place of the plaster, the craftsmen shaped thin, 3/32-inch (2.38 mm) copper sheets against the underside of these negative wood forms. These shaped copper sheets were then moved to the lead forms for finish hammering.

Rather than begin with the body of the statue, construction started with her right arm and torch and, next, with her head. This sequencing took advantage of two world's fairs in the 1870s, the Centennial in Philadelphia in 1876 and the Universal Exposition in Paris in 1878. Inclusion of the statue, or a portion thereof, in the two world's fairs was perfectly fitting. World's fairs were demonstrations of national progress and international coopera- tion, often following periods of unrest, ether domestic or inter- national. The writers Edmond and Jules de Goncourt skeptically commented during the 1867 Universal Exposition that Paris was "inundated with people collected to celebrate the fraternization of the Universe." For the host country, a world's fair provided an opportunity to confirm its self-confidence and its standing inter- nationally and to display its accomplishments. Exhibitors from all nations appreciated the "peaceful competition" of a well-at- tended international fair to make their goods known to people around the world. The French Exposition of 1878 followed the Franco-Prussian War and the turmoil of the early 1870s; the idea for an American Centennial Exhibition came on the heels of the Civil War. The Centennial Exhibition served not only to celebrate the nation's independence but also to publicly affirm the union of the states and to display to the world the Union's innovations and accomplishments. As the Civil War major general Daniel Sickles explained in Paris in 1875, "our Centennial anniversary will af- ford a happy opportunity to bury all that is painful in the past and to inaugurate a new and grander epoch in our history." The Statue of Liberty, celebrating both international friendship and the founding and achievements of the United States, was well suited to this event.

It was important that the statue, which was announced as "a commemorative monument of the Centennial anniversary of the United States independence," be represented in America in some

The arm and torch display at the 1876 Centennial Exhibition in Philadelphia. © Musée des arts et métiers–Cnam, Paris. Photograph by S. Pelly.

fashion during the nation's centennial celebration. John Forney, who spoke at the inaugural banquet for the fundraising campaign, gave Bartholdi and the Franco-American Union the idea of exhibiting a portion of the statue in Philadelphia's Centennial Exhibition. As Centennial Commissioner to Great Britain and Continental Europe, Forney sought the participation of France in the Philadelphia exhibition, and he persuaded his friends to assume a role. Laboulaye and fellow Franco-American Union members Oscar de Lafayette, Charles Dietz-Monin, and Louis Wolowski joined the committee organized to oversee the involvement of France in the exhibition. For his part, Bartholdi submitted numerous pieces demonstrating both the range of his work and affection for the United States: two oil paintings of California from his visit in 1871 and four bronze sculptures for display in the French section of the Art Gallery. In addition, Bartholdi submitted two works for the park grounds. The first of these was a large bronze sculptural fountain, which was assigned the most prominent position on the grounds, at the center of the plaza inside the park entrance between the Main and Machinery Buildings. The second was the right arm and torch of the Statue of Liberty.

Unfortunately, this portion arrived after the opening of the Centennial and was, as a consequence, omitted from the visitor's guide to the exhibition. The symbolism of the statue was also not entirely understood. Although some reports identified the torch as a part of a planned illuminated statue of Liberty Enlightening the World, others referred to it as the Colossal Arm or the Bartholdi Electric Light. This colossal arm and torch, moreover, turned out to be only one of the many colossal works of art and industry exhibited. Many of the heroic statues were predictably patriotic; Christopher Columbus upon his discovery of the New World, William Penn explaining the original plan of Philadelphia, Rev. John Witherspoon urging fellow representatives of the Continental Congress to sign the Declaration of Independence, assuring them that he would rather die "by the hand of the executioner than desert at this crisis the sacred cause of my country," Robert Livingston as chancellor of the State of New York, in which position he administered the oath of office to George Washington, and Abraham Lincoln signing the Emancipation Proclamation. The fair ground and exhibition buildings were themselves record-setting in size.

At the same time, other figures of liberty were associated with the fair in Philadelphia. Liberty was featured on the certificates of capital stock issued to help finance the exhibition. A fifty-foot-high painting in the Main Building featured Columbia with a raised staff supporting a liberty cap, and a statue of Columbia was erected above the dome of the Art Gallery. While Bartholdi must have been disappointed that his display did not receive special recognition, he likely gained confidence in the impression of the United States he had formed during his first visit five years earlier. Liberty figures were fundamental to the nation's identity, he had observed in 1871, and everything is big in America. Besides, the display of the torch was a success nonetheless, attracting exhibition visitors and also acquainting them with Bartholdi. Visitors entered the arm to climb an internal ladder to the balcony encircling

The Centennial Fourth—Illumination of Madison Square, New York. From a sketch by E. A. Abbey, 1876. The canvas painting of the statue can be seen on the building at the far side of the square. George A. Kubler Collection, Cooper-Hewitt, National Design Museum, Smithsonian Institution. Photograph by Matt Flynn.

the flame. From this platform, they could admire the balustrade, with its corn motif, and gain a sense of the statue's outward-reaching enlightenment.

Although the arm and torch did not arrive at the exhibition until September, Bartholdi found another way to associate the statue with the Centennial during the Fourth of July celebrations that summer. New York was planning a grand torchlight procession for the evening of the third and early hours of the fourth of July, with flags and patriotic bunting draped on buildings along the route. Bartholdi arranged for an enormous painting depicting the Statue of Liberty, which had been exhibited in Paris at the Opera, to be shipped from France. This canvas panorama, by Jean-Baptiste Lavastre, was hung on a building at Madison Square Park, and, as Bartholdi had hoped, the lighting of the painting during the evening's celebration was greeted with much enthusiasm.

Most important, Americans were starting to show their support for a statue of liberty in 1876. "The statue will be commemorative of our Centennial and the traditional friendship between the two great nations," a review of the canvas painting explained. The statue "is no longer a mere project but has passed into the domain of reality."

9

THE AMERICAN COMMITTEE AND THE FRENCH ENGINEERS

The arm and torch at the Centennial Exhibition confirmed that the idea for a statue was already taking form in France. During his second visit to the United States, in the summer and fall of 1876, Bartholdi looked for other opportunities to publicize the statue. One such occasion was the unveiling of a statue of the Marquis de Lafayette, also designed by Bartholdi. The French government had commissioned the Lafayette statue as an expression of gratitude for the aid raised in New York during the Franco-Prussian War. Scheduled to coincide with Lafayette's birthday celebration on September 6, the festive ceremony in Union Square Park placed the young hero in the company of statues of George Washington and Abraham Lincoln. Bartholdi took advantage of this event, which focused attention on the alliance between the two nations, to remind people about the Statue of Liberty. This grand statue planned for the New York Harbor, he assured his audience, would commemorate the independence Lafayette had helped make possible and testify the friendship Lafayette had established.

A number of groups invited Bartholdi to attend their meetings that fall. Speaking at a gathering of the New England Society commemorating the 250th anniversary of the pilgrims' landing at Plymouth—for which Richard Morris Hunt and John Quincy Adams Ward designed a monument—Bartholdi expounded on how the liberty statue related to the pilgrims' experience. The French people, he explained, thought "to erect a Statue of Liberty at the entrance of this great country . . . as a personification of hospitality to all great ideas and to all sufferings." His own sense of longing and suffering, caused by the war in France, likely strengthened his empathy with the immigrant and pilgrim experience and enabled him to capture this meaning in his design.

Bartholdi sought to both build a sense of anticipation for the statue and convince Americans that it was time to begin their own planning for it. In this effort he was joined by Laboulaye, who, from France, wrote letters to his many contacts in the United States requesting that they initiate a fundraising effort on American soil. Two groups in particular, Bartholdi and Laboulaye believed, had reason to associate themselves with this monument. The first was the community of French businessmen in New York that had raised funds for the erection of Bartholdi's Lafayette statue. The second group consisted of members of the Union League, primarily in New York and Philadelphia. The Union League had been organized during the Civil War to assist the Union cause and its broad mission included the support of art, considered an important element of education, along with nationalism. In New York, the members of the Union League Club were among the founders of the Metropolitan Museum of Art. When Laboulaye wrote to members of the Union League, asking them to form an American Committee of the Franco-American Union, they agreed. They held Laboulaye in high regard; moreover, this statue of liberty meshed perfectly with the interests of the Union League. The American Committee initially planned to have branches in several cities but activities eventually centered in New York.

Members of the committee branches were exceptionally influential and energetic men. Many were businessmen, politicians, or newspaper journalists and publishers; some already had ties to France. John Forney, a man of many activities and connections, was representative of the type of person involved in the committee. In addition to being the publisher of several newspapers at various times, including the *Press* of Philadelphia and the *Washington Daily Union,* Forney was involved in politics. He served as clerk of the U.S. House of Representatives in the 1850s and in 1861, with the support of President Lincoln, was chosen secretary of the U.S. Senate, a position he held until 1868. William M. Evarts, who became chairman of the American Committee in New York, was another member with notable credentials. He served as the U.S. attorney general under President Andrew Johnson, as secretary of state under President Hayes, and as a U.S. senator, sponsoring the Judiciary Act of 1891, which created the federal courts of appeal. Evarts had spent time in Paris following the end of the Franco-Prussian War, when the French people were struggling to realize their own "new birth of freedom."

One young committee member, nineteen-year-old Theodore Roosevelt, was destined to become twenty-sixth president of the United States. The statue may have appealed to Roosevelt's patriotic bent; he also understood that self-government could not be taken for granted. As a young politician, he urged his fellow citizens to embrace a spirit of public service and called attention to the effect of their decisions on future generations. "So it is peculiarly incumbent on us here today," Roosevelt told a crowd during a Fourth of July celebration in 1886, the year the statue was unveiled, "to act throughout our lives as to leave our children a heritage, for which we will receive their blessing." As president, he would encourage the federal government to take an active role in national concerns such as conservation of natural resources and heritage. During his second term in office, Congress passed the Antiquities Act of 1906, establishing presidential authority to proclaim national monuments, a status that was conferred on the Statue of Liberty in 1924.

Shortly after the American Committee was organized in late 1876, the statue received federal support, a necessary first step. With the assistance of President Grant, the American Committee succeeded in obtaining the designation of federal land for the monument. A joint resolution, passed by the U.S. Congress and signed by Grant on March 3, 1877, authorized the President of the United States to prepare a site for and accept the statue when presented by France. The President, it continued, shall cause the statue "to be inaugurated with such ceremonies as will serve to testify the gratitude of our people for this expressive and felicitous memorial of the sympathy of our sister republic." Designation of the island site was left to the new president, Rutherford B. Hayes, who agreed with the selection of the French-American Union, Bedloe's Island. With the site secure and the government's acceptance of the statue certain, the committee felt confident about the work that remained, namely raising funds, preparing the site, and building a pedestal for the statue.

Back in Paris, following his return from the Centennial Exhibition in 1876, Bartholdi focused his attention on the construction of a second portion of the statue. The arm and torch had been moved to New York, where it would be displayed in Madison Square Park for the next several years. For the upcoming world's fair in Paris, therefore, Bartholdi decided to complete the head and shoulders of the statue. This portion, over 30 feet (5.3 m) high, was finished in time for exhibition on the grounds of the Universal Exposition in 1878. The display got off to a promising start already on its way to the fairgrounds. As a team of twelve horses drew the cart from the Gaget, Gauthier & Co. workshop to the grounds at Champ-de-Mars, the immense head of the statue seemed to nod to those it passed by on its way. Encountering this scene as the cart rolled through the Arc de Triomphe and along the Champs-Élysées, people instinctively raised their hats, calling out "Vive la République!" The press estimated that a crowd of fifteen hundred sang "La Marseillaise" as the liberty head passed through the center of Paris. "Despite oneself," an observer wrote of that day, "one felt compelled to tip one's hat and pay her respect." Similar to the arm and torch in Philadelphia, the interior of the statue head was made accessible to the public during the fair. Visitors were able to climb to a viewing platform, positioned at the level of the crown openings.

The two portions of the statue were built with the assistance of Viollet-le-Duc, who likely offered advice on the repoussé work that shaped the copper exterior as well as on the construction of the structural frame for each portion. Both the arm and torch and the head were constructed with light metal frameworks on the inside to shape and support these portions. It is not known exactly where or how Viollet-le-Duc intended to transition from the metal construction in the upper portions of the statue to masonry and sand. He was not able to work further on the project, because in 1879 he suddenly became ill. In September of that year he died at the age of sixty-five.

Despite the controversial position Viollet-le-Duc had assumed in the architecture profession in France, or perhaps because of it, he left his mark on the direction of architecture and is considered by architects today as "one of the most important influences" of the second half of the nineteenth century. Through his emphasis on rational design as the basis for incorporating new materials into contemporary architecture he fostered progressive theory and practice, which enabled a shift over the following decades to Modern architecture, with its discussion of logical functional and structural design.

As a consequence of Viollet-le-Duc's sudden death, Bartholdi was unexpectedly in need of a designer for the structure of the main body of the statue before its construction had even begun. The Franco-American Union fundraising campaign, meanwhile, was finally approaching its goal. After the first year of fundraising, events had shifted from elaborate banquets to more modest and broad endeavors. The statue's image was made available for mementos and as a logo. Bartholdi also offered the statue for reproduction to manufacturers for miniatures, along with a limited edition of autographed 3-foot-high (1 m) terra-cotta statues. Perhaps most appreciated by the public was the decision to issue tickets for entry to the Gaget, Gauthier & Co. workshop. An estimated three hundred thousand people, Bartholdi later reported, viewed the workshop activity.

In the summer of 1879 the Franco-American Union obtained permission from the government to organize a national lottery, which helped bring the fundraising to a conclusion. Among the many prizes offered were a few works of art donated by artists, including Bartholdi's former instructor Antoine Étex. In July 1880, nearly five years after its inaugural banquet, the Franco-American Union reached its fundraising objective. Altogether more than 100,000 individuals, 181 towns, and 10 chambers of commerce contributed to the making of the statue. Various amounts have been reported for the total; 400,000 francs (approximately $250,000) appears to be the amount raised while additional contributions were received as materials, such as the copper that was donated for the statue and nonreimbursed costs, including Bartholdi's time and expenses.

Further progress on the statue was assured in 1880 when Bartholdi secured a new designer for the support structure, the engineer-builder Alexandre-Gustave Eiffel. Bartholdi and Eiffel had little in common and the two designers probably did not know each other on a social basis. However, Eiffel had established a reputation for innovation and talent by the late 1870s. His work was featured at the Universal Exposition in Paris in 1878; he also built the central pavilion at the Exposition, along with two other pavilions.

Eiffel had attended the École Centrale des Arts et Manufacturers in Paris, a relatively new engineering school that opened in 1829 in response to a growing awareness that the industrial age required young men to be trained for the industrial sciences. The school's three-year program had nurtured Eiffel's practical inclination and provided him with engineering as well as management

Alexandre-Gustave Eiffel. Library of Congress, Prints and Photographs Division, LC-B2-5504-5A.

skills. On receiving his diploma in 1855, Eiffel heeded the advice of his mother, whose sense for business alerted her to metalwork as a business of the future, and found employment with a foundry that manufactured, among other things, railway engines and tracks. The choice was a wise one, for this job launched his career. At the age of twenty-six Eiffel was given responsibility for the fabrication and erection of the iron structure on his first bridge, the Bordeaux Bridge.

Eiffel had the good fortune of entering the industry in an era of both tremendous railway network expansion and growing use of metal. In France, the miles of railway track leapt from around 300 miles (500 km) in 1840 to close to 10,000 miles (16,000 km) by 1870 and continued to increase again after the Franco-Prussian War, approaching 17,000 miles (27,000 km) in 1881. The new lines of track inevitably required railway bridges and viaducts to efficiently cross the rivers and ravines they encountered. At the same time, iron was gradually displacing the traditional structural materials of wood and stone. Eiffel rapidly gained experience with railway projects, and in 1866 he opened his own business. He soon began to expand the business, taking a partner with a mind for theory to complement his practical acumen.

Each successful project encouraged another, as railroad companies dared to ask for more demanding design and construction projects. Construction technique was as important as design, in that staging could not be used to support a long span built across a deep ravine. Instead, methods had to be developed to temporarily support the long extensions of a viaduct until they obtained their permanent support; in cantilever type construction, two halves of a span would be built out from two end piers concurrently and joined in the center. Eiffel's attention to construction details and methods helped ensure the economic viability of these long-span structures and, matched with the efficient designs his office developed, placed Eiffel in the forefront of the transition to metal construction. In 1872 he received his first commission outside of France, and by the late 1870s he had established a reputation as one of the premier builders in all of Europe. He was mastering record-setting and innovative projects, both in size and method of construction.

Although his forte was bridges and viaducts, Eiffel also worked on building projects. These included gasworks, covered markets, pavilions, a large Bon Marché department store, a synagogue, a church, a bank, a school, a social club, and a railway station. For the Universal Exposition in Paris in 1878, Eiffel obtained the commission for the main entrance hall and three domes for the central pavilion, in addition to a large pavilion for the City of Paris and another pavilion for the Parisian Gas Company. Drawings and models of his work from the past two decades were featured in France's display in the exposition, to showcase the nation's progress in this modern industry.

Bartholdi may already have been aware of the engineer's work. Modern metal bridge construction held a certain fascination for him and in his journal he remarked on some of the bridges he saw. He admired metal bridges for their "fantastically bold and ingenious" construction. One bridge in the United States near St. Louis made a particularly strong impression. "More extraordinary than all the others," Bartholdi wrote in a letter to his mother, this bridge seemed "to be made of matches and thread. Nevertheless, when you are on it, you see with what care and skill the capacity of the materials it utilizes."

In 1880, when Eiffel agreed to design the structure for the Statue of Liberty, his office had recently completed the design for the Garabit Viaduct to bridge the Truyère River in France. Eiffel had been asked to span the Truyère River with a scheme similar to the one his former partner, Théophile Seyrig, had developed a few years before to cross the Douro River in Portugal. Seyrig's viaduct received particular notice because of its unusual design for a 520-foot (160 m) arch span and its surprising economy. The scheme proposed for crossing the Truyère River extended a total length of 1,853 feet (565 m) and included a 54-foot-wide (165 m) arch rising to the exceptional height of 400 feet (122 m) above the valley. To complete this difficult design commission, Eiffel hired a gifted young engineer, only two years out of school, Maurice Koechlin.

Born in Alsace, Koechlin had relocated to Switzerland after the Franco-Prussian War and studied at the Swiss Federal Polytechnique (ETH Zurich). He became a student of Karl Culmann, a professor whose development of a method of static analysis combined calculation and graphics to improve, and simplify, the design of metal structures such as railway bridges. Koechlin analyzed the structure for the Garabit Viaduct using Culmann's method. His design resulted in a progressive, efficient system that was admired as well for its visual aesthetic. Compared to previous constructions, the structure's trussed pier and box beam systems had greater strength and resistance to wind, a critical concern highlighted by frequent bridge collapses.

When Eiffel's office began work on the support structure for the liberty statue, Koechlin employed the new analytical method and developed a framework resembling that of a tall viaduct pier. The design consists of a main vertical truss tower formed of four corner columns with diagonals in both vertical and horizontal planes; the cross-bracing elements were referred to as *des croix de Saint-André* (crosses of Saint André), an old term in house construction for the crossing of two timber logs. On each side of this central tower, and supported by it, an outer vertical truss was roughly fitted to follow the shape of the statue. A separate trussed structure was connected at the statue's upper right side to support the raised arm.

Koechlin and his colleagues carefully considered the wind forces to which the large surface area of the statue might be subjected in New York Harbor. There was little information on wind available in the 1880s, so the engineers assumed the largest wind pressure generally used for viaduct design. They applied this pressure to the full surface area of the statue in the primary directions, at the front and the back and at either side. In addition, they considered the possibility of the wind pressure originating from an intermediate direction, namely, on the diagonal. Designing for wind in the diagonal direction was not yet common in engineering practice but was particularly important because it resulted in the largest forces at the base of the truss tower. Well into the twentieth century engineers were still learning to include this load condition.

The engineers also had to develop a method for attaching the sculpted copper sheets to the truss structure. They knew that the thin copper skin of the statue would flex as strong winds pressed on it or as the heat of the sun caused the metal to expand. The elaborate folding of the suppliant drapery, which helped stiffen the individual copper sheets, conveniently accommodated movement by providing the overall exterior form with elasticity and a system for distributing stresses. Similarly, the attachment of the copper skin to the truss structure needed to provide support for the copper figure yet accommodate some movement. A completely rigid system of connection would have caused stresses to build and to crack the

The support structure under construction in Paris in 1881. Musée Bartholdi, Colmar. Reproduction by C. Kempf.

skin. The system that Eiffel's office developed to solve this problem introduced flexibility into the connection between the copper skin and the truss structure by incorporating an intermediate layer of connecting bars. The outermost component of the layered system consists of a mesh of metal straps shaped to fit against the copper skin. These straps are loosely attached to the skin by intermittent short copper sleeves, referred to as "saddles." The saddles permit the mesh and skin to move, during expansion under the heat of the sun, for example. The engineers then interposed flat iron bars between the skin and the truss structure to support these saddles, holding them in place. Because each iron bar projects from the truss to connect to a saddle at a different position on the sculpted figure, each required individual shaping. Although labor-intensive, this layered system formed a remarkably effective means of support.

At the same time, the engineers were concerned that moisture from the salty spray of the sea would set in motion a cycle of corrosion if the iron and copper elements were in direct contact. Dealing with this secondary aspect of the design proved to be especially difficult. It appears that in some locations small pieces of fabric soaked in an anticorrosive red lead pigment were placed between the iron and copper (since these materials deteriorated, there is some uncertainty about the methods used).

Eiffel rarely talked about the design for the support of the statue, almost slighting its importance. Nonetheless, he did take satisfaction in the statue's successful performance. "Despite conditions of strict economies that the circumstances imposed," he later wrote, "the work has well resisted the formidable storms that have assailed it."

For Eiffel's office, the statue's structural design fit into a continuum of development. Advancing the office's ideas for structural form, the freestanding structure can be seen as a forerunner of the 976-foot-tall (300 m) Eiffel Tower. Romantic notions of a 1,000-foot (or a 300-meter) tower had circulated since the start of the industrial age but had never been realistically followed. In 1884, Koechlin, together with another engineer in the office, Emile Nouguier, decided to pursue the idea. They had no commission for such a project; however, the upcoming exposition planned by the government to commemorate the centennial of the French Revolution offered a setting for a symbolic tower. They determined that a three-hundred-meter tower could be built and drew up preliminary plans. With input from architect Stephen Sauvestre, the design concept for a trussed tower gained acceptance in Eiffel's office, was agreed to by the officials in charge of the exposition, and was constructed in time for the Universal Exposition of 1889. Although a connection with the Seven Wonders of the Ancient World was not emphasized, occasional references were made by the designers, including Eiffel, to the Pharos at Alexandria and the "charm inherent in the colossal." Founded on the inspiration of past achievement, the two progressive metal structures, the concealed framework of the Statue of Liberty and the exposed Eiffel Tower, took advantage of the century's development of new structural materials and advanced computational techniques. These two towers pointed toward a modern way of thought in structural design, in which wind forces are resisted not by supplying mass but by the design of a strong and stiff lightweight structure.

By changing the support system for the liberty statue from masonry construction to lightweight metal, the engineers had enabled Bartholdi to change his plans for fabrication and erection of the statue. Bartholdi had initially expected to build the interior support for the copper form in place on Bedloe's Island. But metal framing could be disassembled and transported from Paris to New York. It was preferable to construct the entire statue in Paris, to ensure that every detail of the statue's construction was accurately accounted for before it was sent to the United States. The decision was made, accordingly, to erect the iron truss tower in a yard next to the Gaget, Gauthier & Co. workshop and attach, with temporary connections, the sculpted copper sheets forming the statue. Each iron and copper piece could then be marked to identify its position, making construction at Bedloe's Island simpler and quicker. This plan had the additional advantage of allowing the people of France, who had paid for the statue, to observe its construction.

The two portions of the statue, the arm and torch and the head, were already complete; now the body could start to take shape. Erection of the truss tower began in 1881, and the labor-intensive work of crafting full-size molds for hammering thin copper sheets proceeded. In October of that year a grand opening ceremony was arranged to mark the placement of the first pieces of sculpted copper for the main body. In the yard outside the Gaget, Gauthier &

Co. workshop the first rivet was ceremoniously placed by the U.S. minister to France, Levi P. Morton.

The opening ceremony was scheduled to coincide with celebrations of the centennial anniversary of the victory at Yorktown. "France and America have, during the last few days," Morton recounted in an address to the gathering in the foundry yard, "joined in a celebration of the crowning victory of their allied armies. Today we raise a monument to the liberty they secured." Morton also

On October 24, 1881, the U.S. minister to France, Levi P. Morton, placed the "first" rivet to mark the beginning of construction of the main body of the statue. Musée Bartholdi, Colmar. Reproduction by C. Kempf.

acknowledged Bartholdi and Laboulaye's dedication to the statue, which symbolized the friendship between France and the United States. "The illustrious names of Lafayette, Rochambeau, Noailles, and others . . . have been household words in the Republic of the New World since their ancestors gave their blood and treasure so freely to secure its independence. To this illustrious roll may now be added the names of Laboulaye and Bartholdi." It was no doubt a moment of deep satisfaction for the two men. Progress on the statue, it appeared at the moment, was on track to move smoothly forward.

10

HUNT DESIGNS
A PEDESTAL

The placement of the first rivet in the statue in Paris prompted the American Committee, whose activity had subsided in the late 1870s, to begin making plans for construction on Bedloe's Island. The committee solicited proposals from architects and, based on a preliminary scheme submitted for its review, commissioned Richard Morris Hunt to design the pedestal for the statue.

By the time of his selection in late 1881, Hunt had become one of the most highly esteemed architects in America. His work included the Studio Building, where he had his office and atelier. This was the first building in New York designed to accommodate artists, providing individual studios, exhibition space, and living quarters. John La Farge was one of the initial artists to establish his studio here when the building opened in 1858, as was Frederic Edwin Church; Albert Bierstadt and Winslow Homer acquired studios later. The Studio Building was both a design and a financial success, having been fully occupied since its opening. Similarly successful was Hunt's design for Stuyvesant Apartments, considered the first apartment building in New York on its completion in 1870. The concept and design of this twenty-unit, five-story building reflected Hunt's training in France; the style is regarded as inspired by Viollet-le-Duc. In the same period Hunt designed the Presbyterian Hospital, a large facility that opened in 1872, and the acclaimed Lenox Library, the construction of which began in the summer of 1871. It is understandable, given the activity of Hunt's architecture practice, that Bartholdi found Hunt rather pleased with himself when they met in August 1871.

Hunt also designed the tallest office tower in New York, the Tribune Building. Completed in 1875, this 260-foot-high (79 m) tower was one of the first elevator structures in the city. Hunt's work included homes for members of the American Committee and the Union League, among other clients. The extent of his experience with public monuments, moreover, was unusual, especially for an architect known for his building designs. The fact that Hunt was a fellow member of the Union League Club and acquainted with the American Committee members on a personal basis further increased the desirability of his selection. In addition, Hunt's family background had the respect of the Union League. His grandfather had fought in the militia during the Revolution and served as Vermont's lieutenant governor; his father had served in Vermont's state legislature and in the U.S. House of Representatives. Friends of the Hunt family included the renowned champion of Union integrity, Daniel Webster of New England, who sought to cultivate "a truly national spirit." In a dramatic speech, considered by the U.S. Senate as the most famous speech in its history, Webster concluded his response to an argument in favor of states' sovereignty with the long-remembered phrase, "Liberty *and* Union, now and forever, one and inseparable!" Hunt's personal background, moreover, was certain to please the sponsors of the liberty statue on the other side of the Atlantic.

According to a *New York Times* article, Hunt's initial proposal in late 1881 anticipated a relatively simple granite shaft of great height, 180 feet. But as Hunt began to focus on the project Bartholdi sent him sketches suggesting either a broad stepped base with a short pedestal or a tall tower with an embedded colonnade motif to enliven the large expanse of surface area. Hunt seems to have taken these ideas seriously; he also understood the ancient heritage of colossal sculpture and Bartholdi's linking of the statue with the Seven Wonders of the Ancient World. There was, in fact, a compelling model for the pedestal among the Seven Wonders, after which Hunt named his early designs for the pedestal. Built in approximately the same period as the Colossus of Rhodes, the Pharos at Alexandria had served to mark the shore and harbor of the ancient Egyptian city. Acclaimed in its time for its tremendous height, at least 300 feet (92 m) tall—equivalent to a modern thirty-story apartment building—the impressive structure comprised three sections. The lowest tier was square in plan, the middle tier was of octagonal shape, and the short upper tier was formed as a circular shaft. At each of the two transition levels the wall from the tier below extended a few feet above the transition to enclose a 360-degree balcony, abundantly decorated with sculpture. Along the height of the two lower tiers, series of windows are believed to have punctured the solid walls. Images of the Pharos on Alexandrian coins also led to one interpretation (today generally discarded) of the "windows" not as openings but as round shields hung on the exterior. The base of the tower may have been protected from the sea by a high wall that surrounded it at some distance. Accordingly, the structure's base and entrance door were raised above the level of the surrounding wall, and steps led from ground level to the door. It is known that a statue stood above the roof of the tower; however, there remains some uncertainty regarding its identity. According to early writings about the Pharos, this statue depicted Zeus holding a thunderbolt in his arm. A plaque recorded the dedication of the Pharos to Zeus Soter (Zeus the Savior) "for the safety of those who sail the seas."

Several centuries following its construction, probably in the first century A.D., the Pharos was transformed from a marker to a lighthouse by the addition of a light near its top. Creating this light, of course, would not have been a simple matter. It may have been accomplished with an oil fire that was kept burning near the base of the structure and a series of reflective metal sheets conveying the light of the flame to the top tier. With this additional feature, the Pharos at Alexandria, already revered in the ancient world, became the exemplary lighthouse in Roman times and gave its name "pharos" to lighthouses built thereafter. Soundly constructed, it stood for more than a millennium until earthquakes damaged and finally destroyed it in the fourteenth century. Besides its practical function for seafarers, the lighthouse held spiritual meaning, serving as a guiding beacon metaphorically. And, as with all of the Seven Wonders, the Pharos at Alexandria embodied a sense of piety. In building these wondrous edifices the people meant to demonstrate that they lived in harmony with their gods.

The Isle of Pharos and the city of Alexandria nicely paralleled

Bedloe's Island and New York. Indeed, the similarities between the setting of the Pharos and that of the Statue of Liberty were astonishing. To begin with, the relationship of the Isle of Pharos to Alexandria, as it projected beyond the city at its harbor, approximated the position of Bedloe's Island in the harbor off New York. On shore, the protective sea wall that surrounded the Pharos resembled the existing fort wall on Bedloe's Island. One could find similarities between ancient Alexandria and nineteenth-century New York, as well. Founded by Alexander the Great in the third century B.C., Alexandria grew into a vibrant city, drawing people from far away to form an agglomeration of cultures and religions. As with New York, a competitive spirit stimulated Alexandria's focus on commerce; at the same time, the gateway city developed into a prominent cultural and intellectual center of the Mediterranean region.

Hunt no doubt recognized the similarities between the Pharos at Alexandria and the project for Bedloe's Island. His ideas for the pedestal derived from his knowledge of the Pharos, together with his training in classical architecture. Having determined that a tall pedestal was appropriate for the liberty monument, he shaped a three-tiered structure with diminishing dimension, each tier slightly narrower than the one below. He contemplated a cylindrical form for the entire structure; referring again to the Pharos, he considered an octagonal form for one tier. In the end he opted for a square plan for all three tiers but chamfered the uppermost one so that it has, in effect, eight sides; four short sides at the corners in addition to the four main sides. Following the Pharos model, he raised the pedestal and its door above the level of the top of the wall, a feature that lent it the dignity that ancient Roman temples had achieved in a similar fashion.

Development of a design for the pedestal took several years as Hunt explored different schemes that ranged from tapering towers reminiscent of what he had seen along the coastlines during his grand tour to stark classical structures with smooth surfaces and formal elements. Intertwining the various models and influences for his design, he studied a wide variety of form and decoration, along with varying shapes and sizes of openings and colonnades. He preferred a tall pedestal. The American Committee, on the contrary, could not be reconciled to the scale of pedestal he proposed, or with the cost. Moreover, the notion that the pedestal had an association with the Seven Wonders must have disconcerted, rather than appealed to, the committee. Hunt's schemes, titled *Pharos I* and *Pharos II*, were rejected as too costly in 1883 and 1884.

By 1883 the American Committee was anxious about the expense for a couple of reasons. First, it had discovered that raising funds would be more difficult than initially anticipated, and, second, it had realized that construction costs would exceed original projections. Although the design for the pedestal was still uncertain in 1883, the committee had started work at Bedloe's Island to prepare for the pedestal construction. Excavation for a massive 15-foot-deep (4.6 m) foundation, which grew from 64 feet (19.7 m) square to 91 feet (28 m) square as the pedestal design developed, began in April 1883. By May 1884 the foundation, together with a pyramidal base for the pedestal, was complete.

During this time Hunt developed new schemes for the pedestal, while complying with the Committee's request that its height be reduced. The design that was finally agreed on in the summer of 1884 retained the impressive verticality of the Pharos but not its name. With a height of 89 feet (27.1 m), the pedestal was certain to raise the statue adequately to be seen from a distance. At the same time, the new design for the middle tier transformed the previously ambiguous colonnade element into a well-defined, central, recessed porch, referred to as a "loggia." To emphasize the separate surfaces of the central porch and the side walls, Hunt used smooth stone for the porch and roughened stone at the sides. The use of roughened stone, or rustication, was a traditional method of increasing visual interest. The two distinct surfaces create a richness of texture and also provide transitional continuity between the rough stone face of the existing fort wall and the smooth metal finish of the copper statue. Hunt may have intended as well to relate the pedestal to the rusticated granite piers of the recently completed Brooklyn Bridge located nearby in the bay.

The proportions and placement of the porch suggest that Hunt discovered a strong character for the middle tier in the example of American buildings. It was desirable, after all, to interpret ancient sources in a manner consistent with American tradition, and his familiarity with buildings connected to the nation's formative history likely influenced his work. One such example, seen in Newport, Rhode Island, where Hunt spent a considerable amount of time, was the Colony House. It was from the porch of the Colony House

The porch, or loggia, is the central element of the pedestal design. Library of Congress, Prints and Photographs Division, Historic American Engineering Record. Photograph by Jet Lowe.

that the Declaration of Independence was read to townspeople in 1776. A few years later, when Washington visited Newport to confer with Rochambeau, who was settled there with his troops, Washington was entertained by his French hosts in the great hall of the Colony House. The building design included an early-eighteenth-century American interpretation of the front portico, a common classical element, with shortened columns set on high pedestals.

Another building firmly associated with the birth of the nation, with which Hunt was well familiar, was the old Federal Hall in New York, site of Hunt and Ward's statue of George Washington. It was here, on the building's second-story front porch, that Washington's inauguration as the country's first president took place in April 1789 (see chapter 6). The porch, with its Doric columns, was enmeshed in the creation of the nation; and, with the Washington statue unveiled in 1883, Federal Hall was forefront in Hunt's thoughts at the time that he was studying alternative schemes for the liberty monument.

With Hunt's reconfiguration of the middle tier the pedestal became an active footing for the statue and a complementary symbol. The porch brings to mind the inauguration of the nation's first president; likewise, it strengthens the welcoming nature of the statue, as the poet Edmund Clarence Stedman depicted in his verse "Liberty Enlightening the World":

> Enter! there are no bars
> Across your pathway set:
> Enter at Freedom's porch,
> For you I lift my torch.

On top of the middle tier Hunt extended the cornice well beyond the plane of the pedestal wall to widen the promenade of the viewing area above. Rising from this platform is the uppermost and smallest tier, neatly matched to the statue's copper base. A doorway at the upper tier, as at the lower tier, is capped with a triangular pediment.

Adapting these classical design elements to the Pharos-inspired structure, Hunt set the tone and established a significant setting for the historical liberty statue—the primary purpose of the pedestal. Nevertheless, he wished to identify the pedestal with the United States and the preservation of the Union that the Union League celebrated. To do so, he planned two features. The first of these was a horizontal band of shields, which he placed around the lowest tier. These shields resemble the ones at the top of the Arc de Triomphe in Paris, as well as the bronze dedicatory shields of the Parthenon in Athens, a favorite source for neoclassical design.

They may also have referred to the possible shields of the Pharos at Alexandria. Hunt and American Committee members agreed that engraving each shield with the coat of arms of one state or territory would be an ideal way of associating the individual states and territories with the monument. Such an association offered a fundraising opportunity, as the state legislatures might be asked to contribute to this state-specific design feature. The idea also had symbolic merit; all the states of the Union were a home for liberty. However, the continual growth of the Union—in 1889, there were four new states—presented a difficulty, as did the limited show of interest on the part of the states. The second contemporary reference Hunt considered was a dedicatory inscription in the area below the central porch.

Had these two features been incorporated, the pedestal would have embodied a continuity of architectural history from ancient Alexandria, Greece, and Rome up to the time of the monument's unveiling in 1886. And yet such specific reference to the states and territories and to the date of unveiling might have worked against the statue's suggestion of movement, which has enabled the liberty figure to progress with the Union, as it has grown in size and as its citizens' understanding of liberty has continued to evolve.

By the time a design for the pedestal was accepted by the American Committee in the summer of 1884, the statue had seemingly come to life in the rue de Chazelles near the Parc Monceau in Paris. Parisians had watched the progress of construction for close to three years, since the first rivet was ceremoniously placed by the U.S. minister to France, Levi P. Morton. Equal in height to a fourteen- or fifteen-story building, if there had been one in Paris, the statue now towered over the six-story houses of the city. The construction of the iron truss tower and copper sculptural form was, as described in *American Architect and Building News*, "an industrial *tour de force*" in the 1880s. The truss tower, the tallest metal structure built to date, may have hinted at the transition to a scale and type of structure that was soon to follow—the first skyscraper rose in Chicago in this same period.

The Statue of Liberty also surpassed other examples of national statuary. The statue from which she claimed the title of world's tallest was the 86-foot (27 m) figure of the Hermannsdenkmal in Germany, which had been completed in 1875. Brandishing a sword, Germany's patriotic liberty statue symbolized the end of a long history of incursions by foreigners and celebrated the German states' unification and growing strength. The Germanic tribal chief Arminius, credited with liberating the interior of Germany from Roman oppression in A.D. 9, was selected for the statue. The choice was not surprising for a national monument. The contrast between the two statues, however, both in copper and unveiled about a decade apart, is striking. Built in the tradition of patriotic statuary, the Hermannsdenkmal armed warrior rebukes the oppression of the past; the Statue of Liberty, meanwhile, focuses on a vision of life that liberation has made possible. The American liberty statue, in addition, reflects a sense of common humanity many people felt at the time, irrespective of international tension and war. As one nineteenth-century critic optimistically predicted, the art of the future will translate "into harmonious form the irresistible feeling which draws the world toward unity." The alternative perspective on freedom and national identity that the Statue of Liberty conveys is rooted in this frame of mind.

Shortly after the statue was finished in Paris, Victor Hugo came to see her. Hugo had fled France in 1851, when Louis Napoleon tightened his control over individual liberties and expanded his presidential authority, before declaring himself Emperor Napoleon III. During his nineteen years in exile Hugo lent his voice to political and social causes, both in France and around the world. By the time he returned to France in 1870, after nearly twenty years, he was considered a spokesperson for individual liberty, political amnesty, and international peace. He had actively supported the Lincoln medal following Lincoln's assassination; catching sight of an American flag on his return to Paris in 1870, he hailed the "banner of stars," which speaks to the people of France of "a great principle; the liberty of every race and the fraternity of all." Visiting the statue in Paris in 1884, a year before his death, Hugo was moved by the sight of this monument demonstrating the common ideals of the people of two nations. "This beautiful work of art . . . will constitute a lasting pledge of peace between France and America," he concluded. "It is good that this has been done."

To mark the completion of the statue, Bartholdi and the Franco-American Union planned a ceremony worthy of the important event. The date selected was July 4, 1884. The occasion would also include the official presentation of the statue to the United States. The Gaget, Gauthier & Co. yard and the streets and buildings of the neighborhood were decorated with French and American flags. People crowded into the yard, filled the streets outside, and climbed to neighboring rooftops to participate in some fashion in the event, while a band played the national anthems of the United States and France. Morton, who had ceremoniously placed the first rivet in 1881, now accepted the statue on behalf of U.S. president Chester A. Arthur. Morton had been instructed by his government, he told the crowd, to assure the sponsors of the statue and "the French nation that the American people responded with all their hearts to the sentiments of friendship." Morton hoped, he concluded, "that the statue would remain for all time an emblem of the imperishable sympathies uniting both countries."

There was one person missing on this day of heartfelt celebration. In May 1883, while the statue was still rising in Paris, the man who had shepherded the liberty project through political and fundraising obstacles from design to construction, had died at the age of seventy-two. The loss of Édouard Laboulaye was an especially painful blow. Laboulaye had remained personally committed to the project over the last eighteen years of his life, and it is doubtful that any other person could have conceived and pursued the idea of a statue as he had. Indeed, the chances are slight that anyone in France, or elsewhere, would have seriously considered building a colossal monument as a gift to the United States and confidently presented this seemingly excessive suggestion to the public, asking it to finance a monument to a memory one hundred years past. It is equally unlikely that this same person would have had the connections, from artists to presidents, to bring together the many people necessary to accomplish the task and been able to sustain their motivation. Exuding an irresistible enthusiasm, Édouard Laboulaye, a distinctly suitable advocate for a statue promulgating the ideals of justice and liberty, had seized a moment in history and quietly left his mark.

Although Laboulaye did not live to see his ambition for a monument completed, he could take comfort in knowing that he had played a part in the advancement of liberty. He had witnessed the abolition of slavery in the United States and worked to see this movement spread to other parts of the world. He had been an advocate of worker's rights and women's rights (women's rights activist Susan B. Anthony was among those who made a point of attending his funeral), and he had assisted his country as it rose

The Statue of Liberty towered over the buildings of the 17th arrondissement in the early 1880s. On July 4, 1884, the statue was formally presented to the United States. Musée Bartholdi, Colmar. Reproduction by C. Kempf.

from the brutality and defeat of war to initiate a government based on respect for individual liberties. The statue he had conceived at a time of great uncertainty, during the empire of Napoleon III and shortly following the assassination of an American president, was becoming a reality. "In a century the centenary of independence will be celebrated again," he once told the statue's supporters. "We shall then be only forgotten dust. . . . But this statue will remain. It will be the memorial of this festival, the visible proof of our affection. Symbol of a friendship which braves the storms of time, it will stand there unshaken." This statue, he believed, would long endure as a symbol of shared aspirations and international friendship.

11

FUNDRAISING AND A VISIONARY SONNET

In the summer of 1884, the liberty monument was nearing completion. Construction of the foundation and pedestal base were complete. A design for the pedestal had been selected, and its construction would soon begin. The details of the sculptural copper form and the inner support structure had been worked out as the statue was built in Paris. To a casual observer, it appeared that "the moment" after the acceptance of the statue by Levi P. Morton on behalf of the United States, "the workmen will begin to take it to pieces for transport to America." There, continued an article in the *London Daily News*, which complimented the project as both a meaningful monument and a work of art, "it will be riveted together again to stand for eternity."

Left unspoken at the presentation ceremony in Paris, however, was an uneasy feeling that had overshadowed the statue's construction for the past few years. Following the initial success of the American Committee in obtaining a site on Bedloe's Island, progress in the United States had stalled in the late 1870s. Although the idea of a statue was received with enthusiasm by some Americans, there remained numerous obstacles to its realization.

One factor that contributed to the hesitant response the statue encountered was the timing of the project. In the years after the Civil War Americans favored realistic statuary, commemorating military and political heroes and events in American history, over allegorical statuary. The economic condition in the 1870s was also not favorable for what many perceived as a superfluous expenditure. The country had entered a depression in 1873, and newspaper editors asked why Americans should spend money on a statue with no particular purpose at a time when workers faced wage cuts or unemployment and families were struggling financially. Government funds for construction and monument projects were already committed, and privately financed projects were having difficulty meeting their goals. Even a monument dedicated to George Washington, the obelisk in Washington, D.C., by architect Robert Mills, was at a standstill. It would require a total of thirty-six years for the obelisk to be completed, partly due to a shortage of funds.

In the 1870s, many Americans doubted that the statue would actually be completed in France. When the arm and torch were on display in Philadelphia during the Centennial Exhibition, an article in the *New York Times* reported that Americans were being asked to donate funds to complete the statue; that is, if Americans wanted to receive more than one arm from France, they would need to fund the construction themselves. But "no true patriot," the article asserted, "can countenance any such expenditure for bronze females in the present state of our finances." In response to skepticism of this kind, the American Committee had allowed its activity to slip into a lull for several years while work continued in France.

Raising the necessary funds in France had similarly taken longer than anticipated, requiring the subscription campaign to continue for five years. The halting progress of fundraising in the United States, however, caused greater distress. Notwithstanding rumors in the United States, there was no longer any doubt that the statue would be built. Now, the looming concern in France was whether the statue would have a home—and a purpose. Mutterings against disassembling the statue to ship it to the United States, where it was thought to be unwanted, may have convinced a group of American residents in Paris to propose a replacement statue. With the support of Morton, the group announced in September 1884 that it planned to erect a smaller reproduction of the Statue of Liberty to demonstrate Americans' appreciation while honoring Bartholdi's design. The necessary funds were raised by the following September, and Morton had the opportunity to present the planned quarter-scale reproduction to the French capital on behalf of the American residents of Paris. The initial site for the statue was the Place des Etats Unis.

Another factor contributing to the American Committee's difficulty in raising funds was the problem Americans had understanding the reasons for the gift. The people of the United States and France had a tradition of gift exchange, but this was usually connected with a particular event. The Lafayette statue Bartholdi designed as a sign of appreciation for New Yorkers' aid during the Franco-Prussian War was such a gift. The scale and prominence of the proposed liberty statue added to people's discomfort with the idea. It "could not possibly be a free gift," people assumed; the idea itself seemed "Frenchy and fanciful."

The request that Americans provide the pedestal for the statue compounded the confusion. Few Americans perceived the value of making the project a collaborative effort between the people of the two nations. Nor did they recognize this opportunity for providing a symbolic solid footing for liberty in the United States. "We catch ourselves," one writer in *Harper's New Monthly Magazine* commented in 1878, "wishing that M. Bartholdi and our French cousins had 'gone the whole figure' while they were about it, and given us statue and pedestal at once." Even as newspaper and magazine articles began to show increased support for the statue, they acknowledged a sense of bewilderment with the gift. Americans should receive this "symbolic and significant gift . . . in the spirit of the offering," George William Curtis wrote in *Harper's New Monthly Magazine* in 1885. "It may not be the 'American way' to send an allegorical statue to another country in sentimental recognition of an ancient alliance, but it is the French way."

The statue was not what "public-spirited capitalists" considered a "safe aesthetic investment," a newspaper article explained. People were uncertain how a colossal female figure, prominently exhibited in the harbor, would look, and how it would reflect on its sponsors. It is possible that they were also aware of the changes taking place in the art world and in public taste, concurrent with a broadening public audience for art. In the two decades that intervened between Laboulaye's suggestion of a statue and its completion in New York, both the subject of art and the manner of its expression were undergoing a transformation that was quite controversial at the time. The tradition of great painting, in which artists "looked to the heights," as Eugène Delacroix explained in 1859, to express and inspire ideas, was receding during the second half of the nineteenth century. Artists began to eschew the depiction of the ideal and the potential of human nobility and sought instead to reveal the reality of human nature and "the modern spirit" of the people. When asked about the progress of art in France in 1886, the painter and friend of Bartholdi Jean-Léon Gérôme replied that "it is not easy to say whether the change has been for the better or the worse." The first large exhibition of impressionist painters in the United States was received with similar ambivalence. Monet, Pissaro, Manet, and other painters who "adhere to the principles of the school" of impressionism, were represented. But, as an article in the *Boston Daily Globe* acknowledged "these principles are very little understood here." In the early to mid-1880s, this climate of uncertainty made it difficult to appraise the design of the Statue of Liberty. A few newspaper and magazine articles commended Bartholdi for the statue's artistic merit; others criticized the design. Most reviewers chose to overlook the artistic aspect of the statue altogether and to focus on its meanings.

Fundraising efforts were also hampered by the fact that a variety of projects were competing for donors' funds; many churches, hospitals, universities, and libraries built in this period depended on private support. There were also other national subscriptions, for projects such as the statue of Henry Wadsworth Longfellow for Washington, D.C., following his death in March 1882.

The American Committee, despite the influence and connections of its members, also had difficulty obtaining government funds for the project. Western and rural representatives in Congress, resentful of what they understood to be the Eastern establishment, were not inclined to fund the statue. Northerners who still associated France with the perceived pro-Confederate position of Napoleon III during the Civil War greeted the idea of a gift with skepticism. In addition, jealousies between states were blamed for legislators' opposition to appropriating funds. Some congressmen agreed with the argument, made by Representative Richard P. Bland of Missouri, that the statue was "a local affair, in which only New-York was interested." Only in September 1886, when the statue was nearly complete, did Congress agree to provide $56,500 "to properly execute the inauguration ceremonies."

Another factor working against the statue was a growing sense that development of an American school of art necessitated establishing cultural independence from Europe. American culture was founded on classical and European culture, and many people looked to France and England for examples. But as confidence in the growth and endurance of the United States as a nation strengthened, a movement emerged not only to develop new manners of expression reflecting the national character but also to support American artists. As part of this movement, the selection of Italian-born Constantino Brumidi to decorate the Capitol had been harshly criticized, in spite of his strong identification with the United States as a naturalized citizen.

In late 1882, nearly a year after commissioning Richard Morris Hunt to design the pedestal, the American Committee renewed its fundraising effort in earnest. It still could not find clear or convincing terms to convey the meaning of the statue. In its *Appeal to the People of the United States in Behalf of the Great Statue, Liberty Enlightening the World*—published by the *Evening Post,* where Carl Schurz was now editor in charge of politics and foreign relations—the American Committee unwisely repeated a reference to the statue as "an impressive ornament to the entrance of the commercial metropolis of the Union." Linking liberty with commerce and prosperity dated back to the nation's early years and was entrenched by the 1870s. But this was certainly an uninspiring means of capturing the attention of the nation. It also neglected to emphasize that the statue was a gift and a symbol for all Americans, not only residents of New York.

Explaining that the Franco-American Union specifically requested that funds be "raised by the whole people," the American Committee reached out to the public, albeit largely in the New York area. A fundraising event at the Academy of Music in November 1882 proved a promising start. Members of the American Committee wrote to Bartholdi about the event, knowing that he was anxiously waiting for the committee to resume its activities. Bartholdi, in turn, showed the optimistic letters he received from American Committee members to the newspapers, hoping that their exposure would assure the French people that the statue was appreciated and welcomed by Americans. The American Committee indeed had considerable success. It organized benefit art fairs, lectures, public balls, concerts, and amateur theatricals, for which friends and family members were recruited. Six-inch- and twelve-inch-high tin models of the statue were sold, along with lithographs and a short book by Bartholdi about his design. A wide variety of groups responded to the committee's appeal, from Civil War veterans and the Sons of the Revolution, to trade associations and school teachers. Businesses and individuals sent contributions as well. One schoolgirl included a note with her contribution, recommending that the committee ask every schoolchild throughout the country to donate one penny. The committee gratefully reported her idea, together with the observation that if every American sent a small amount, the necessary funds—now estimated at $250,000—would soon be raised.

As the statue's image slowly became known and its relevance for the nation gained credence, the symbolism of a triumphal figure holding forth the lamp of liberty began to touch a chord. Among those who unexpectedly found themselves inspired by the symbolism of the statue was a young woman from New York, Emma Lazarus. Descended of Jewish immigrants of the seventeenth century, the Lazarus family had long-established roots in America. By the time Emma Lazarus was born in 1849 her family was "well-known in the best society of the city" and part of a Sephardic community that felt itself quite distant from recent immigrants. Her family was close-knit and encouraged her talents as a writer, arranging for the publication of her first book of poetry when Lazarus was seventeen. In her twenties Lazarus made the acquaintance of a large number of writers and editors, while developing her own skills. She wrote poetry in blank verse, a play, a novel and a short story, essays, and art criticism for newspapers. For the *American Hebrew* she introduced "An Epistle to the Hebrews," a weekly column in late 1882 and early 1883.

In the early 1880s Lazarus joined the debate among writers about American literary identity, adamant that American writers no longer relied on the muses of Europe but instead now influenced English authors. Her friend Edmund Clarence Stedman took up her argument, while pointing to a source of America's cultural vitality: immigrants. "Here are the emigrants or descendants of every people in Europe,—to go no further," Stedman wrote in *Scribner's Monthly* in 1881, "and all their languages, and customs, and traditions, and modes of feeling, at one time or another, have come with them. Hence our unconscious habitude of variety. . . . There is a ferment in new blood."

In the fall of 1883 Lazarus was drawn into the fundraising campaign for the liberty monument by way of a benefit art exhibition organized by the American Committee at the National Academy of Art in New York. This was expected to be an exceptionally large exhibition of art loaned from private collectors and distinguished art galleries. Paintings, many publicly shown for the first time in the United States, would be on view, along with antique prints, missals and antique books, coins, miniatures, china, ceramics, stained glass, musical instruments, rare lace and fans, embroideries, jewelry and silver, costumes of various nations, arms and armor, furniture, metal work, and examples of oriental art and American Indian art. John La Farge, Joseph Pulitzer, and Carl Schurz volunteered on the executive committee responsible for organizing the event; Richard Morris Hunt served as the chairman of the committee on insurance.

Known in New York circles for her poetry, Lazarus was asked to contribute a poem for the auction of original works of art and literary manuscripts that was planned as part of the exhibition. She may already have heard about the exhibition during its planning; she was a member of a social club in Newport to which Hunt and La Farge belonged, and her father was a member of the Union League Club. Lazarus declined at first, explaining that she could not simply write a poem about a statue. But by coincidence she was immersed in another cause at the moment, a cause that evoked the emotion she subsequently bestowed on the liberty statue. A rise in anti-Semitism in the late 1870s had culminated in a rash of pogroms in Russia in the early 1880s. Appalled by the violence of these riots and by the acquiescence of Russian officials, people in Europe and America protested against the pogroms and held public demonstrations. Lazarus had not previously been involved in humanitarian activities, but as other writers started to speak out against the atrocities, she joined in their effort. She rebuked in harsh terms not only Russia but much of Europe.

When refugees began inundating the shelters in New York, Lazarus took an interest in the conditions in which they lived, visiting Ward's Island in the East River where many were temporarily housed once the shelters in New York filled. Deeply affected by this exposure, Lazarus discerned her twofold mission. First, she would work to improve the lives of these immigrants, in particular through support of vocational training. Second, anticipating further violence and acknowledging local concern that New York could not absorb greater numbers of refugees, she would advocate the settlement of Jewish refuges in Palestine. To this end, she organized the Society for the Improvement and Colonization of East European Jews. According to one biographer, Lazarus was the first American to advocate the creation of a Jewish state in Palestine.

Lazarus's mixed reaction to the refugees with whom she came into contact during the early 1880s furnished the material from which she would compose her sonnet for the Statue of Liberty. Coming from "the cream of the monied aristocracy," she was astounded by the abysmal condition of the "huddled masses" she witnessed, a sight she had never before imagined. At the same time, she was overwhelmed with empathy for these poor and wearied refugees, which led her to envision the liberty statue in a manner similar to Bartholdi when he described the statue "at the entrance of this great country" as "a personification of hospitality to all great ideas and to all sufferings." The loss of Alsace had quickened Bartholdi's longing for liberty; in a similar manner, Lazarus's contact with individuals who were denied civil and religious rights and forced into degrading circumstances substantiated liberty as fundamental to dignified human life. Extending the experience of the Russian immigrants to that of all newcomers, she penned a sonnet that skillfully brought together the past, present, and future, offering compassion and hope while displaying her pride in the horizon that America offers.

> "The New Colossus"
> Not like the brazen giant of Greek fame,
> With conquering limbs astride from land to land,
> Here at our sea-washed, sunset gates shall stand
> A mighty woman, with a torch, whose flame
> Is the imprisoned lightning, and her name
> Mother of Exiles. From her beacon-hand
> Glows world-wide welcome; her mild eyes command
> The air-bridged harbor that twin-cities frame.
>
> "Keep, ancient lands, your storied pomp!" cries she,
> With silent lips. "Give me your tired, your poor,
> Your huddled masses, yearning to breathe free;
> The wretched refuse of your teeming shore—
> Send these, the homeless, tempest-tost to me—
> I lift my lamp beside the golden door!"

As her title conveys, Lazarus was well aware of Bartholdi's association of his statue with the Colossus of Rhodes. Similarly, her two opening lines clearly refer to the image of the Colossus of Rhodes standing with legs apart, spanning over the entry to the harbor, thus establishing a context and a scale for the subject of her verse. Although less direct, her depiction of "imprisoned lightning" may refer to the descriptions of Zeus, the supreme Greek god who ruled the sky and was often shown holding a thunderbolt, placed at the summit of the Pharos at Alexandria.

Lazarus did not record the meaning of her allusions, but she likely realized that they could encompass both antiquity and the life of the revolutionary generation. She was undoubtedly familiar with the poetic descriptions of Benjamin Franklin and his experiments with electricity and lightning, such as the motto an adoring public applied to him during his years in France: Franklin "snatched lightning from the sky and the scepter from tyrants." By drawing "down the fire from heaven," his discoveries had given people in the eighteenth century a sense of control through reason, freeing them, as his contemporary John Adams explained, from the "panic, terror, and superstitious horror" that the unknown nature of thunderstorms previously instilled. A century later, the perceived connection between scientific and political progress was reiterated in a commemorative address at the statue's unveiling: "When Franklin drew the lightning from the clouds, he little dreamed that in the evolution of science his discovery would illuminate the torch of Liberty for France and America."

Lazarus likely also realized that her personal reaction to the "huddled masses, yearning to breathe free" reflected the revolutionary generation's view of the nation as an asylum from oppression. The more radical Thomas Paine was not alone when he insisted on this purpose, exclaiming, "O! receive the fugitive, and prepare in time an asylum for mankind." James Madison, too, had voiced his conviction that inherent in the United States' achievement of independence from oppression was the offer of "asylum to the persecuted and oppressed of every nation and religion."

In Lazarus's sonnet the Statue of Liberty gained an active yet mild character that appealed to Americans. Also appealing was the interpretation of this "Mother of Exiles," welcoming weary travelers to shore. After talking with Bartholdi in 1875, John Forney explained to his readers, "The artist's thought is that all the nations may see by day the figure of Liberty welcoming them to the United States, and follow her shining welcome in the darkest hours of their despair." This meaning of the statue, highlighted in Lazarus's sonnet, took on increased significance as immigration surged in the two decades following its unveiling. In 1903 the sonnet was inscribed on a plaque and attached to the pedestal by Lazarus's friend Georgina Schuyler. Lazarus did not live to see her verse rendered into a dedicatory inscription; she died of illness the year following the statue's unveiling.

The reception that opened the art exhibition featured a reading of "The New Colossus." In addition, Charles Gounod's hymn to liberty, composed for the reception at the Paris Opera in 1876, was performed by orchestra and singers, and former president Ulysses S. Grant delivered an address of welcome, declaring the exhibition open. Considering the significance of the collection of artwork loaned for display, the exhibition would have been noteworthy in any case. It attracted additional attention for an unrelated reason: midway through the month-long exhibit, the executive committee voted to keep the exhibition open on Sundays, with a reduced admission fee for this day. This decision risked violating the city's ordinance prohibiting "shows" from being open on Sundays. The art director for the exhibition, F. Hopkinson Smith, insisted, however, that not only did an art exhibit differ from a show, but the decision to remain open on Sundays was essential to making the exhibit accessible to working people. It was appropriate, moreover, in that the art exhibit served an educational purpose, and education was second only to religious activity. Acknowledging that the organizers' action strayed from accepted practice regarding Sunday activities, Smith urged museums and libraries across the country to adopt a similar policy. The nation, he asserted, can affirm the depth of meaning of the Statue of Liberty by allowing the rays of her "beneficent torch" to enlighten our customs and bylaws. Smith and the executive committee managed to defend their position and the exhibition succeeded in drawing people from a cross section of society. With the largest attendance on Sundays, the exhibition attracted over forty thousand visitors during the busy holiday month of December and netted over twelve thousand dollars, a respectable sum "in these hard times," commented the *New York Times.*

The amounts raised through its numerous fundraising events

were less than the American Committee hoped for but adequate to fund the start of construction at Bedloe's Island. In 1883 the committee retained Charles Pomeroy Stone to manage construction at the site as well as design the foundation for the pedestal. Stone was an experienced engineer who had trained at West Point, served in various capacities in the U.S. military, and led a scientific expedition in Mexico prior to the American Civil War. More recently, Stone had spent thirteen years assisting with the modernization of the Egyptian army, during which time he gained command of the French language and exposure to colossal statuary. Charles C. Schneider, a civil engineer known for his work on bridges, assisted Stone with design and inspection, in particular on the anchorage system for the statue. To build the pedestal, David H. King Jr. offered the services of his construction company without profit.

Work on the 15-foot-deep (4.6 m) foundation, measuring 91 feet (28 m) on each side, proceeded without unusual difficulty. Above this a pyramidal pedestal base, referred to as the above-ground portion of the foundation, was constructed. This portion, which decreased in steps from a base width of 91 feet (28 m) to 67 feet (20.6 m) at the top, was "said to be the largest solid mass of concrete above ground in the world." Passageways at ground level were incorporated into the construction, and in the center of the stepped foundation the workers formed a vertical shaft for location of a stairway or elevator. This stepped structure reached nearly 38 feet (11.7 m) above ground but would largely be hidden by landscaping. Stone took great care with the construction, including the regular sampling of concrete for compression strength. This measure was important to ensure consistent good quality throughout but added to the total cost of the foundation, which reached nearly ninety-four thousand dollars.

Soon after Hunt's design was approved in the summer of 1884, the cornerstone for the pedestal was laid with Masonic rites. Building the pedestal involved the construction of another massive concrete structure, tapering from a plan dimension of 65 feet to 43 feet (20 m to 13.2 m). A vertical access shaft was formed in its center and a framework of steel beams was cast into the concrete to serve as an anchoring mechanism for Eiffel's truss tower. The metal tower would be subject to enormous forces caused by wind pressure against the large surface area of the statue. The engineers in Eiffel's office had calculated the maximum uplift forces that each of the four corners of the tower might experience, and they may have recommended a system for securing the corners of the tower. But the details of the design were left to Stone, who decided to take advantage of the availability of structural steel, which was just beginning to replace iron in building construction in the 1880s. The anchoring framework that he built consists of two horizontal grids of steel beams, one grid embedded into the pedestal at its top and the other sixty feet below, connected by long steel vertical members acting as anchor bolts. The lower horizontal grid anchors the frame into the mass of the pedestal and the upper grid supports the iron tower of the statue. Secured to the uppermost horizontal plane of this anchoring system, the statue would be certain to remain stable during the fiercest windstorms.

This is, at least, what the completed structure promised. But in March 1885, while construction of the pedestal was underway, the American Committee ran out of funds. Only $182,000 had been raised since the committee first opened its fundraising campaign in 1877, and less than $3,000 remained. An additional $100,000 was needed, the committee estimated, to complete the work at the site, which included finishing the pedestal and erecting the statue. The committee had no choice; on March 13, 1885, it announced that "work upon the pedestal at Bedloe's Island is suspended for lack of funds to continue it."

Worries about the project's successful conclusion, which had remained in the background for a decade, now came to the fore. The considerable efforts of the past twenty years—the fundraising work of the committee, the many benefit events, the donations large and small, in the United States and France, the tireless dedication of Bartholdi and Laboulaye, and the design and construction of the 151-foot-tall (46 m) statue in Paris—were all thrown into question. Moreover, at the moment that work on the pedestal was suspended, the statue was being disassembled and crated in France, in preparation for its shipment to the United States. Facing the prospect of being unable to accept this gift from the French people, the American Committee beseeched the public to help "prevent so painful and humiliating a catastrophe." In a "final appeal" to the nation, in particular to the people of the state and of the city of New York, who had subscribed more than 90 percent of the funds raised to that point, the committee concluded: "We ask you in the name of glorious memories, in the name of our country, in the name of civilization and of art, not to neglect this last opportunity for securing to yourselves and to the Nation an imperishable glory."

Three days after the suspension of work was reported, Joseph Pulitzer, owner of the *New York World* newspaper, issued a response. The *World,* Pulitzer announced, would organize its own subscription campaign and would raise the hundred thousand dollars needed to complete the statue. Pulitzer had attempted once before, in 1883, shortly after he purchased the *World,* to sponsor a fundraising drive for construction of the pedestal. At the time, however, he had neither the personal influence nor the readership necessary for its pursuit. He had instead contributed to the American Committee's efforts by serving on the executive committee that organized the Art Loan Exhibition of December 1883.

Pulitzer's personal experience may have animated his interest in the statue. He had arrived in the United States from Hungary in 1864, without money, connections, or even knowledge of the English language. The Union army provided him employment for about a year, but at the conclusion of the war he found himself unemployed in New York. Stories about St. Louis took him to that city, where he settled in a German-speaking community and embarked on a course of self-improvement and learning. He studied law, American history, and government, and in 1868 he obtained employment with the German-language *Westliche Post* as a newspaper reporter.

One of the directors at the *Westliche Post* was a man active in politics, Carl Schurz. Perhaps with Schurz's encouragement, or through his example, Joseph Pulitzer soon became involved in politics himself. In 1869, at the age of twenty-two, Pulitzer was elected to the Missouri legislature. He remained committed to journalism as well, and when an opportunity came his way in 1878 to purchase and merge two city newspapers, forming the St. Louis *Post-Dispatch,* he commenced his career as a newspaper publisher. A few years later, he expanded his terrain with the purchase of the *New York World,* a paper that was suffering from a declining circulation. Pulitzer immediately sought the paper's revival by establishing a strong, compelling voice for the paper—the voice, he declared, of the people. He argued that a newspaper should not only report events but also become an active participant in them, and he thrived on challenges.

When news of the crisis facing the American Committee surfaced in 1885, Pulitzer was alarmed by the situation and motivated by the cause. He zealously addressed his readers and predicted their success. "*We must raise the money!*" Pulitzer proclaimed in the *World*. "The $250,000 that the making of the statue cost was paid in by the masses of the French people—by the working men, the tradesmen, the shopgirls, the artisans—by all." This is the people's statue, he reiterated. "It is . . . a gift of the whole people of France to the whole people of America."

Public monuments were often claimed to be the work of the public, as opposed to the select group that sponsored the monument. In the case of the Statue of Liberty it was especially fitting that this claim should be made a reality, as Pulitzer asserted. Not only was the statue intended to represent liberty for all, but the war that established the nation's independence had distinguished itself as a war of the people, in contrast to a war of governments foisted on the people.

Pulitzer promised to print each donor's name in his paper, and when donations were accompanied by personal notes, he published these, too. "There is no other stage-manager like him," a contemporary said of Pulitzer. However, Pulitzer seems to have sincerely believed in the statue and the ideals she embodied, and four years later he dedicated the new building he constructed for the *World* to "liberty and justice." Pulitzer's fundraising methods were effective, and in a short five months' time over 120,000 people responded to his appeal. Single donations reached as high as $2,500, yet the bulk of the funds came from donations less than one dollar. Pulitzer was rewarded for his efforts with a dramatic rise in the circulation of his paper and the prestige of conducting a spectacularly successful campaign. The fundraising drive, now an exciting affair, motivated people to plan their own benefit events. There were benefit horse races, boxing matches, and amateur minstrel performances. Amateur nines participated in baseball games, whether between businessmen or political groups; in Bridgeport, Connecticut, the mayor served as umpire in a game between the board of alderman and the city council. The enthusiasm was infectious and other papers, even some of the *World*'s competitors in New York, got in the spirit, offering editorial support or contributions.

As funds accumulated that summer Pulitzer sent them on to the

American Committee so work on the pedestal could resume. Construction at Bedloe's Island brought the project to life in full view of New Yorkers and other visitors. People became aware of the activity of workers on Bedloe's Island and saw the enormous concrete structure rising far above the fort walls. Tourist boats took people out to the island to observe the construction underway. The growing presence of the monument on this side of the Atlantic underscored the relevance and urgency of the American Committee and the *World*'s fundraising efforts. And on August 11, 1885, Pulitzer announced that the *World* had reached its goal. Completion of the statue was at last assured.

While the campaign was still underway, in June 1885, the French military ship the *Isère* arrived at Bedloe's Island after twenty-six days at sea. Laden with over 210 wooden crates weighing more than 150 tons, the *Isère* brought the now much-anticipated gift from the people of France. The Franco-American Union had allowed the statue to remain standing in the rue de Chazelles for over half a year following its completion, knowing that preparations in New York were far from complete. Beginning in January 1885, the copper statue and the iron truss tower were slowly disassembled in the work yard at Gaget, Gauthier & Co. Each copper piece of the skin, each iron member of the structural frame, and each connecting bar was labeled for reassembly on Bedloe's Island and carefully packed for shipment. The crates filled seventy railroad containers, which transported them from Paris to the port at Rouen, where a government ship waited to carry the fragile cargo across the ocean. When the *Isère* reached the North American coast in June, over one hundred ships rushed out to accompany it during the last leg of its voyage. Some newspaper reports still made reference to the statue as the "most elaborate and rather eccentric gift" of modern times, but there was no longer any question about Americans' enthusiasm for the statue from France.

Bartholdi made a trip to New York later that year, to meet with Stone and explain his suggestions for carrying out the complex reassembly work. Bartholdi had expected to find the granite-faced pedestal complete and attention turned to the intricate assembly of the support tower and copper figure. This phase of the work, however, was postponed until the spring.

As predicted, construction of the statue presented numerous challenges of its own. Some of the metal pieces had suffered dam-

With the placement of the last rivet, *Frank Leslie's Illustrated Newspaper* wrote in October 1886, "the modern Pharos and noblest colossus in the world will stand complete" ("M. Bartholdi's Mighty Statue," October 9, 1886). © Musée des arts et métiers–Cnam, Paris. Photograph by S. Pelly.

age during crating and transport and required reworking; others were mislabeled and needed identification. In addition, the broad base of the pedestal precluded the use of scaffolding to support workers as they pieced the copper sheets together with thousands of rivets. To deal with this condition, a method was devised for securing the workers by rope to the inner frame and lowering them down along the surface of the copper skin. These suspended workmen, who "remind one of the Lilliputians swarming over Gulliver in the picture-books," as *Frank Leslie's Illustrated Newspaper* described the sight, caused some alarm among observers. But the construction proceeded without any fatalities and in good time.

By that fall, the statue's twenty-one-year journey from conception to realization neared its conclusion. On October 23, 1886, the last copper sheet was riveted into position at the heel of the right foot. Set on her pedestal on Bedloe's Island, the Statue of Liberty rose higher than any of the buildings of New York. Rising 151 feet 1 inch (46 m) from her feet to the tip of her torch and measuring 35 feet (10.8 m) across at her waist, this colossal emblem of liberty was ready to be presented to the nation.

12

THE UNVEILING

The inauguration of a public monument was often a grand occasion. The Yorktown Monument, for instance, drew representatives from France and from each of the original thirteen states. The ceremony planned for the Statue of Liberty, therefore, reached for grandeur to acknowledge the work's unique significance. A parade through the streets of New York, a naval procession in the harbor, and speeches at Bedloe's Island all served to mark the nation's acceptance of the gift from France and to commemorate the ideals and proud birth of the nation that the statue honors. A cold drizzle the day of the festivities diminished their sparkle and caused the evening's fireworks to be cancelled; however, it did not detract from the celebration. On the morning of October 28, 1886, eager spectators thronged the city's sidewalks, occupied windows and balconies along Broadway, gathered on rooftops, and even perched themselves on lampposts and telegraph poles. Estimates of the number of spectators for the event ranged from several hundred thousand to one million. Presiding over the ceremony was Stephen Grover Cleveland, president of the United States.

The parade began on Fifth Avenue near 57th Street and ended in lower Manhattan, covering a distance of close to five miles. Accompanied by his cabinet ministers, President Cleveland commenced the procession at about ten o'clock in the morning. Escorted by a detachment of cavalry and a battalion of the army's Old Guard, "looking extremely ferocious in their great bear-skin caps," his carriage traveled down Fifth Avenue from 57th to 30th Street, where the parade route shifted to Madison Avenue. Reaching Madison Square Park at 26th Street, Cleveland took his place on the reviewing stand erected for the occasion. Madison Square had previously been a focal point for the statue. It was on a building bordering Madison Square Park that Bartholdi arranged for the large canvas painting to be displayed during the Centennial celebrations in July 1876. The arm and torch that Bartholdi brought to the Centennial Exhibition in Philadelphia had also been displayed in Madison Square Park, from 1877 to 1882, at which time it was returned to France to complete the statue in Paris.

Among those waiting for Cleveland at the reviewing stand were Lieutenant General Philip Sheridan, senior commanders of the army and navy, the governor of New York, the diplomatic corps, and members of the American Committee. Richard Butler, the secretary of the American Committee, introduced each member of the French delegation to the president, beginning with Bartholdi and Ferdinand de Lesseps. Known on both sides of the Atlantic as the man responsible for building the Suez Canal, Lesseps had filled the position of president of the Franco-American Union left vacant by Édouard Laboulaye in 1883.

President Cleveland stood for over two hours as the procession passed by the reviewing stand. Groups had joined the parade from side streets as it made its way from 57th Street to Madison Square Park, and the line was now several miles long. There to celebrate the unveiling were army regiments and the Engineer Corps, city militia, the National Guard of New York and of New Jersey, over one thousand marines of the Naval Brigade, police battalions, military veterans, and ex-prisoners of war. Brooklyn, Newark, Philadelphia, and a number of other cities were represented by their troops, firemen, and boisterous brass bands. The veteran volunteer firemen and their old ladder trucks were reported to have "commanded the heartiest interest." One of the old fire engines displayed a small reproduction of the Statue of Liberty, while a newer ladder truck carried two young women, one of whom was dressed as Liberty. Her companion represented America. "With tinted skin and carrying a bow and arrow," the *New York Times* reported, this young woman looked "for all the world like a handsome Indian maiden."

Many civic organizations and foreign societies, in particular the French societies, were also part of the parade. From Indiana, members of the Knights of Pythias, an international fraternal order dedicated to promoting universal peace, joined the line. The public schoolchildren of New York and Brooklyn had been given the day off to participate in the celebration, as had New York university students, who added their school spirit to the revelry, chanting "C-O-L-U-M-B-I-A" or "B-A-R-T-H-O-L-D-I" as they proceeded along the route.

Charles P. Stone, who organized the parade and served as its grand marshal, led the procession down Fifth Avenue from Madison Square to Washington Square in Greenwich Village (where a statue of Garibaldi was erected in 1888). Here it turned onto Broadway and progressed south in the direction of Battery Park. The parade took a short detour just past New York City Hall, onto Park Row, known as Newspaper Row. The purpose of the detour was to acknowledge the important role of the *World* in realizing this day. The procession passed through an arch, decorated by greenery, that the *World* had erected in front of its building.

As the festivities moved past Wall Street on the way to Battery Park, young men at the Stock Exchange, which, unlike the Produce Exchange, had not closed for the day, leaned out the windows and began to unreel spools of ticker tape, letting them drift onto the crowds below. More and more tape filled the air as the enthusiastic youths were joined by their elders, and the celebratory effect was such that the tradition of the ticker tape parade was established that day.

Capping the symbolism of the spectacular procession was George Washington's carriage, drawn by eight horses and conducted by the Sons of the Revolution. "The whole history," of the Statue of Liberty, the New York *Independent* enthused, "from the arrival of Lafayette down to the first proposal to build the monument, and throughout its actual development, has risen above all grades and degrees of ordinary interest, and comes into the regions of romance."

In the afternoon attention turned to the statue itself. Crowds filled the streets around the harbor, and vessels of all sorts—excursion steamers, yachts, rowboats, tugboats, barges, and seven men-of-war—flying a wide assortment of flags, testified to the universal and peaceful appeal of the statue. On Cleveland's arrival at

Bedloe's Island, the speeches planned for the day began. Following an opening prayer, Lesseps spoke on behalf of the Franco-American Union. With his thoughts now occupied by his plans for a Panama Canal, he congratulated Americans on their commitment to progress. In landing beneath the rays of the statue, he professed, "people will know that they have reached a land where individual initiative is developed in all its power; where progress is a religion; where great fortunes become popular by the charity they bestow and by encouraging instruction and science and casting their influence into the future."

The chairman of the American Committee, Senator William M. Evarts, spoke next, presenting "the united work of the two republics" to the people of the United States. Taking a breath in the middle of his address, he was understood to have completed his speech. The signal was given, and Bartholdi, together with Richard Butler and David H. King Jr., whose firm built the pedestal and erected the statue, let the veil fall from her face. A "huge shock of sound" erupted as a thunderous cacophony of salutes from steamer whistles, brass bands, and booming guns, together with clouds of smoke from the cannonade, engulfed the statue for the next half hour. What Evarts "might have said had he spoken out of the fullness of his heart at that moment," remarked a *New York Times* reporter, with regard to this interruption in Evarts' prepared speech, "will never be known, because he sat down."

Once a semblance of calm returned, the president was introduced to accept the statue. Cleveland began by distinguishing this statue from others of the past. Unlike those statues "representative of a fierce and warlike god, filled with wrath and vengeance . . . we contemplate [in this statue] our own peaceful deity keeping watch before the open gates of America." Her light will not shine on these shores only, Cleveland continued, but reflected on "the shores of our sister Republic . . . shall pierce the darkness of ignorance and man's oppression until Liberty Enlightens the World."

Next, the French minister to the United States, W. Albert Lefaivre, spoke about the "impressive import" of the inauguration of the statue. "For it is one of those" events, he emphasized, "which form an epoch in history." To Americans, the statue represents the "noble efforts and glorious triumphs" of the country's first century; "to other nations, it eloquently affirms human dignity." Bartholdi then came forward to take a bow. The crowd shouted for a speech, but Bartholdi was uncomfortable about speaking in this setting and declined.

Chauncey M. Depew, president of the Union League Club and the invited orator at the unveiling ceremony, brought the series of speeches to a close with the commemorative address. This was the longest of the speeches and covered the history of friendship between the people of the United States and France, recalling Lafayette and the other Frenchmen "who fought for us in our first struggle." Turning to the statue, he pointed out that "in all ages the achievements of man and his aspirations have been represented in symbols." This statue "rises toward the heavens to illustrate an idea . . . which fired the farmer's gun at Lexington and razed the Bastille in Paris; which inspired the charter in the cabin of the Mayflower and the Declaration of Independence from the Continental Congress." However, he noted, "the development of Liberty was impossible while she was shackled to the slave." Although the "sacrifice for freedom" during the American Civil War was terrible, "the results," Depew assured his listeners, are "immeasurably great." He then examined the French alliance during the War for Independence, which "overcame improbabilities impossible in fiction." Depew concluded by calling on Washington and Lafayette: "I devoutly believe that from the unseen and unknown the two great souls have come to participate. . . . The spirit-voices of Washington and Lafayette join in the glad acclaim of France and the United States to Liberty Enlightening the World."

With these words the speeches came to an end. According to Richard Butler, the American Committee had considered including the reading of a poem, "Liberty," composed for the occasion by S. Miller Hageman. It decided not to, Butler explained in a preface to the subsequent printing of the poem by Hageman, due to the "severe inclemency of the occasion, the extreme length of the programme," and the length of the poem itself. Following a brief benediction, the air filled again with thunderous salutes as a mad dash for the boats brought the day's revelry to a close. At a reception that evening Bartholdi expressed a feeling of deep satisfaction with the outcome of his many years of labor. Any "troubles and difficulties" he had experienced along the way, the *New York Times* reported him saying, were amply compensated for by "one single minute of 'this great day.'"

In the midst of the great day's celebration, one group of participants had voiced a complaint. In a boat in the harbor, members of the New York State Woman's Suffrage Association "denounce[ed] the ceremonies just witnessed as a farce." The members came in protest of women's exclusion from America's political liberties. How, they asked, could liberty, personified here as a woman, be celebrated when the "unalienable rights" the Declaration of Independence proclaimed for all were selectively applied? Activists campaigned for equality in the workplace and in marriage, for admission to public universities, and for the right to vote, which they considered linked with women's social and legal status as citizens. When Congress passed the Fourteenth Amendment to the Constitution in 1866, providing states with incentive to extend voting rights to all *male* citizens, they suffered a painful blow. Although numerous congressmen presented petitions from their constituents requesting that suffrage be extended to women, this suggestion was either not taken seriously by many in Congress or rejected, largely out of fear of change. Opponents of women's suffrage worried about the degrading effect a role in public life would have on women and the "shock which the whole social fabric must receive." In addition, Representative Stevenson Archer of Maryland warned in 1872, if the barrier to political participation is broken down even further in this way, then not only will the age minimum rightly be challenged but the country will also soon be obliged to let everyone, even "Bushmen vote, if fate ever brings them to our shores." It would not be until 1920, when the Nineteenth Amendment to the Constitution was ratified, that the federal government established the right for women to vote. A few years later, in 1924, Native Americans, another group notably denied equality before the law, gained citizenship.

For those who have been excluded in some way from the promise of liberty and justice, celebration of these rights can be a painful reminder of their own restricted status. And as many African Americans discovered in the 1860s and 1870s, obtaining freedom from slavery and the right to vote fell far short of gaining protection under the law and equality of opportunity. The sense of anticipation that accompanied the conclusion of the Civil War had largely devolved into a state of disillusion. Many African Americans shared the disappointment voiced by the women protestors, unable to see their place in the promise of freedom and justice the statue represented. An article and an editorial printed less than a month apart in the *Cleveland Gazette,* an African American news-paper, reflect the mixed response of the community to the statue. The paper's report about the unveiling ceremony expressed appreciation for the statue, "a free gift of respect and good will from the people of France. . . . It may well rank with the wonders of the world, for in design and achievement it is a model of sublime conception, nobly wrought out." But the later editorial, echoing the tone of the women protestors, exclaimed: "'Liberty Enlightening the World,' indeed! The expression makes us sick. This Government is a howling farce. It can not or rather *does not* protect its citizens within its *own* borders. . . . The idea of the 'liberty' of this country, 'enlightening the world,' or even Patagonia, is ridiculous in the extreme."

But society's attitudes and prejudices can change with time, and the laws governing society can follow suit. In the history of the nation our participatory system of government has gradually become increasingly democratic, as property qualifications and race and gender restrictions have been eliminated. This possibility for change gives substance to America's sense of optimism about the future. It is evidence that the rule of law guiding the national community is fluid and vibrant, adjusting to the character of the age. This is the mental attitude that the suggested movement of the Statue of Liberty represents. She is not locked into place in the life of the eighteenth century. Although defined by her steady composure, she is ready to advance with the realities of the life of her people. The statue, people rejoiced on her unveiling, was more than the eighth wonder of the world; she was a wonder of the modern age, reflecting a new way of life.

Drawing on a range of sources, from ancient to American, the design of this heroic work of art renders a powerful image, the elements of which the eye can easily comprehend. One need not look beyond the raised torch or the date engraved on the tablet clasped in her hand to appreciate her statement. Yet if one chooses to do so, the past comes alive, endowing this monument with a history of remarkable achievements. We can imagine Benjamin Franklin pondering the sun rising on the nation, the youthful Lafayette inspired by the American pursuit of liberty, or George Washington standing on the second-story porch solemnly taking the oath of office. We can recall the revolutionaries who held forth the light of liberty and the framers of the constitution who shouldered weighty ambitions and responsibilities as they attempted to craft a lasting experiment in self-government. This historical past reminds us that the statue's meanings are not abstract but are founded in examples of individual commitment.

The experience of the United States affirms that the founders' experiment in self-government based on ideals of liberty was reasonable and admirable, and other republics across the globe have magnified the breadth of the revolutionary generation's endeavor. Yet this achievement does not rest in the past. As President Cleveland acknowledged during the unveiling ceremony in October 1886, the light the statue holds aloft demands our constant attention. "We will not forget that Liberty has here made her home," he assured his audience, "nor shall her chosen altar be neglected. Willing votaries shall keep its fires alive." A half-century later, on the occasion of the statue's fiftieth anniversary, President Franklin D. Roosevelt restated this responsibility. The "covenant between ourselves and our most cherished convictions has not been broken," he declared, and we will carry forward freedom and peace "by making them living facts in a living present." It is in this sense that the Statue of Liberty is far grander than a commemorative memorial. Finding her footing in the past, she looks to the future and represents an ongoing process that is never complete or static. As the founders took the risk of asking all citizens to share in their mission for a government, so Liberty offers her light, her passion, her wisdom, her experience formed of history, and her law of guidance for us to make of what we will.

The ideals she embodies and the identity she asks us to reflect on form the substance of her lasting relevance. Ruminating on the meaning the liberty statue would have for Americans at a reception held for Bartholdi in 1885, Chauncey Depew suggested that she would perpetually present the question, "What is liberty?" In the United States, he observed, liberty has been founded on the people's freedom to participate in the public life of the nation. It is indeed as participants and sovereigns in the life of the nation that each generation must enable the statue to advance, making the choices that will keep her vision of individual dignity alive.

The idea in France for a monument to independence and liberty was born of anxiety during a critical period in American history. Victory for the Union during the Civil War entailed not only the end of hostilities but also the reestablishment of liberties, liberties

The statue celebrates the history and achievements of the United States with emblems of liberty that are meaningful to people around the world. Library of Congress, Prints and Photographs Division, Historic American Engineering Record. Photograph by Jet Lowe.

Americans cherished and admirers longed for. Recognizing the exceptional importance of the nation's "experiment" with representative democratic government and with the challenges it faced, Abraham Lincoln eloquently placed this in a historical and global context in his Gettysburg Address. Only through our dedication, he concluded, will we ensure that the nation "shall have a new birth of freedom—and that government of the people, by the people, for the people, shall not perish from the earth."

As the portrait medal presented by the French people to Mary Todd Lincoln praised, President Lincoln "saved the Republic" and reestablished order without sacrificing liberty. Those seeking reform in France took the colossal leap from sponsoring a medal to building a monument because they agreed with the assertions of Lincoln, and before him, Jefferson, regarding the interconnection of people around the world. They honored the vision of life on which the American nation was founded and celebrated its enduring pursuit of this vision. As Bartholdi composed a liberty figure and Hunt formed a pedestal they followed the example of Lincoln's words, placing the experience of the United States in timeless universal language. The design of the monument did not attempt to memorialize an individual or glorify a particular victory along the lines of a traditional patriotic monument; it did not matter whether one stood on the side of the North or the South, the colonists or the British, to which political party one belonged, or even on which continent one lived. The singularly American liberty figure, devoid of nationalistic hubris, embraced all who shared her aspirations. From the organizers and the artists to the working people in both countries with no expectation of ever setting eyes on her, the collective effort that shaped the Statue of Liberty demonstrated people's faith in striving for a better life, animated by her principles.

In the years since her completion, the statue has gained importance in the United States as a national monument and icon, and her image has become familiar and uniquely meaningful around the world. Her individual features have coalesced into a new emblem of liberty, which speaks to diverse groups of people and to a broad range of aspirations. Interpretations of her meaning have been varied and changing; she continues to be both treasured as a symbol of possibility and thanksgiving and employed as a tool of criticism. The inability of the statue to fulfill her promises has inevitably been held against her. In a similar manner, Lincoln and others whose "championship of humanity" has had limited, or dismayingly slow, effect have been subject to criticism. Certainly, the gates of America are not as open as Cleveland suggested in 1886; even Bartholdi was surprised by the scrutiny he and his luggage received when he arrived in 1871. And when, people have asked as they point to the statue, will America walk in the light of her torch to break through the darkness and open the path of new life to all people?

In this duality of meaning we see the fullness of character that enriches the design of the statue. While Bartholdi and Laboulaye sought to celebrate the achievements of the American democratic republic with this liberty figure, their own disappointments and aspirations imbued the statue with a spiritual sense of longing and confidence: longing for her ideals to be fully attained; and confidence in the belief that, with the guidance of her light, progress is possible.

The enduring relevance of the statue is demonstrated by the diverse interpretations of her image. Her presence and her many meanings seem quite natural to us today. So much so, in fact, that we tend to overlook the journey of her creation. Yet we should recall the achievement of the twenty-one-year journey from conception to unveiling. For it was through an extraordinary meeting of sources, talents, personal devotion, and circumstances that this monument came into being in the nineteenth century. It is verily a matter of good fortune that we have present among us this lady of liberty—a lasting tribute to liberty, as Bartholdi rejoiced, "grand as the idea which it embodies."

Notes

Introduction

1 *Statue dimensions* Survey measurements taken during the renovation in the 1980s vary slightly from those recorded by the sculptor. According to Bartholdi, the statue measures 151 feet 1 inch (46 m) and the total height with the pedestal is 305 feet 1 inch (93 m). In *Restoring the Statue of Liberty* (New York, 1986), 99, Richard Seth Hayden and Thierry W. Despont, with Nadine M. Post, report that survey measurements found the statue to be 152 feet 2 inches (46.4 m) and the total height 306 feet 8 inches (93.5 m).

3 *"lay a foundation"* "James Wilson, Pennsylvania Ratifying Convention, 11 December 1787," in Philip B. Kurland and Ralph Lerner, eds., *The Founders' Constitution,* vol. 1, *Major Themes* (Chicago, 1987), 231.

"a constitutional republic" Abraham Lincoln, "Message to Congress in Special Session," July 4, 1861, in U.S. Congress, *House Journal,* 37th Cong., 1st sess., July 5, 1861.

"thus practically put an end" Ibid.

4 *"How great is the emotion"* Édouard Laboulaye to John Bigelow, quoted in Hertha Pauli and E. B. Ashton, *I Lift My Lamp: The Way of a Symbol* (New York, 1948), 9.

"grand as the idea" Frederic Auguste Bartholdi, *The Statue of Liberty Enlightening the World,* trans. Allen Thorndike Rice (New York, 1885), 19.

"Like all Americans" Theodore Roosevelt, speech at Fourth of July celebration, July 4, 1886, Dickinson, Dakota Territory, in Hermann Hagedorn, *Roosevelt in the Bad Lands* (Boston, 1921), 410.

5 *"models of antiquity"* Thomas Jefferson to Pierre Charles L'Enfant, April 10, 1791, in Saul K. Padover, ed., *Thomas Jefferson and the National Capitol, 1783–1818* (Washington, D.C., 1946), 59.

"asylum for the persecuted" Common Sense, rev. ed., in *Thomas Paine: Collected Writings,* ed. Eric Foner (New York, 1995), 23.

6 *"Keep, ancient lands"* Emma Lazarus, "The New Colossus," in *The Poems of Emma Lazarus* (Boston, 1888), 1:203.

"open gates" Stephen Grover Cleveland, speech at the unveiling ceremony, October 28, 1886, Bedloe's Island, in "The Statue Unveiled," *New York Times,* October 29, 1886.

"Such a work as this" Kinsley Twining, "The Inauguration of the Bartholdi Statue," *The Independent . . . Devoted to the Consideration of Politics, Social and Economic Tendencies, History, Literature, and the Arts* (New York), November 4, 1886.

7 *"liberty and peace"* Franklin D. Roosevelt, speech at the fiftieth-anniversary celebration, October 28, 1886, Bedloe's Island, "Roosevelt's Address at the Statue of Liberty," *New York Times,* October 29, 1936.

"In each generation" Ibid.

"One is never cured" Édouard Laboulaye [René Lefebvre, pseud.], *Paris en Amérique,* 14th ed. (Paris, 1865), 417. Translated by the author.

1. The Idea

8 *"Four score and seven"* Abraham Lincoln, "Gettysburg Address: Hay Copy," November 1863, Abraham Lincoln Papers at the Library of Congress, Manuscript Division, Washington, D.C., http://memory.loc.gov/cgi-bin/query/r?ammem/mal:@field(DOCID+@lit(d4356600)).

9 *"experiment of self-government"* Thomas Jefferson to Joseph Priestley, June 19, 1802, in Thomas Jefferson, *The Works of Thomas Jefferson,* ed. Paul Leicester Ford (New York, 1905), 9:381. The term "experiment" was widely used to describe the new system of representative government in the United States.

"monstrous injustice" Abraham Lincoln, speech in Peoria, Illinois, October 16, 1854, in *The Collected Works of Abraham Lincoln,* ed. Roy P. Basler (New Brunswick, 1953–55), 2:255.

"deprives our republican example" Ibid.

"the whole family of man" Abraham Lincoln, "Message to Congress in Special Session," July 4, 1861, in U.S. Congress, *House Journal,* 37th Cong., 1st sess., July 5, 1861.

"as slaves of the foreigner" Giuseppe Garibaldi, order disbanding his army, July 31, 1849, in George Macaulay Trevelyan, *Garibaldi's Defense of the Roman Republic* (London, 1912), 277.

"Let free men religiously" Italian declaration of support for President Lincoln, in Carl Sandburg, *Abraham Lincoln: The War Years,* vol. 2 (New York, 1939), 510–11.

10   *"Prosperity to you"* Ibid.

    "to the two hundred members" John Bigelow, *Some Recollections of the Late Edouard Laboulaye* (New York, [1888]), 6.

    "was far greater" Ibid.

11   *"Therefore we wait"* Édouard Laboulaye, *Professor Laboulaye, the Great Friend of America, on the Presidential Election: The Election of the President of the United States,* trans. U.S. Department of State (Washington, D.C., 1864), 14.

12   *"Mr. Lincoln had come to"* Norman B. Judd to William H. Seward, May 2, 1865, in *Appendix to Diplomatic Correspondence of 1865: The Assassination of Abraham Lincoln, Late President of the United States of America* (Washington, D.C., 1866), 496. A revised edition of this appendix was printed by the U.S. Department of State in 1867; the page numbers cited here refer to the 1866 edition.

13   *"heart-felt sympathy . . . preserved"* Address of condolence presented by members of the Prussian House of Deputies to Norman B. Judd, May 1, 1865, Berlin, in *Appendix to Diplomatic Correspondence of 1865,* 489.

    "a martyr of the great" Appended remarks by the Polish members to the address of condolence presented by members of the Prussian House of Deputies to Judd, May 1, 1865, Berlin, in *Appendix to Diplomatic Correspondence of 1865,* 491.

    "has assumed proportions" William Edward Johnston [Malakoff, pseud.], "Our Paris Correspondence," *New York Times,* May 28, 1865.

    "expressions of sympathy" John Bigelow to William H. Seward, May 10, 1865, in *Appendix to Diplomatic Correspondence of 1865,* 68.

    "struck with stupor" The Perfect Union Masonic Lodge, Orient of Confolens, to John Bigelow, June 1, 1865, in *Appendix to Diplomatic Correspondence of 1865,* 56.

    "is the sorrow of all" Edward Talbot to John Bigelow, May 10, 1865, in *Appendix to Diplomatic Correspondence of 1865,* 58.

    "At the termination" William Edward Johnston [Malakoff, pseud.], "Interesting from Paris," *New York Times,* May 16, 1865.

    "I had no idea" John Bigelow to William H. Seward, April 28, 1865, in *Appendix to Diplomatic Correspondence of 1865,* 67.

14   *"veil[ing] the statue of the law"* Édouard Laboulaye [René Lefebvre, pseud.], *Paris in America,* trans. Mary L. Booth (New York, 1863), 74.

    Competition of 1848 Brief descriptions of the entries of the twenty finalists are included in the appendix to Albert Boime's "The Second Republic's Contest for the Figure of the Republic," *The Art Bulletin* 53 (March 1971): 82. The entry referred to is identified as entry 311, finalist 10, by A. Hesse.

    Dinner party of 1865 Frederic Auguste Bartholdi recorded the events of this gathering in *The Statue of Liberty Enlightening the World,* trans. Allen Thorndike Rice (New York, 1885), 12–14. Writing in 1885, he stated that the gathering occurred twenty years earlier but did not provide a date. The summer of 1865 was indicated in a few reports about the statue, such as

James B. Townsend's "The Statue of 'Liberty,'" *Frank Leslie's Popular Monthly*, August 1885, 130.

15 *"principle of 'liberty to all'"* "Fragment on the Constitution and the Union," in Abraham Lincoln, *The Collected Works of Abraham Lincoln*, ed. Roy P. Basler (New Brunswick, 1953–55), 4:169.

"emblematic of Liberty" U.S. Congress, *House Journal*, 2nd Cong., 1st sess., March 24, 1792.

"very natural" Bartholdi, *Statue of Liberty*, 14.

"built by united effort" Ibid.

2. A Champion of Liberty

17 *"Bliss was it"* William Wordsworth, *The Prelude: The Four Texts (1798, 1799, 1805, 1850)*, ed. Jonathan Wordsworth (London, 1995), 441.

18 *"régime of improvisations"* Alfred Cobban, *A History of Modern France*, vol. 1, *Old Régime and Revolution, 1715–1799*, 3rd ed. (London, 1990), 256.

19 *"We find the desire"* Alexis de Tocqueville, *The Old Régime and the French Revolution*, trans. Stuart Gilbert (1858; New York, 1955), 209.

20 *"In one night"* Victor Hugo, quoted in Elihu B. Washburne, *Recollections of a Minister to France, 1869–1877* (New York, 1889), 1:35.

"Although the political horizon" William Edward Johnston, *Memoirs of "Malakoff": Being Extracts from the Correspondence and Papers of the Late William Edward Johnston*, ed. Robert M. Johnston (London, 1906), 11.

"Liberty and public order!" Édouard Laboulaye, *Paris en Amérique*, 14th ed. (Paris, 1865), 139–40. Translated by the author, based on the translation by Mary L. Booth as *Paris in America* (New York, 1863), 129.

"One might see them" Ibid.

"time of ferment" Gordon Wright, *France in Modern Times: From the Enlightenment to the Present*, 4th ed. (New York, 1981), 95.

21 *"yoked . . . to the despotic"* Alexis de Tocqueville, letter to the editor, *Times* (London), December 11, 1851, in John Stone and Stephen Mennell, eds., *Alexis de Tocqueville on Democracy, Revolution, and Society: Selected Writings* (Chicago, 1980), 279.

"connecting link" "Gratitude to Lafayette," in U.S. Congress, Senate, *Register of Debates in Congress*, 18th Cong., 2nd sess., December 21, 1824.

Lafayette's political activities For a detailed discussion of Lafayette's activities in the 1820s see Lloyd Kramer's *Lafayette in Two Worlds: Public Cultures and Personal Identities in an Age of Revolutions* (Chapel Hill, 1996).

22 *"for only freedom"* Tocqueville, *Old Régime and the French Revolution*, xiv.

"He considered the past" Gustave de Beaumont, *Memoir, Letters and Remains of Alexis de Tocqueville*, quoted in Stone and Mennell, eds., intro-

duction to *Alexis de Tocqueville on Democracy, Revolution, and Society,* 18.

"*the spirit of modern societies*" Édouard Laboulaye, *L'État et ses limites: suivi d'essais politiques,* 2nd ed. (Paris, 1863), 28.

23 "*repository of the sacred*" Saul K. Padover, ed., *Thomas Jefferson and the National Capitol, 1783–1818* (Washington, D.C., 1946), 460–61.

"*be lighted up*" Ibid.

"*incendiary*" William Edward Johnston [Malakoff, pseud.], "Affairs in France," *New-York Daily Times,* December 13, 1856.

"*At last . . . made the discovery*" Ibid.

"*infecting undergraduates*" Joyce Appleby, *Capitalism and a New Social Order* (New York, 1984), 2.

25 "*one of the most distinguished*" Washburne, *Recollections of a Minister,* 2:319.

Hunt's admiration for Laboulaye Catherine Clinton Howland Hunt, "Biography of Richard Morris Hunt," transcribed by Jonathon Hunt, Richard Morris Hunt Collection, Octagon, Museum of the American Architectural Foundation, Washington, D.C.

"*keep[ing] alive in France*" John Bigelow, introduction to *Autobiography of Benjamin Franklin,* ed. John Bigelow (Philadelphia, 1869), 55–56.

"*two illustrious chiefs*" Emilio Castelar, "The Republican Movement in Europe," part 2, *Harper's New Monthly Magazine,* July 1872, 218.

"*one of the most original*" "News of the Day," *New York Tribune,* January 1, 1864.

"*in the shape of a magnetic*" John W. Forney, *Letters from Europe* (Philadelphia, 1867), 158.

"*I have had leisure*" William Seward to John Bigelow, March 31, 1863, in John Bigelow, *Retrospections of an Active Life* (New York, 1909–13), 1:617.

26 "*a people intoxicated*" Édouard Laboulaye, *Paris en Amérique,* 334. Translated by the author.

"*By its grace of style*" Castelar, "Republican Movement in Europe," 218.

"*So great was the demand*" Miss Robbins, "Edward Laboulaye," *Appletons' Journal of Popular Literature, Science, and Art,* September 4, 1869, 84–85.

"*An ignorant democracy*" Edmond Dreyfus-Brisac, "Édouard Laboulaye," *Revue internationale de l'enseignement* 5 (June 1883): 599.

"*gave liberty not only*" Édouard Laboulaye, preface to *Histoire des Etats-Unis* (Paris, 1868; facsimile of the third edition. Boston, 2006), 2:x. Translated by the author.

27 "*Only a virtuous people*" Benjamin Franklin to the abbés Chalut and Arnaud, April 17, 1787, in Benjamin Franklin, *The Works of Benjamin Franklin,* ed. Jared Sparks, vol. 10 (Boston, 1844), 297.

"*I soon felt myself*" François-Jean Chastellux, *Travels in North America, in the Years 1780, 1781, and 1782,* trans. Howard C. Rice Jr. (Chapel Hill, 1963), 1:106.

28 *"Washington . . . resembles"* Laboulaye, preface to *Histoire des États-Unis,* 2:x. Translated by the author.

"in the best of all works" Benjamin Franklin to David Hartley, July 5, 1785, in Benjamin Franklin, *Private Correspondence of Benjamin Franklin,* ed. William Temple Franklin (London, 1833), 1:185.

"an old man with gray" Benjamin Franklin to Mary Hewson, January 12, 1777, in Benjamin Franklin, *The Complete Works of Benjamin Franklin,* ed. John Bigelow, vol. 6 (New York, 1888), 53.

"perhaps few strangers" Benjamin Franklin to an unidentified recipient, October 25, 1779, in Benjamin Franklin, *Complete Works of Benjamin Franklin,* 470–71.

"of which copies upon copies" Benjamin Franklin to Sarah Bache, June 3, 1779, in Benjamin Franklin, *Complete Works of Benjamin Franklin,* 418.

"may be truly said" Ibid.

"respect and esteem of all" Benjamin Franklin to Margaret Stevenson, January 25, 1779, in Benjamin Franklin, *Complete Works of Benjamin Franklin,* 300.

29 *"the confidence we put"* Comte de Vergennes to Chevalier de la Luzerne, February 14, 1781, in Francis Wharton, ed., *The Revolutionary Diplomatic Correspondence of the United States* (Washington, D.C., 1889), 4:256.

"relieve the pecuniary" Ibid.

"poured a flood of light" Comte de Mirabeau, speech at the National Assembly of France, June 11, 1790, Paris, in Benjamin Franklin, *The Works of Benjamin Franklin,* ed. Jared Sparks, vol. 1 (Chicago, 1882), 592.

"each citizen [be] master" Campaign poster for 1864 Paris election, *Journal des Débats,* March 8, 1864, quoted in Gray, *Interpreting American Democracy,* 104.

"a positive passion" John Adams to Mercy Warren, April 16, 1776, in Philip B. Kurland and Ralph Lerner, eds., *The Founders' Constitution,* vol. 1, *Major Themes* (Chicago, 1987), 670.

"Of all the enemies" James Madison, "Political Observations," April 20, 1795, in Lance Banning, ed., *Liberty and Order: The First American Party Struggle* (Indianapolis, 2004), 166.

30 *"to form a more perfect"* Preamble to the United States Constitution.

31 *"A republic, if you can"* "James McHenry: Anecdotes," in Max Farrand, ed., *The Records of the Federal Convention of 1787,* vol. 3 (New Haven, 1911), 85.

32 *"vicissitudes of [his] hopes"* James Madison, *Notes of Debates in the Federal Convention of 1787, Reported by James Madison* (Athens, Ohio, [1966]), 659.

3. Bonds of Friendship

33 *"Vulgarity and violence"* Philip Hone, *The Diary of Philip Hone, 1828–1851,* ed. Bayard Tuckerman (New York, 1889), 2:87.

34 *"bleeding Kansas"* "Political," *New York Daily Times,* September 12, 1856. By 1856 the meaning of this phrase was widely understood.

"crime against Kansas" Charles Sumner, speech in the U.S. Senate, May 19, 1856, Washington, D.C., *Appendix to the Congressional Globe,* 34th Cong., 1st sess., 531.

"In vain do we condemn" Ibid., 534.

"rape of a virgin Territory" Ibid., 530.

35 *"the harlot, Slavery"* Ibid.

"gold-mounted, bearing" Édouard Laboulaye, speech at the International Anti-Slavery Conference, August 27, 1887, Paris, in *Special Report of the Anti-Slavery Conference* (London, [1868]), 30.

"No wonder that the Chief" *New-York Daily Tribune,* March 10, 1857.

36 *"the right of property"* Roger B. Taney, Opinion of the Court, *The Case of Dred Scott in the United States Supreme Court* (New York, 1860), 37–38.

"our Declaration of Independence" Abraham Lincoln, speech in reply to Stephen Douglas, June 26, 1857, Springfield, Ill., in *The Collected Works of Abraham Lincoln,* ed. Roy P. Basler (New Brunswick, 1953–55), 2:404.

"an evil not to be extended" Abraham Lincoln, address at the Cooper Institute, February 27, 1860, New York, in Harold Holzer, *Lincoln at Cooper Union: The Speech That Made Abraham Lincoln President* (New York, 2004), 267.

"assailed, and sneered at" Abraham Lincoln, speech in reply to Stephen Douglas, June 26, 1857, Springfield, Ill., *Collected Works of Abraham Lincoln,* 2:404.

"It is now no child's" Abraham Lincoln to H. L. Pierce and others, April 6, 1859, *Complete Works of Abraham Lincoln,* ed. John G. Nicolay and John Hay, vol. 1 (New York, 1894), 533.

37 *"counterfeit logic which concludes"* Abraham Lincoln, speech in reply to Stephen Douglas, June 26, 1857, Springfield, Ill., *Collected Works of Abraham Lincoln,* 2:405.

"Pronounced the most ultra" "From Washington," *New York Times,* June 5, 1860.

"madness for slavery" Charles Sumner, speech in the U. S. Senate, June 4, 1860, Washington, D.C., in "From Washington," *New York Times,* June 5, 1860.

"is treated with kindness" James Buchanan, Third Annual Message to Congress on the State of the Union, December 19, 1859, U.S. Congress, *House Journal,* 36th Cong., 1st sess., February 9, 1860, 200.

"the barbarism of Slavery" Charles Sumner, speech in the U. S. Senate, June 4, 1860, Washington, D.C., in "From Washington," *New York Times,* June 5, 1860.

38 *"great, and free"* William Edward Johnston [Malakoff, pseud.], "Secession Abroad," *New York Times,* January 15, 1861.

"this war is not prosecuted" Resolution passed by the Senate, *Congressional Globe,* Senate, 37th Cong., 1st sess., July 25, 1861, 257.

"In the European view" William Edward Johnston [Malakoff, pseud.], "Our Rebellion Abroad," *New York Times,* May 5, 1861.

"half-measures satisfy nobody" La Presse, October 1862, quoted in Lynn M. Case and Warren F. Spencer, *The United States and France: Civil War Diplomacy* (Philadelphia, 1970), 331.

"In simple truth" "Reply of Agenor de Gasparin, Edouard Laboulaye, Henri Martin, Augustin Gochin to the Letter of the Loyal National League," trans. John Austin Stevens Jr., Pamphlets Issued by the Loyal Publication Society, pamphlet no. 41 (New York, 1864), 5.

"friends of justice" Augustin Cochin, quoted in Mary L. Booth, translator's preface to *The Results of Emancipation* by Augustin Cochin (Boston, 1863), vi.

"Mr. Lincoln should be accused" "Reply of Agenor de Gasparin," 5.

"strong enough to survive" Ibid., 12.

39 *"besieged with complaints"* Edouard Thouvenal to Henri Mercier, October 3, 1861, in Case and Spencer, *United States and France,* 171.

"entreating the Emperor" John Bigelow to William H. Seward, October 25, 1861, in Case and Spencer, *United States and France,* 179.

"have at times been clouds" Édouard Laboulaye, quoted in John Bigelow, *Some Recollections of the Late Edouard Laboulaye* (New York, [1888]), 18. Translated by the author.

"democratic-republican government" John Bigelow, speech at Fourth of July celebration, July 4, 1865, Paris, in John Bigelow, *Retrospections of an Active Life* (New York, 1909–1913), 3:106.

"has now acquired" Ibid.

"appear[ed] never to tire" William Edward Johnston [Malakoff, pseud.], "Interesting from Paris," *New York Times,* May 16, 1865.

40 *"the greatest and most honest"* Letter to Mrs. Lincoln, presented to the U.S. minister at Paris after Lincoln's death, in *Appendix to Diplomatic Correspondence of 1865,* 66.

"I noticed how many" John W. Forney, *Letters from Europe* (Philadelphia, 1867), 194.

"one of those feasts" William Edward Johnston [Malakoff, pseud.], in Robert M. Johnston, ed., *Memoirs of "Malakoff": Being Extracts from the Correspondence and Papers of the late William Edward Johnston* (London, 1906), 529.

"What now will result from" Édouard Laboulaye, speech at the International Anti-Slavery Conference, August 26, 1887, Paris, in *Special Report of the Anti-Slavery Conference,* 3.

"*we serve his [God's] interests*" Édouard Laboulaye, speech at the International Anti-Slavery Conference, August 27, 1887, Paris, in *Special Report of the Anti-Slavery Conference*, 32.

41 "*that wonderful command*" William Edward Johnston [Malakoff, pseud.], Johnston, ed., *Memoirs of "Malakoff*," 530.

"*avoided the [censorship] law*" Ibid.

"*romantic devotion*" Kinsley Twining, "The Inauguration of the Bartholdi Statue," *Independent*, November 4, 1886.

"*revealed to [Americans]*" Ibid.

42 "*Never had so noble*" Marie-Joseph-Paul-Yves-Roch-Gilbert du Motier, Marquis de Lafayette, *Mémoires, Correspondance et Manuscrits du Général Lafayette*, Publiés par sa famille, vol. 1 (Paris, 1837), 9. Translation from Charlesmagne Tower, *The Marquis de La Fayette in the American Revolution* (Philadelphia, 1895), 1:17.

"*his zeal, courage*" Henry Laurens to Louis XVI, October 22, 1778, in Marie-Joseph-Paul-Yves-Roch-Gilbert du Motier, Marquis de Lafayette, *Memoirs, Correspondence and Manuscripts of General Lafayette, Published by His Family*, vol. 1 (London, 1837), 235.

"*most sweet tempered*" Nathanael Greene to Catherine Greene, November 20, 1777, in Nathanael Greene, *The Papers of General Nathanael Greene*, ed. Richard K. Showman, vol. 2 (Chapel Hill, 1980), 200. Written as "temperd" in the original.

"*Our General is a man*" Marquis de Lafayette to the Duc d'Ayen, December 16, 1777, in Lafayette, *Mémoires*, 131–32. Translated by the author.

"*connecting link*" "Gratitude to Lafayette," in U.S. Congress, Senate, *Register of Debates in Congress*, December 21, 1824.

44 "*I have never seen*" Armand Louis de Gontaut Biron, Duc de Lauzun, *Memoirs of the Duc de Lauzun*, trans. C. K. Scott Moncrieff (1928; reprint, New York, 1969), 204.

"*May this immense temple*" From Lafayette's reply to the committee of Congress appointed to receive him on December 11, 1784, in Continental Congress, *Journals of the Continental Congress, 1774–1789*, ed. Worthington C. Ford et al. (Washington, 1904–37), 27:684.

45 "*delirium into which*" Thomas Jefferson to Richard Rush, October 13, 1824, in Thomas Jefferson, *The Works of Thomas Jefferson*, ed. Paul Leicester Ford (New York, 1905), 12:380.

"*Indeed I fear*" Thomas Jefferson to the Marquis de Lafayette, September 3, 1824, in Jefferson, *The Works of Thomas Jefferson*, 12:376.

Portraits of Lafayette and Washington These two portraits hang today in the House Chamber, one on each side of the Speaker's rostrum.

46 "*winning kindness*" Edward Livingston, speech in the U.S. House of Representatives, January 20, 1824, Washington, D.C., *Annals of Congress*, 18th Cong., 1st sess., 1102.

4. The French Sculptor

47   "*a goodly array of excellent*" "France to America," *Scribner's Monthly,* June 1877, 130.

Salon of Nieuwerkerke Robert Belot and Daniel Bermond, *Bartholdi* (Paris, 2004), 133.

"*generous impulses must be*" "Science and Art," *Christian Advocate,* May 7, 1885.

51   "*perfectly recovered*" Frédéric Auguste Bartholdi to Émile Jacob, quoted in Belot and Bermond, *Bartholdi,* 71. Translated by the author.

"*infinity*" Frederic Auguste Bartholdi, *Statue of Liberty Enlightening the World,* trans. Allen Thorndike Rice (New York, 1885), 36.

"*If I have had some*" Frédéric Auguste Bartholdi, in Gilbert Meyer, "L'art graphique d'Auguste Bartholdi," *Annuaire de la Société d'histoire et d'archéologie de Colmar* (1979), quoted in Belot and Bermond, *Bartholdi,* 89. Translated by the author.

Bartholdi's visit to Rome For a description of Bartholdi's tour of Italy see Belot and Bermond, *Bartholdi,* 125–26.

53   "*seems to have been reserved*" Margaret Stokes, "The Corona Radiata and the Crown of Thorns," *The Art-Journal* 44 (September 1882): 265.

54   "*Weak Governments often*" Napoleon III, speech at Arras, August, 27, 1867, "European Intelligence," *New York Times,* August 28, 1867.

"*The energy and rapidity*" Empress Eugénie to the Prussian ambassador at Paris, in Wolfgang Schivelbusch, *The Culture of Defeat: On National Trauma, Mourning, and Recovery,* trans. Jefferson Chase (New York, 2003), 107.

55   *War to distract the French army* Geoffrey Wawro, *The Franco-Prussian War* (Cambridge, 2003), 29.

56   *War costs of twelve billion francs* Geoffrey Wawro reports this figure in *Franco-Prussian War,* 310.

57   "*How great was my surprise*" Elihu B. Washburne, *Recollections of a Minister, 1869–1877* (New York, 1889), 2:31, 44.

"*We must wipe out*" Doctrine of a Commune leader, in [William Edward Johnston,] "European News by Mail," *New York Times,* July 7, 1871.

58   "*Rue Vavin—what a surprise*" Frédéric Auguste Bartholdi, *Journal,* May 30, 1871, trans. Rodman Gilder, Frédéric Auguste Bartholdi Papers, Manuscripts and Archives Division, The New York Public Library, Astor, Lenox and Tilden Foundations.

"*But . . . no rubbish inside*" Ibid.

59   "*proud struggle*" Frédéric Auguste Bartholdi to the mayor of Belfort, 1872, Archives municipales de Belfort, quoted in Belot and Bermond, *Bartholdi,* 196. Translated by the author.

"*this work of art*" Ernest Bosc, "Le Salon," *Encyclopédie d'Architecture* 1 (1872): 90. Translated by the author.

60   "*moderately pillaged*" Édouard Laboulaye to John Bigelow, July 28, 1871,

in John Bigelow, *Some Recollections of the Late Edouard Laboulaye* (New York, [1888]), 67. Translated by the author.

5. Bartholdi's Tour of America and the American Architect

62 *"I have confidence"* "A French View of Grant," *New York Times*, October 15, 1868.

"too scanty!!" Frédéric Auguste Bartholdi, *Journal*, July 2, 1871, Frédéric Auguste Bartholdi Papers, Manuscripts and Archives Division, The New York Public Library, Astor, Lenox and Tilden Foundations.

"there [was] no formality" Frédéric Auguste Bartholdi to Charlotte Bartholdi, July 21, 1871, Frédéric Auguste Bartholdi Papers.

"loves the arts" Frédéric Auguste Bartholdi, *Journal*, July 5, 1871, Frédéric Auguste Bartholdi Papers.

"from its new birth" Carl Schurz, "Charles Sumner," *Boston Globe*, April 30, 1874.

"The fate of Slavery" Charles Sumner to William Wetmore Story, January 1, 1864, in Henry James, *William Wetmore Story and His Friends*, vol. 2 (Boston, 1904), 158.

63 *"the token of victory"* George Washington to the Marquis de Lafayette, August 11, 1790, *The Papers of George Washington*, Presidential Series, ed. Dorothy Twohig, vol. 6 (Charlottesville, 1996), 233.

"make Philadelphia his chosen" John W. Forney, "Col. Forney's Letters," *The Press* (Philadelphia), April 26, 1875.

"In this I have sought" Edward Dalton Marchant to unidentified recipient, May 24, 1863, in Robert Wilson Torchia, *The Collections of the Union League of Philadelphia*, vol. 1, *Portraits of the Presidents of the United States of America* (Philadelphia, 2005), 18.

"the window from which" Frédéric Auguste Bartholdi, *Journal*, July 11, 1871, Frédéric Auguste Bartholdi Papers.

64 *"Painters had found it difficult"* Benjamin Franklin, in James Madison, *Notes of Debates in the Federal Convention of 1787, Reported by James Madison* (Athens, Ohio, [1966]), 659.

65 *"celebrating the one hundredth"* H. R. 1478, March 3, 1871, *Senate Journal*, 41st Cong., 3rd sess., 457. Mistakenly written as "industrial" exhibition.

66 *"We have met"* Excerpt from Perry's dispatch to Major General William Henry Harrison, September 10, 1813: "We have met the enemy and they are ours: Two Ships, two Brigs, one Schooner and one Sloop." William S. Dudley, ed., *The Naval War of 1812: A Documentary History*, vol. 2 (Washington, D.C., 1992), 553.

67 *"of substance and social"* William Francklyn Paris, "Richard Morris Hunt: First Secretary and Third President of the Institute," part 1, *Journal of the American Institute of Architects* 24 (December 1955): 244.

"pleased with himself" Frédéric Auguste Bartholdi, *Journal*, August 6, 1871, Frédéric Auguste Bartholdi Papers.

68 *Hunt's grand tour* The description of Hunt's grand tour is largely based on Catherine Clinton Howland Hunt's "Biography of Richard Morris Hunt," which incorporates Richard Morris Hunt's journal entries (transcribed by Jonathon Hunt, Richard Morris Hunt Collection, Octagon, Museum of the American Architectural Foundation, Washington, D.C.) and Paul R. Baker's biography of Hunt, *Richard Morris Hunt* (Cambridge, Mass., 1980).

71 *"dean of the profession"* Louis H. Sullivan, *The Autobiography of an Idea* (New York, 1956), 190.

72 *"so essential to good work"* Richard M. Hunt, "Paper on the Architectural Exhibit of the Centennial Exhibition," *American Institute of Architects, Proceedings of the Tenth Annual Convention* 10 (1876), 38.

"the do-nothing policy" William F. M. Arny, testimony to the U.S. Senate, January 17, 1860, Select Committee on the Harper's Ferry Invasion, *Report*, 36th Cong., 1st sess., 1860, 88.

73 *"to see a plan adopted"* George Washington to Robert Morris, April 12, 1786, *The Papers of George Washington*, Confederation Series, ed. W. W. Abbott and Dorothy Twohig, vol. 4 (Charlottesville, 1995), 16.

"treason, advising and conspiring" "The Virginia Rebellion," *New York Times*, November 1, 1859.

"madman" From the *Albany Evening Journal*, in "The Harper's Ferry Rebellion," *New York Times*, October 20, 1859. Brown was widely referred to as insane and a fanatic.

"whilst bearing a flag" "The Negro Insurrection," *New York Times*, October 19, 1859.

"consideration and kindness" Lewis W. Washington, paraphrased in "Harper's Ferry Rebellion," *New York Times*.

"cause of human freedom" John Brown, quoted by Benjamin Mills, master of the armory at Harpers Ferry, in "Harper's Ferry Rebellion," *New York Times*.

"settlement of that question" Henry David Thoreau, *A Plea for Captain John Brown* (Boston, 1969), 32.

"they are leading old John" Henry Wadsworth Longfellow, diary entry, December 2, 1859, in Thomas Wentworth Higginson, *Henry Wadsworth Longfellow* (Boston, 1902), 271.

"to plead his cause" Thoreau, *Plea for Captain John Brown*, 31.

"when you plant, or bury" Ibid., 10.

74 *"I kneel with tears"* Victor Hugo, "To the United States of America," December 2, 1859, in Victor Hugo, *Actes et Paroles*, vol. 2, *Pendant l'Exil, 1852–1870*, 2nd ed. (Paris, 1875), 237.

"Do you suppose that" Henry Ward Beecher, sermon at Plymouth Church, October 30, 1859, Brooklyn, quoted in "The Virginia Rebellion," *New York Times*, November 1, 1859.

"the speech that made" Harold Holzer's subtitle for his book *Lincoln at Cooper Union: The Speech That Made Abraham Lincoln President* (New

York, 2004). Holzer also credits the photograph of Lincoln taken by Mathew Brady on the day of the speech as an important element in the presidential campaign.

74   *"the great champion"* William Cullen Bryant, introducing Lincoln at the Cooper Institute, February 27, 1860, New York, quoted in Charles H. Brown, *William Cullen Bryant* (New York, 1971), 410.

"assemblage of the intellect" New York Tribune, February 28, 1860, quoted in Brown, *William Cullen Bryant,* 411.

"the precise fact upon which" Abraham Lincoln, address at the Cooper Institute, February 27, 1860, New York, in Holzer, *Lincoln at Cooper Union,* 283.

"slavery is morally right" Ibid., 282.

"be slandered from our duty" Ibid., 284.

75   *Hunt's interest in a military career* Baker, *Richard Morris Hunt,* 17.

Hunt's plan to raise a flag Baker, *Richard Morris Hunt,* 126.

Hunt's meeting with William L. Dayton Baker, *Richard Morris Hunt,* 127.

76   *"slow to smite and swift"* William Cullen Bryant, ["The Death of Lincoln"], from lines 1, 2, 11, and 12, in *Poetical Tributes to the Memory of Abraham Lincoln* (Philadelphia, 1865), 13. The punctuation of the poem has not been followed here.

77   *"marble column"* Continental Congress, October 24, 1781, *Journals of the Continental Congress, 1774–1789,* ed. Worthington C. Ford et al. (Washington, D.C., 1904–37), 21:1081.

"The very air" George William Curtis, *An Address at the Unveiling of the Statue of Washington, Upon the Spot Where He Took the Oath as First President of the United States* (New York, 1883), 28.

Federal Hall The existing building was designated a national historic site in 1939 and established as the Federal Hall National Monument in 1955.

78   *"getting [his] bearings"* Frédéric Auguste Bartholdi to Charlotte Bartholdi, June 24, 1871, Frédéric Auguste Bartholdi Papers.

"more American than all" Frédéric Auguste Bartholdi, *Journal,* August 14, 1871, Frédéric Auguste Bartholdi Papers.

79   *where Indians are encamped* Frédéric Auguste Bartholdi to Charlotte Bartholdi, August 29, 1871, Frédéric Auguste Bartholdi Papers.

"Here . . . novels and all other" Frédéric Auguste Bartholdi to Charlotte Bartholdi, August 22, 1871, Frédéric Auguste Bartholdi Papers.

"magnificent fruits" Frédéric Auguste Bartholdi to Charlotte Bartholdi, August 29, 1871, Frédéric Auguste Bartholdi Papers.

"furious search for gold" Ibid.

"enormously productive" Ibid.

"These colossi are superb" Frédéric Auguste Bartholdi, *Journal,* September 1, 1871, Frédéric Auguste Bartholdi Papers.

"When you observe the attention" Frédéric Auguste Bartholdi to Charlotte Bartholdi, September 11, 1871, Frédéric Auguste Bartholdi Papers.

80 *"My country, right or wrong."'* Carl Schurz, debate in the U.S. Senate, *Congressional Globe,* 42nd Cong., 2nd sess., February 29, 1872, 1287.

"Ideals are like stars" Carl Schurz, "True Americanism," speech in Faneuil Hall, April 18, 1859, Boston, in *Speeches of Carl Schurz* (Philadelphia, 1865), 54. Schurz dedicated this collection to the Union League of Philadelphia.

"vast country" Frédéric Auguste Bartholdi to Charlotte Bartholdi, July 2, 1871, Frédéric Auguste Bartholdi Papers.

81 *"take root immediately"* Ibid.

"is sure to be a long" Ibid.

"may end up not just" Frédéric Auguste Bartholdi to Laboulaye, July 15, 1871, in Christian Blanchet and Bertrand Dard, *The Statue of Liberty: The First Hundred Years,* trans. Bernard A. Weisberger (New York, 1985), 184n6.

6. Washington, D.C., as a National Symbol

82 *sister republics* The term "sister republic" was used by the U.S. Congress when it authorized the designation of a site for the proposed monument in 1877. U.S. Congress, Senate, Committee on Foreign Relations, *Compilation of Reports of Committee on Foreign Relations, 1789–1901.* Vol. 4. 56th Cong., 2nd sess., 1901, 58.

83 *"operations in Kansas"* "Forty-First Congress," *New York Times,* January 19, 1871.

"by force, intimidation, or threat" "An act to enforce the provisions of the fourteenth amendment to the Constitution of the United States, and for other purposes," H. R. 320, 42nd Cong., 1st sess., April 10, 1871.

84 *"We are re-laying the very"* Willard Warner, speech in the U.S. Senate, March 3, 1871, Washington, D.C., *Appendix to the Congressional Globe,* 41st Cong., 3rd sess., 269. Written "relaying" in the original.

"The government had refused" Daniel J. Morrell, speech at the closing ceremonies of the Centennial Exhibition, November 10, 1876, Philadelphia, in *Frank Leslie's Illustrated Historical Register of the Centennial Exposition 1876,* facsimile with a new introduction by Richard Kenin (New York, 1974), 315.

"hardly open to things" Frédéric Auguste Bartholdi to Charlotte Bartholdi, June 24, 1871, Frédéric Auguste Bartholdi Papers.

"pained" Frédéric Auguste Bartholdi, *Journal,* June 29, 1871, Frédéric Auguste Bartholdi Papers.

85 *"It commanded respect"* Frédéric Auguste Bartholdi to Charlotte Bartholdi, July 9, 1871, Frédéric Auguste Bartholdi Papers.

"first plans" John La Farge Jr., *The Manner is Ordinary* (New York, 1954), 14. The recollections of La Farge's son are imprecise with regard to dates and names. He gives the date as 1876, but if Bartholdi worked on his first

plans at Newport, as La Farge *fils* remembered, it had to be during Bartholdi's visits with the La Farge family in 1871.

86   *"If people see the Capitol"* Abraham Lincoln, July 1863, quoted in John Eaton, *Grant, Lincoln and the Freedmen: Reminiscences of the Civil War,* in collaboration with Ethel Osgood Mason (New York, 1907), 89.

87   *"a sense of the really"* Pierre Charles L'Enfant, "First report to the President, March 26, 1791," in Elizabeth S. Kite, *L'Enfant and Washington, 1791–1792* (Baltimore, 1929), 17.

     "The immense lay-out" Frédéric Auguste Bartholdi to Charlotte Bartholdi, July 4, 1871, Frédéric Auguste Bartholdi Papers.

89   *"the approbation of thousands"* Thomas Jefferson to Pierre Charles L'Enfant, April 10, 1791, in Saul K. Padover, *Thomas Jefferson and the National Capitol, 1783–1818* (Washington, D.C., 1946), 59.

90   *"For every eventuality"* Victor Hugo, *Oeuvres Complètes, Océan, Tas de Pierres,* quoted in Graham Robb, *Victor Hugo* (New York, 1998), 70.

     "painted in all their Deformity" John Adams to John Quincy Adams, May 18, 1781, in L. H. Butterfield and Marc Friedlaender, eds., *Adams Family Correspondence,* vol. 4 (Cambridge, Mass., 1873), 117.

     "Natural law is stamped" Cicero, *Oratio pro Milone,* in Benjamin Rush, "The Influence of Physical Causes upon the Moral Faculty," in *The Selected Writings of Benjamin Rush,* ed. Dagobert D. Runes (New York, 1947), 181. Translation from Carl J. Richard, *The Founders and the Classics* (Cambridge, Mass., 1994), 219n40.

     "wanting nothing but a fresh" Livy [Titus Livius], *The History of Rome from Its Foundation,* books 1 to 5, *The Early History of Rome,* trans. Aubrey De Sélincourt (New York, 1971), 42.

     "Fathers" Ibid., 43.

     "greatness of antiquity" A. C. Gierlew, *Breve om Italien* (1807), 2:52–55, quoted in Christian Elling, *Rome: The Biography of Her Architecture from Bernini to Thorvaldsen,* trans. Bob and Inge Gosney (Boulder, 1975), 515.

     Lazarus in Rome Bette Roth Young includes many of Lazarus's letters from Europe describing her impressions and experiences in *Emma Lazarus in Her World: Life and Letters* (Philadelphia, 1995).

91   *"so close to Antiquity"* Frédéric Auguste Bartholdi, travel notebook, Musée Bartholdi, Colmar, quoted in Robert Belot and Daniel Bermond, *Bartholdi* (Paris, 2004), 125. Translated by the author.

     "glorious golden falcon" Dashiell Hammett, *The Maltese Falcon* (New York, 1930), 105.

92   *"is the visible sign"* Eugène-Emmanuel Viollet-le-Duc, "Introduction," *Encyclopédie d'Architecture* 1 (1872): 1. Translated by the author.

93   *"Americanized capitals might"* George C. Hazelton Jr., *The National Capitol: Its Architecture, Art, and History* (New York, 1902), 185.

96   *Constantino Brumidi* Brumidi's biographical information is difficult to confirm; the sketch given here is based on Vivien Green Fryd, *Art and Empire:*

The Politics of Ethnicity in the United States Capitol, 1815–1860 (Athens, Ohio, 2001), 129, and Hazelton, *National Capitol,* 95.

"armed Liberty" Thomas Crawford to Montgomery C. Meigs, October [18], 1855, quoted in Hazelton, *National Capitol,* 65.

97   *"The whole [is] intended"* Charles Bulfinch to unidentified recipient, June 22, 1825, in Hazelton, *National Capitol,* 87.

Greenough statue The statue of Washington has since been moved to the National Museum of American History.

"Washington was too prudent" Philip Hone, *The Diary of Philip Hone, 1828–1851,* ed. Bayard Tuckerman (New York, 1889), 2:216.

"that grand resort" Ibid.

98   *"a colossal statue"* Édouard Laboulaye, speech at the Grand Hôtel du Louvre, November 6, 1875, Paris, quoted in Belot and Bermond, *Bartholdi,* 289. Translated by the author.

7. *Bartholdi's Design*

99   *"Everyone has heard"* John Romer and Elizabeth Romer, *The Seven Wonders of the World* (London, 1995), vii.

100   *"very remarkable piece"* Frederic Auguste Bartholdi, *The Statue of Liberty Enlightening the World,* trans. Allen Thorndike Rice (New York, 1885), 38.

"Soldiers! From the height" Peter A. Clayton, "The Great Pyramid of Giza," in *The Seven Wonders of the Ancient World,* ed. Peter A. Clayton and Martin J. Price (London, 1988), 33.

101   *"high to heaven"* Anthologia Palatina, vol. 6, no. 171, in *The Greek Anthology,* vol. 1, trans. William R. Paton (Cambridge, 1916), 387.

"fantastic legend" Bartholdi, *Statue of Liberty,* 38.

"The Colossus of American" "Report of a dinner in New York City in honor of John Adams," *Whitestown Gazette,* October 31, 1797, quoted in Alfred F. Young, *The Democratic Republicans of New York: The Origins, 1763–1797* (Chapel Hill, 1967), 581.

102   *"the best site"* Frédéric Auguste Bartholdi, *Journal,* June 22, 1871, Frédéric Auguste Bartholdi Papers.

"site favorable by its own" Bartholdi, *Statue of Liberty,* 41.

"site is superb!" Frédéric Auguste Bartholdi, *Journal,* July 1, 1871, Frédéric Auguste Bartholdi Papers.

103   *"the site will not be difficult"* Bartholdi, *Journal,* July 18, 1871, Frédéric Auguste Bartholdi Papers.

"an evilly disposed newspaper" Bartholdi, *Statue of Liberty,* 37.

105   *"vestal fire of Freedom"* John Quincy Adams, "Oration on the Life and Character of Gilbert Motier de la Fayette," in U. S. Congress, *House Journal,* 23rd Cong., 2nd sess., December 31, 1834. Adams served in Congress for seventeen years, from 1831 to 1848, following his term as the sixth president of the United States.

106 "*saved the Republic without veiling*" Inscription on the medal presented to Mary Todd Lincoln. See chapter 1.

"*was the inspiration*" Frédéric Auguste Bartholdi quoted in "Arrival of M. Bartholdi," *New York Times,* November 5, 1885.

107 "*is as unavoidable*" Louis Ménard's criticism of Bartholdi's design, paraphrased in "Vol. XVI of 'L'Art,'" *Scribner's Monthly,* August 1879, 631.

108 "*Considered merely*" Thomas Paine, "Rights of Man," in Paine, *Thomas Paine: Collected Writings,* ed. Eric Foner (New York, 1995), 548.

109 "*This is not Liberty*" Édouard Laboulaye, speech at the Opera, April 25, 1876, Paris, quoted in Robert Belot and Daniel Bermond, *Bartholdi* (Paris, 2004), 296. Translated by the author.

"*tablets of the law*" Ibid.

111 "*Let weapons yield*" Carl J. Richard, *The Founders and the Classics* (Cambridge, Mass., 1994), 39.

"*the principles promulgated*" "First Inaugural Address—First Edition," January 1861, in Abraham Lincoln, *The Collected Works of Abraham Lincoln,* ed. Roy P. Basler (New Brunswick, 1953–55), 4:258.

"*framed around*" "Fragment on the Constitution and the Union," in Lincoln, *Collected Works,* 4:168–69.

Celebration of the Constitution on July 4 Gary Wills discusses the association of the Constitution with the Fourth of July in *Inventing America: Jefferson's Declaration of Independence* (Garden City, 1978), 338, 348.

"*lines once so familiar*" George William Curtis, "Editor's Easy Chair," *Harper's New Monthly Magazine,* January 1887, 318.

112 "*The fathers in glory*" Ibid. The verse, titled "Welcome Lafayette," was written by Charles Sprague in August 1824.

Speculation on design Portions of the story of the statue are generally agreed on; some of the conclusions and associations made in this text, however, are original to this work. These include the association of the design with Marchant's painting of Lincoln, with Franklin's story of the rising sun, and with the creation story.

114 "*The drapery is both massive*" "Bartholdi's Great Statue," *London Daily News,* July 3, 1884, reprinted in the *New York Times,* July 14, 1884.

"*simplicity of its pose*" Louis Ménard, quoted in "Vol. XVI of 'L'Art,'" *Scribner's Monthly,* August 1879, 631.

115 "*kindly and impassable glance*" Bartholdi, *Statue of Liberty,* 36.

116 "*it is a vehicle of life*" Woodrow Wilson, *Constitutional Government in the United States* (New York, 1908), 69.

8. *The Statue Takes Shape*

117 "*moral order*" Elihu B. Washburne, *Recollections of a Minister to France, 1869–1877,* 2 vols. (New York, 1889), 2:298.

118 "*government of the Republic*" "The Proposed Laboulaye Amendment,"

January 28, 1875, *Journal Officiel,* January 29, 1875, quoted in Frank Maloy Anderson, *The Constitutions and Other Select Documents Illustrative of the History of France, 1789–1907,* 2nd ed. (1908; New York, 1967), 633.

119 *"a ferment of intellectual"* Eugène-Emmanuel Viollet-le-Duc, *Lectures on Architecture,* trans. Benjamin Bucknall (1881; New York, 1987), 2:161.

121 *"I find that the French"* John W. Forney, "Col. Forney's Letters," *The Press* (Philadelphia), January 25, 1875.

"a lively interest" Ibid.

"You have founded" Jules Favre to Elihu B. Washburne, September 8, 1870, in Washburne, *Recollections of a Minister,* 1:121.

122 *"America and France are sisters"* Address by a delegation of French citizens to the U.S. minister, September 8, 1870, Paris, in Washburne, *Recollections of a Minister,* 1:124.

"In fulfilling today" Elihu B. Washburne, address to Oscar de La Fayette, December 9, 1874, Paris, in Washburne, *Recollections of a Minister,* 2:306.

"a most favorable impression" Washburne, *Recollections of a Minister,* 2:308.

123 *"colossal statue"* Franco-American Union subscription appeal, reproduced in André Gschaedler, *True Light on the Statue of Liberty and its Creator* (Narberth, Penn., 1966), facing page 42.

"our enthusiasm in France" Franco-American Union to Ulysses S. Grant, October 26, 1875, in Robert Belot and Daniel Bermond, *Bartholdi* (Paris, 2004), 283. Translated by the author.

124 *"sealed by the blood"* Franco-American Union subscription appeal, in Gschaedler, *True Light on the Statue.* Written as "forfathers" in the original.

"trifling" Ibid.

Attendance at the inaugural banquet Most reports indicate that President MacMahon did not attend the event.

"these precious memories" Édouard Laboulaye, speech at the Opera, April 25, 1876, Paris, quoted in Gschaedler, *True Light on the Statue,* 39.

"The events of the evening" John W. Forney, *A Centennial Commissioner in Europe, 1874–1876* (Philadelphia, 1876), 370.

125 *"struck the rock"* Forney, *Centennial Commissioner in Europe,* 370–71.

"wit and pathos" Ibid.

"His words excited" Ibid.

"American freedom" Édouard Laboulaye, quoted in "The Franco-American Fete," *New York Times,* April 26, 1876.

"will not resemble" Laboulaye, speech at the Grand Hôtel du Louvre, November 6, 1875, Paris, quoted in Belot and Bermond, *Bartholdi,* 289. Translated by the author.

128 *"inundated with people"* Edmond and Jules de Goncourt, *The Goncourt Journals 1851–1870,* ed. and trans. Lewis Galantiere (New York, 1968), 242.

"peaceful competition" John Welsh, speech at the opening of the Centennial Exhibition, May 10, 1876, Philadelphia, in *Frank Leslie's Illustrated Historical Register of the Centennial Exposition 1876* (New York, 1974), 76.

"our Centennial anniversary" Daniel E. Sickles, quoted in Forney, *Centennial Commissioner in Europe*, 194.

"a commemorative monument" Franco-American Union subscription appeal, in Gschaedler, *True Light on the Statue*.

129 *Bartholdi's fountain at the Centennial* This fountain now stands in Bartholdi Park in Washington, D.C.

"by the hand of the executioner" David Walker Woods, *John Witherspoon* (New York, 1906), 218.

132 *"The statue will be commemorative"* "The Liberty Colossus," *Daily Graphic* (New York), June 2, 1876.

9. The American Committee and the French Engineers

134 *"to erect a Statue"* Frédéric Auguste Bartholdi, text for speech to the New England Society, December 22, 1876, New York, private collection, quoted in Janet Headley, "Bartholdi's Second American Visit: The Philadelphia Exhibition (1876)," in Pierre Provoyeur and June Hargrove, eds., *Liberty: The French–American Statue in Art and History* (New York, 1986), 146.

135 *"new birth of freedom"* Abraham Lincoln, "Gettysburg Address: Hay Copy," November 1863, Abraham Lincoln Papers at the Library of Congress, Manuscript Division, Washington, D.C., http://memory.loc.gov/cgi-bin/query/r?ammem/mal:@field(DOCID+@lit(d4356600)).

"So it is peculiarly" Theodore Roosevelt, speech at Fourth of July celebration, July 4, 1886, Dickinson, Dakota Territory, in Hermann Hagedorn, *Roosevelt in the Bad Lands* (Boston, 1921), 407–10.

"to be inaugurated" U.S. Congress, Senate, Committee on Foreign Relations, *Compilation of Reports of Committee on Foreign Relations, 1789–1901*, vol. 1, 56th Cong., 2nd sess., 1901, 4:59.

136 *"Vive la République!"* Robert Belot and Daniel Bermond, *Bartholdi* (Paris, 2004), 329.

"Despite oneself one felt" A personal journal, June 28, 1878, quoted in Belot and Bermond, *Bartholdi*, 329. Translated by the author.

"one of the most important" Banister Fletcher, *A History of Architecture*, 18th ed., rev. J. C. Palmes (New York, 1975), 1191.

139 *Railway track in France* These figures are given in kilometers by Bernard Marrey in *Gustave Eiffel: Une Entreprise Exemplaire* (Paris, 1989), 28–29.

140 *"fantastically bold and ingenious"* Frédéric Auguste Bartholdi to Charlotte Bartholdi, September 11, 1871, Frédéric Auguste Bartholdi Papers.

"More extraordinary than all" Ibid.

143 *Deterioration due to corrosion* During the 1980s' renovation the iron bars were replaced by ferallium flat bars and stainless steel curved mesh bars, insulated from the copper skin by teflon tape. Richard Seth Hayden and Thierry W. Despont, with Nadine M. Post, *Restoring the Statue of Liberty* (New York, 1986), 76.

"Despite conditions of strict" Alexandre-Gustave Eiffel, "Généalogie de la famille Eiffel," *Biographie industrielle et scientifique* (unpublished, 1922), quoted in Michel Carmona, *Eiffel* (Paris, 2002), 219.

144 *"charm inherent in the colossal"* Alexandre-Gustave Eiffel, reply to criticism of the tower, in *Le Temps*, February 14, 1887, quoted in Joseph Harriss, *The Tallest Tower: Eiffel and the Belle Epoque* (Boston, 1975), 25.

145 *"France and America have"* Levi P. Morton, quoted in "Bartholdi's Statue of Liberty," *New York Times*, October 25, 1881.

146 *"The illustrious names"* Ibid.

10. Hunt Designs a Pedestal

147 *Occupants of the Studio Building* Paul R. Baker lists many of the artists who took studios in the building in *Richard Morris Hunt* (Cambridge, Mass, 1980), 95–97.

Stuyvesant Apartments Sarah Bradford Landau and Carl W. Condit refer to Viollet-le-Duc in discussing the influences on this design in *Rise of the New York Skyscraper, 1865–1913* (New Haven, 1996), 17.

148 *"a truly national spirit"* Daniel Webster to James Pleasants Jr., March 6, 1830, in Daniel Webster, *The Private Correspondence of Daniel Webster*, ed. Fletcher Webster, vol. 1 (Boston, 1857), 493.

"Liberty and Union, now" Daniel Webster, reply to Robert Y. Hayne (January 26, 1830, U.S. Congress, Senate, *Register of Debates in Congress*, 21st Cong., 1st sess., January 27, 1830.

Hunt's initial pedestal proposal The scheme is briefly described in a short article, "Bartholdi's Statue of Liberty," *New York Times*, December 7, 1881.

149 *"for the safety of those"* Peter A. Clayton, "The Pharos at Alexandria," in *The Seven Wonders of the Ancient World*, ed. Clayton and Martin J. Price (London, 1988), 144.

150 *Hunt's designs for the pedestal* Susan R. Stein includes illustrations of many of the schemes considered by Hunt's office in "Richard Morris Hunt and the Pedestal" in *Liberty: The French–American Statue in Art and History*, ed. Pierre Provoyeur and June Hargrove (New York, 1986).

153 *"Enter! there are no"* Edmund Clarence Stedman, "Liberty Enlightening the World," *Harper's Weekly*, October 30, 1886, lines 35–38.

154 *"an industrial tour de force"* "Bartholdi's Statue of Liberty," *American Architect and Building News*, September 15, 1883, 126.

155 *"into harmonious form"* Theophile Thoré [W. Bürger, pseud.], "Des tendencies de l'art au XIXe siècle," quoted in Joseph C. Sloane, *French Paint-*

ing between the Past and the Present: Artists, Critics, and Traditions, from 1848 to 1870 (Princeton, 1951), 65.

"banner of stars . . . a great" Victor Hugo, quoted in Elihu B. Washburne, *Recollections of a Minister to France, 1869–1877,* 2 vols. (New York, 1889), 1:137.

"This beautiful work of art" Victor Hugo, *Œuvres Complètes de Victor Hugo, Actes et Paroles,* vol. 4, *Depuis l'Exil, 1876–1885* (Paris, n.d.), 199. Translated by the author.

156 *"the French nation"* "Bartholdi's Statue Presented," *New York Times,* July 5, 1884.

158 *"In a century the centenary"* Édouard Laboulaye, speech at the Opera, April 25, 1876, Paris, quoted in Frederic Auguste Bartholdi, *Statue of Liberty Enlightening the World,* trans. Allen Thorndike Rice (New York, 1885), 57.

11. Fundraising and a Visionary Sonnet

159 *"the moment the workmen"* "Bartholdi's Great Statue," *London Daily News,* July 3, 1884, reprinted in the *New York Times,* July 14, 1884.

160 *"no true patriot"* "The French Statue," *New York Times,* September 29, 1876.

161 *"could not possibly"* "Bartholdi Complimented," *New York Times,* November 15, 1885.

"Frenchy and fanciful" George William Curtis, "Editor's Easy Chair," *Harper's New Monthly Magazine,* September 1889, 636.

"We catch ourselves" Charles Carroll, "New York in Summer," *Harper's New Monthly Magazine,* October 1878, 695.

"symbolic and significant gift" George William Curtis, "Editor's Easy Chair," *Harper's New Monthly Magazine,* February 1885, 484.

"It may not be" Ibid.

"public-spirited capitalists" "The Statue of Liberty," *New York Times,* August 5, 1884.

162 *"looked to the heights"* Eugène Delacroix to Alexandre Dumas, 1859, quoted in Joseph C. Sloane, *French Painting between the Past and the Present: Artists, Critics, and Traditions, from 1848 to 1870* (Princeton, 1951), 22.

"the modern spirit" Theophile Thoré [W. Bürger, pseud.], quoted in Sloane, *French Painting between the Past and the Present,* 38n8.

"it is not easy to say" Gérôme, quoted in "American Artists Speak," *Boston Daily Globe,* April 28, 1886.

"adhere to the principles" Howard's Gossip, *Boston Daily Globe,* March 31, 1886.

"these principles are very little" Ibid.

"a local affair" "What Congress is Doing," *New York Times,* July 2, 1886.

162 *"to properly execute"* "They Must Be Invited," *Washington Post,* September 10, 1886.

163 *"an impressive ornament"* American Committee, *An Appeal to the People of the United States, in Behalf of the Great Statue, Liberty Enlightening the World,* rev. ed. (1882; New York, 1884), 6.

"raised by the whole people" "The Bartholdi Statue," *New York Times,* November 29, 1882.

164 *"well-known in the best"* "In Memory of Emma Lazarus," *New York Times,* May 6, 1903.

"Here are the emigrants" Edmund Clarence Stedman, "Poetry in America," *Scribner's Monthly,* August 1881, 542.

165 *Lazarus family club memberships* Bette Roth Young, *Emma Lazarus in Her World: Life and Letters* (Philadelphia, 1995), 6–7.

Lazarus's political activity For a discussion of Lazarus's political interests and activities, see Esther Schor's biography, *Emma Lazarus,* Jewish Encounters (New York, 2006) and Young's *Emma Lazarus in Her World.* Schor refers to Lazarus as the first American to advocate a Jewish homeland in Palestine (*Emma Lazarus,* 159).

166 *"the cream of the monied"* Abraham Cahan, *The Education of Abraham Cahan,* trans. Leon Stein, Abraham P. Conan, and Lynn Davison (Philadelphia, 1969), 354.

"huddled masses" From Emma Lazarus, "The New Colossus," in *Catalogue of the Pedestal Fund Art Loan Exhibition,* 9.

"at the entrance of this" Frédéric Auguste Bartholdi, text for speech to the New England Society, December 22, 1876, New York, private collection, quoted in Janet Headley, "Bartholdi's Second American Visit," in Pierre Provoyeur and June Hargrove, eds., *Liberty: The French-American Statue in Art and History* (New York, 1986), 146.

The New Colossus Emma Lazarus, "The New Colossus," in *Catalogue of the Pedestal Fund,* 9. The punctuation of the catalogue printing (namely the use of quotation marks at the beginning of spoken lines) has not been followed here.

167 *"snatched lightning"* Charles Francis Adams, *The Life of John Adams: Second President of the United States,* vol. 1 (Boston, 1856), 662.

"down the fire from heaven" Sydney George Fisher, *The True Benjamin Franklin* (Philadelphia, 1899), 274.

"panic, terror" John Adams, article in the *Boston Patriot,* May 15, 1811, quoted in Adams, *Life of John Adams,* 662.

"When Franklin drew" Chauncey M. Depew, commemorative address at the unveiling ceremony, "Our Lady of Freedom," *Chicago Daily Tribune,* October 29, 1886.

"O! receive the fugitive" Thomas Paine, "Common Sense," rev. ed., in Paine, *Thomas Paine: Collected Writings,* ed. Eric Foner (New York, 1995), 36.

"asylum to the persecuted" "Memorial and Remonstrance against Reli-

gious Assessments" (1785), in James Madison, *The Complete Madison: His Basic Writings,* ed. Saul K. Padover (New York, 1953), 303.

"The artist's thought" John W. Forney, "Col. Forney's Letters," *The Press* (Philadelphia), April 26, 1875.

168 *"beneficent torch"* "Sunday Art Openings," *Washington Post,* December 26, 1883.

"in these hard times" Editorial, *New York Times,* January 3, 1884.

169 *"said to be the largest"* "Massive Base for the Statue," *New York Times,* May 20, 1884.

Cost of the foundation This figure includes the cost of excavation, construction and inspection. "Rearing the Pedestal," *New York Times,* September 1, 1885.

170 *$182,000 raised by March 1885* "The Still Unfinished Pedestal," *New York Times,* March 13, 1885; "The Statue of Liberty," *New York Times,* March 23, 1885.

"work upon the pedestal" "The Still Unfinished Pedestal," *New York Times,* March 13, 1885.

"prevent so painful" "The Statue of Liberty," *New York Times,* March 23, 1885.

"final appeal" Ibid.

"We ask you in the name" Ibid.

172 *"We must raise the money!"* "An Appeal," *New York World,* March 16, 1885.

"There is no other stage-manager" James Creelman, "Joseph Pulitzer— Master Journalist," *Pearson's Magazine* 21 (March 1909): 231.

"liberty and justice" Joseph Pulitzer, editorial in the *World,* 1889, quoted in Creelman, "Joseph Pulitzer," 243.

173 *"most elaborate"* "In Man's Image," *Saturday Evening Post,* March 28, 1885.

175 *"remind one of the Lilliputians"* "M. Bartholdi's Mighty Statue," *Frank Leslie's Illustrated Newspaper,* October 9, 1886.

12. The Unveiling

177 *"looking extremely ferocious"* "World-Lighting Liberty," *New York Tribune,* October 29, 1886.

"commanded the heartiest" "The Great Land Parade," *New York Times,* October 29, 1886.

"With tinted skin" Ibid.

178 *"The whole history"* Kinsley Twining, "The Inauguration of the Bartholdi Statue," *Independent . . . Devoted to the Consideration of Politics, Social and Economic Tendencies, History, Literature, and the Arts* (New York), November 4, 1886.

179 *"people will know that they"* Ferdinand de Lesseps, speech at the unveiling ceremony, October 28, 1886, Bedloe's Island, in "The Statue Unveiled," *New York Times,* October 29, 1886.

"the united work" William Evarts, presentation address at the unveiling ceremony, October 28, 1886, Bedloe's Island, in "Our Lady of Freedom," *Chicago Daily Tribune,* October 29, 1886.

"huge shock of sound" Ibid.

"might have said had he spoken" Ibid.

"representative of a fierce" Stephen Grover Cleveland, speech at the unveiling ceremony, October 28, 1886, Bedloe's Island, in "The Statue Unveiled," *New York Times,* October 29, 1886.

"the shores of our sister" Stephen Grover Cleveland, speech at the unveiling ceremony, October 28, 1886, Bedloe's Island, in "Our Lady of Freedom," *Chicago Daily Tribune,* October 29, 1886.

"impressive import" W. Albert Lafaivre, speech at the unveiling ceremony, October 28, 1886, Bedloe's Island, in American Committee, *Inauguration of the Statue of Liberty Enlightening the World* (New York, 1887), 33.

180 *"who fought for us"* Chauncey M. Depew, commemorative address at the unveiling ceremony, October 28, 1886, Bedloe's Island, in "The Statue Unveiled," *New York Times,* October 29, 1886.

"in all ages the achievements" Ibid.

"the development of Liberty" Chauncey M. Depew, commemorative address at the unveiling ceremony, October 28, 1886, Bedloe's Island, in American Committee, *Inauguration of the Statue of Liberty,* 38.

"overcame improbabilities" Ibid., 39.

"I devoutly believe" Ibid., 59.

"severe inclemency" Richard Butler, preface to S. Miller Hageman, *Liberty, as Delivered by the Goddess at Her Unveiling in the Harbor of New York* (Brooklyn, 1886).

"troubles and difficulties" "French Visitors Dined," *New York Times,* October 29, 1886.

181 *"denounce[ed] the ceremonies"* "They Enter A Protest," *New York Times,* October 29, 1886.

"shock which the whole" Stevenson Archer, speech in the U.S. House of Representatives, May 30, 1872, Washington, D. C., *Appendix to the Congressional Globe,* 42nd Cong., 2nd sess., 640.

"Bushmen vote" Ibid., 633.

182 *"a free gift of respect"* "Enlightening the World," *Cleveland Gazette,* October 30, 1886.

"'Liberty Enlightening the World,' indeed!" Editorial, *Cleveland Gazette,* November 27, 1886.

183 *"We will not forget"* Cleveland, speech at the unveiling ceremony, in "The Statue Unveiled."

"covenant between ourselves" "Roosevelt's Address at the Statue of Liberty," *New York Times,* October 29, 1936.

"What is liberty?" Chauncey M. Depew, speech at the Lotus Club, November 14, 1885, New York, "Bartholdi Complimented," *New York Times,* November 15, 1885.

185 *Meanings of the statue* A number of books and reports discuss the many interpretations and uses of the statue's image since its completion. See Albert Boime, *Hollow Icons: The Politics of Sculpture in Nineteenth-Century France* (Kent, Ohio, 1987), 131–39; Wilton S. Dillon and Neil G. Kotler, eds., *The Statue of Liberty Revisited: Making a Universal Symbol* (Washington, D.C., 1993), 39–114; Pierre Provoyeur and June Hargrove, eds., *Liberty: The French–American Statue in Art and History* (New York, 1986), 230–73; and John Bodnar, Laura Burt, Jennifer Stinson, and Barbara Truesdell, *The Changing Face of the Statue of Liberty,* A Historical Resource Study for the National Park Service, December 2005, www.cesu .umn.edu/documents/ProjectReports/IU/IU_NPS_01_FinalReport.pdf, 47–382.

186 *"championship of humanity"* Franklin D. Roosevelt, address at the Jackson Day Dinner, January 8, 1940, Washington, D.C., *The Public Papers and Addresses of Franklin D. Roosevelt,* 1940 Vol., *War—and Aid to Democracies* (New York, 1941), 30.

"grand as the idea" Frederic Auguste Bartholdi, *The Statue of Liberty Enlightening the World,* trans. Allen Thorndike Rice (New York, 1885), 19.

Bibliography

I consulted several collections dedicated to the statue or its designers. In France, the Musée Bartholdi, located in Bartholdi's family home in Colmar, preserves Bartholdi's papers, photographs, and models, many of which are on display in the museum. The museum also furthers research through publications about Bartholdi's work. The photographer Christian Kempf of Studio K in Colmar is responsible for maintaining the collection's photographs. The Statue of Liberty Collection of the Conservatoire National des Arts et Métiers in Paris contains a large number of photographs, along with original announcements concerning the statue and the Franco–American Union. Complementing these two collections, the Bartholdi Collection of the Bibliothèque du Conservatoire National des Arts et Métiers in Paris contains newspaper clippings from the period of the statue's design and unveiling.

In the United States, my research was assisted by the Richard Morris Hunt Collection of the Octagon, the Museum of the American Architectural Foundation, in Washington, D.C., which preserves Hunt's sketchbooks and a transcript biography of Richard Morris Hunt that was written by his wife, Catherine Clinton Howland Hunt, based on Hunt's journals. The Abraham Lincoln Foundation of the Union League of Philadelphia assisted with information on the Lincoln portrait by Edward Dalton Marchant.

The Frédéric Auguste Bartholdi Papers maintained by the Manuscripts and Archives Division of the New York Public Library, Astor, Lenox and Tilden Foundations, consists of Bartholdi's journal from 1871, when he visited the United States for the first time, and letters Bartholdi wrote to his mother during this trip. The collection includes the English transcriptions of Bartholdi's writings by Rodman Gilder, which are the source of quotations in this book.

SELECTED BOOKS AND ARTICLES CONSULTED

Adams, Charles Francis. *The Life of John Adams: Second President of the United States.* Vol. 1. Boston: Little, Brown, 1856.

Adams, Henry. *The Education of Henry Adams.* New York: Modern Library, 1931.

Adams, Henry, Kathleen A. Foster, Henry A. La Farge, H. Barbara Weinberg, Linnea H. Wren, and James L. Yarnall. *John La Farge.* New York: Abbeville Press, 1987.

American Committee. *An Appeal to the People of the United States, in Behalf of the Great Statue, Liberty Enlightening the World.* 1882. Rev. ed. New York: [private printing], 1884.

——. *Inauguration of the Statue of Liberty Enlightening the World.* New York: D. Appleton, 1887.

Anderson, Frank Maloy. *The Constitutions and Other Select Documents Illustrative of the History of France, 1789–1907.* 1908. 2nd ed. New York: Russell and Russell, 1967.

Anderson, Grace. "Restoring the Statue of Liberty." *Architectural Record* 172 (July 1984): 128–35.

Appendix to Diplomatic Correspondence of 1865. The Assassination of Abraham Lincoln, Late President of the United States of America. Washington, D.C.: GPO, 1866.

Appleby, Joyce. *Capitalism and a New Social Order.* New York: New York University Press, 1984.

Baker, Paul R. *Richard Morris Hunt.* Cambridge: MIT Press, 1980.

Banning, Lance, ed. *Liberty and Order: The First American Party Struggle.* Indianapolis: Liberty Fund, 2004.

Bartholdi, Frederic Auguste. *The Statue of Liberty Enlightening the World.* Translated by Allen Thorndike Rice. New York: North American Review, 1885.

"Bartholdi's Statue of Liberty." *The American Architect and Building News,* September 15, 1883.

Bednar, Michael. *L'Enfant's Legacy: Public Open Spaces in Washington, D.C.* Baltimore: Johns Hopkins University Press, 2006.

Belot, Robert, and Daniel Bermond. *Bartholdi.* Paris: Perrin, 2004.

Bigelow, John. Introduction to *Autobiography of Benjamin Franklin,* edited by John Bigelow. Philadelphia: J. B. Lippincott, 1869.

———. *Retrospections of an Active Life*. 5 vols. New York: Baker and Taylor, 1909–13.

———. *Some Recollections of the Late Edouard Laboulaye*. New York: Privately printed [G. P. Putnam's Sons], [1888].

Blanchet, Christian, and Bertrand Dard. *The Statue of Liberty: The First Hundred Years*. Translated by Bernard A. Weisberger. New York: American Heritage, 1985.

Bodnar, John, Laura Burt, Jennifer Stinson, and Barbara Truesdell. *The Changing Face of the Statue of Liberty*. A Historical Resource Study for the National Park Service. December 2005. www.cesu.umn.edu/documents/ProjectReports/IU/IU_NPS_01_FinalReport.pdf.

Boime, Albert. *Hollow Icons: The Politics of Sculpture in Nineteenth-Century France*. Kent, Ohio: Kent State University Press, 1987.

———. "The Second Republic's Contest for the Figure of the Republic." *The Art Bulletin* 53 (March 1971): 68–83.

Booth, Mary L. Translator's preface to *The Results of Emancipation*, by Augustin Cochin. 2nd ed. Boston: Walker, Wise, 1863.

Bosc, Ernest. "Le Salon." *Encyclopédie d'Architecture* 1 (1872): 90.

Brown, Charles H. *William Cullen Bryant*. New York: Charles Scribner's Sons, 1971.

Brinton, Crane. *A Decade of Revolution, 1789–1799*. New York: Harper and Row, 1934.

Burton, Orville Vernon. *The Age of Lincoln*. New York: Hill and Wang, 2007.

Butterfield, L. H., and Marc Friedlaender, eds. *Adams Family Correspondence*. Vol. 4. Cambridge: Belknap Press / Harvard University Press, 1873.

Cahan, Abraham. *The Education of Abraham Cahan*. Translated by Leon Stein, Abraham P. Conan, and Lynn Davison. Philadelphia: Jewish Publication Society of America, 1969.

Carmona, Michel. *Eiffel*. Paris: Fayard, 2002.

Carroll, Charles. "New York in Summer." *Harper's New Monthly Magazine*, October 1878.

Case, Lynn M., and Warren F. Spencer. *The United States and France: Civil War Diplomacy*. Philadelphia: University of Pennsylvania Press, 1970.

The Case of Dred Scott in the United States Supreme Court. New York: Horace Greeley, 1860.

Castelar, Emilio. "The Republican Movement in Europe." Part 2. *Harper's New Monthly Magazine*, July 1872.

Catalogue of the Pedestal Fund Art Loan Exhibition. New York: National Academy of Design, 1883.

Chastellux, François-Jean. *Travels in North America, in the Years 1780, 1781, and 1782*. Translated by Howard C. Rice Jr. 2 vols. Chapel Hill: University of North Carolina Press, 1963.

Clayton, Peter A., and Martin J. Price, eds. *The Seven Wonders of the Ancient World*. London: Routledge, 1988.

Cliver, E. Blaine. "The Statue of Liberty: Systems within a Structure of Metals." *Bulletin of the Association for Preservation Technology* 18, no. 3 (1986): 12–23.

Cobban, Alfred. *A History of Modern France.* Vol. 1, *Old Régime and Revolution, 1715–1799.* 3rd ed. London: Penguin Books, 1990.

———. *A History of Modern France.* Vol. 2, *From the First Empire to the Second Empire, 1799–1871.* 2nd ed. London: Penguin Books, 1965.

Continental Congress. *Journals of the Continental Congress, 1774–1789.* Edited by Worthington C. Ford et al. Vol. 21. Washington, D.C., 1912.

———. *Journals of the Continental Congress, 1774–1789.* Edited by Worthington C. Ford et al. Vol. 27. Washington, D.C., 1928.

Cortissoz, Royal. *John La Farge: A Memoir and a Study.* 1911. New York: Da Capo Press, 1971.

Craven, Wayne. *Sculpture in America.* Rev. ed. Newark: University of Delaware Press, 1984.

Creelman, James. "Joseph Pulitzer–Master Journalist." *Pearson's Magazine* 21 (March 1909): 229–47.

Curtis, George William. *An Address at the Unveiling of the Statue of Washington, Upon the Spot Where He Took the Oath as First President of the United States.* New York: Harper and Brothers, 1883.

———. "Editor's Easy Chair." *Harper's New Monthly Magazine,* February 1885; September 1885; January 1887; September 1889.

Dillon, Wilton S., and Neil G. Kotler, eds. *The Statue of Liberty Revisited: Making a Universal Symbol.* Washington, D.C.: Smithsonian Institution Press, 1993.

Downing, Antoinette F., and Vincent J. Scully Jr. *The Architectural Heritage of Newport, Rhode Island, 1640–1915.* 2nd ed. New York: Bramhall House, 1967.

Dreyfus-Brisac, Edmond. "Édouard Laboulaye." La Société de l'enseignement supérieur. *Revue internationale de l'enseignement.* Edited by Edmond Dreyfus-Brisac. Vol. 5. Paris: G. Masson, 1883.

Dudley, William S. *The Naval War of 1812: A Documentary History.* Vol. 2. Washington, D.C.: Naval Historical Center, Department of the Navy, 1992.

Eaton, John. *Grant, Lincoln and the Freedmen: Reminiscences of the Civil War.* In collaboration with Ethel Osgood Mason. New York: Longmans, Green, 1907.

"Edouard Laboulaye." *Harper's Weekly.* December 15, 1866.

Elling, Christian. *Rome: The Biography of Her Architecture from Bernini to Thorvaldsen.* Translated by Bob and Inge Gosney. Boulder: Westview Press, 1975.

Farrand, Max, ed. *The Records of the Federal Convention of 1787.* Vol. 3. New Haven: Yale University Press, 1911.

Ferling, John. *A Leap in the Dark.* New York: Oxford University Press, 2003.

Fischer, David Hackett. *Liberty and Freedom: A Visual History of America's Founding Ideas.* New York: Oxford University Press, 2005.

Fisher, Sydney George. *The True Benjamin Franklin.* Philadelphia: J. B. Lippincott, 1899.

Fleming, E. McClung. "The American Image as Indian Princess 1765–1783." *Winterthur Portfolio* 2 (1965): 65–81.

Fletcher, Banister. *A History of Architecture*. 18th ed. Revised by J. C. Palmes. New York: Charles Scribner's Sons, 1975.

Foner, Eric. *Forever Free: The Story of Emancipation and Reconstruction*. New York: Alfred A. Knopf, 2005.

——. *The Story of American Freedom*. New York: W. W. Norton, 1998.

Foner, Eric, and Olivia Mahoney. *America's Reconstruction: People and Politics After the Civil War*. Baton Rouge: Louisiana State University Press, 1997.

Forney, John W. *A Centennial Commissioner in Europe, 1874–1876*. Philadelphia: J. B. Lippincott, 1876.

——. *Letters from Europe*. Philadelphia: T. B. Peterson and Brothers, 1867.

Fox, Nancy Jo. *Liberties with Liberty: The Fascinating History of America's Proudest Symbol*. New York: E. P. Dutton; New York: Museum of American Folk Art, 1986.

"France to America." *Scribner's Monthly*, June 1877.

Frank Leslie's Illustrated Historical Register of the Centennial Exposition 1876. Facsimile with a new introduction by Richard Kenin. New York: Paddington Press, 1974.

Franklin, Benjamin. *The Complete Works of Benjamin Franklin*. Edited by John Bigelow. Vol. 6. New York: G. P. Putnam's Sons, 1888.

——. *Private Correspondence of Benjamin Franklin*. Edited by William Temple Franklin. 2 vols. London: Henry Colburn, 1833.

——. *The Works of Benjamin Franklin*. Edited by Jared Sparks. Vol. 1. Chicago: Townsend MacCoun, 1882.

——. *The Works of Benjamin Franklin*. Edited by Jared Sparks. Vol. 10. Boston: Charles Tappan, 1844.

Fried, Charles. *Modern Liberty and the Limits of Government*. New York: W. W. Norton, 2007.

Fryd, Vivien Green. *Art and Empire: The Politics of Ethnicity in the United States Capitol, 1815–1860*. Athens: Ohio University Press, 2001.

Gasparin, Agenor, de, Edouard Laboulaye, Henri Martin, and Augustin Cochin. *Reply of Agenor de Gasparin, Edouard Laboulaye, Henri Martin, and Augustin Cochin to the Letter of the Loyal National League*. Translated by John Austin Stevens Jr. Pamphlets Issued by the Loyal Publication Society. New York: Loyal Publication Society, 1864.

Gilder, Rodman. *Statue of Liberty Enlightening the World*. New York: New York Trust Company, 1943.

Goncourt, Edmond and Jules, de. *The Goncourt Journals 1851–1870*. Edited and translated by Lewis Galantiere. New York: Greenwood Press, 1968.

Gray, Walter D. *Interpreting American Democracy in France: The Career of Édouard Laboulaye, 1811–1883*. London, Ontario: Associated University Presses; Newark: University of Delaware Press, 1994.

The Greek Anthology. Vol. 1. Translated by William R. Paton. Cambridge: Harvard University Press; London: William Heinemann, 1916.

Greene, Nathanael. *The Papers of General Nathanael Greene*. Edited by Richard K. Showman. Vol. 2. Chapel Hill: University of North Carolina Press, 1980.

Gschaedler, André. *True Light on the Statue of Liberty and Its Creator.* Narberth, Penn.: Livingston, 1966.

Hagedorn, Hermann. *Roosevelt in the Bad Lands.* Boston: Houghton Mifflin, 1921.

Hageman, S. Miller. *Liberty, as Delivered by the Goddess at Her Unveiling in the Harbor of New York.* Brooklyn: [private printing], 1886.

Hammett, Dashiell. *The Maltese Falcon.* New York: Alfred A. Knopf, 1930.

Harriss, Joseph. *The Tallest Tower: Eiffel and the Belle Epoque.* Boston: Houghton Mifflin, 1975.

Hayden, Richard Seth, and Thierry W. Despont. *Restoring the Statue of Liberty.* With Nadine M. Post. New York: McGraw-Hill, 1986.

Hazelton, George C., Jr. *The National Capitol: Its Architecture, Art, and History.* New York: J. F. Taylor, 1902.

Higginson, Thomas Wentworth. *Henry Wadsworth Longfellow.* Boston: Houghton Mifflin, 1902.

Hitchcock, Henry Russell. *The Architecture of H. H. Richardson and His Times.* Rev. ed. Cambridge: MIT Press, 1966.

Holzer, Harold. *Lincoln at Cooper Union: The Speech That Made Abraham Lincoln President.* New York: Simon and Schuster, 2004.

Hone, Philip. *The Diary of Philip Hone, 1828–1851.* Edited by Bayard Tuckerman. 2 vols. New York: Dodd, Mead, 1889.

Hueber, Régis, ed. *Auguste Bartholdi: Desseins . . . Dessins.* Musée Bartholdi. Colmar, France: Editions d'Alsace, 1995.

———, ed. *Bartholdi: Le Lion.* Ville de Colmar / Musée Bartholdi. Colmar, France: L'Imprimerie GRAI, 2004.

———, ed. *D'un album de voyage: Auguste Bartholdi en Egypte (1855–1856).* Colmar, France: Editions d'Alsace, 1990.

Hugo, Victor. *Actes et Paroles.* Vol. 2, *Pendant l'Exil, 1852–1870.* 2nd ed. Paris: Michel Lévy Frères, 1875.

———. *Œuvres Complètes de Victor Hugo, Actes et Paroles.* Vol. 4, *Depuis l'Exil, 1876–1885.* Paris: L. Hébert, n.d.

Hunt, Richard M. "Paper on the Architectural Exhibit of the Centennial Exhibition." American Institute of Architects. *Proceedings of the Tenth Annual Convention* 10 (1876): 34–38.

James, Henry. *William Wetmore Story and His Friends.* Vol. 2. Boston: Houghton, Mifflin, 1904.

Janson, Horst Woldemar. *Nineteenth-Century Sculpture.* New York: Harry N. Abrams, 1985.

Jefferson, Thomas. *The Works of Thomas Jefferson.* Edited by Paul Leicester Ford. 12 vols. New York: G. P. Putnam's Sons, 1904–5.

Johnston, Robert M., ed. *Memoirs of "Malakoff": Being Extracts from the Correspondence and Papers of the late William Edward Johnston.* London: Hutchinson, 1906.

Kennedy, Melvin D. *Lafayette and Slavery: From His Letters to Thomas Clarkson and Granville Sharp.* The American Friends of Lafayette, no. 4 (1950).

Kennon, Donald R., ed. *The United States Capitol: Designing and Decorating a National Icon.* Athens: Ohio University Press, 2000.

Kite, Elizabeth S. *L'Enfant and Washington, 1791–1792.* Baltimore: Johns Hopkins Press, 1929.

Knowlton, Helen M. *Art–Life of William Morris Hunt.* Boston: Little, Brown, 1899.

Kramer, Lloyd. *Lafayette in Two Worlds: Public Cultures and Personal Iden tities in an Age of Revolutions.* Chapel Hill: University of North Carolina Press, 1996.

Kurland, Philip B., and Ralph Lerner, eds. *The Founders' Constitution.* Vol. 1, *Major Themes.* Chicago: University of Chicago Press, 1987.

La Farge, John, Jr. *The Manner is Ordinary.* New York: Harcourt, Brace, 1954.

Laboulaye, Édouard. *Histoire des États-Unis.* Vol. 2. Paris: Charpentier, 1868. A facsimile of the third edition. Boston: Adamant Media, 2006.

———. *L'État et ses limites: suivi d'essais politiques.* 2nd ed. Paris: Charpentier, 1863.

———. [René Lefebvre, pseud.]. *Paris en Amérique.* 14th ed. Paris: Charpentier, 1865.

———. [René Lefebvre, pseud.]. *Paris in America.* Translated by Mary L. Booth. New York: Charles Scribner, 1863.

———. *Professor Laboulaye, the Great Friend of America, on the Presidential Election: The Election of the President of the United States.* Translated by the U.S. Department of State. Washington, D.C.: Union Congressional Committee, 1864.

Lafayette, Marie-Joseph-Paul-Yves-Roch-Gilbert du Motier, Marquis de. *Mémoires, Correspondance et Manuscrits du Général Lafayette. Publiés par sa famille.* Vol. 1. Paris: H. Fournier Ainé, 1837.

———. *Memoirs, Correspondence and Manuscripts of General Lafayette. Published by His Family.* Vol. 1. London: Saunders and Otley, 1837.

Landau, Sarah Bradford, and Carl W. Condit. *Rise of the New York Skyscraper, 1865–1913.* New Haven: Yale University Press, 1996.

Lauzun, Armand Louis de Gontaut Biron, Duc de. *Memoirs of the Duc de Lauzun.* Translated by C. K. Scott Moncrieff. 1928. Reprint, New York: Arno Press, 1969.

Lazarus, Emma. *The Poems of Emma Lazarus.* 2 vols. Boston: Houghton, Mifflin, 1888.

Lemoine, Bertrand. *Gustave Eiffel.* Paris: Fernand Hazan, 1984.

———. "La Statue de la liberté, New York." *L'Architecture D'Aujourd'hui,* no. 246 (September 1986): 39–45.

Le Normand-Romain, Antoinette, et al. *Sculpture: The Adventure of Modern Sculpture in the Nineteenth and Twentieth Centuries.* New York: Rizzoli International, 1986.

Levasseur, Auguste. *Lafayette en Amérique en 1824 et 1825, ou Journal d'un Voyage aux États-Unis.* Paris: Baudouin, 1829.

———. *Lafayette in America in 1824 and 1825: Journal of a Voyage to the United States.* Translated by Alan R. Hoffman. Manchester, New Hampshire: Lafayette Press, 2006.

Lincoln, Abraham. *Abraham Lincoln: Speeches and Writings, 1859–1865.* Edited by Don E. Fehrenbacher. New York: Library of America, 1989.

———. Abraham Lincoln Papers at the Library of Congress. Manuscript Division. Washington, D.C., http://memory.loc.gov/cgi-bin/query/r?ammem/mal:@field(DOCID+@lit(d4356600)).

———. The Collected Works of Abraham Lincoln. Edited by Roy P. Basler. 9 vols. New Brunswick: Rutgers University Press, 1953–55.

———. Complete Works of Abraham Lincoln. Vol. 1. Edited by John G. Nicolay and John Hay. New York: Century, 1894.

Lincolniana: In Memoriam. Boston: William V. Spencer, 1865.

Livy [Titus Livius]. The History of Rome from Its Foundation. Books 1 to 5, The Early History of Rome. Translated by Aubrey De Sélincourt. New York: Penguin, 1971.

Loyrette, Henri. Gustave Eiffel. Translated by Rachel and Susan Gomme. New York: Rizzoli International, 1985.

Luria, Sarah. Capital Speculations: Writing and Building Washington, D.C. Durham: University of New Hampshire Press; Lebanon: University Press of New England, 2006.

MacIntire, Jane Bacon. Lafayette: The Guest of the Nation. Newton, Mass.: Anthony J. Simore Press, 1967.

Madison, James. The Complete Madison: His Basic Writings. Edited by Saul K. Padover. New York: Harper and Brothers, 1953.

———. Notes of Debates in the Federal Convention of 1787, Reported by James Madison. Athens: Ohio University Press, [1966].

Marrey, Bernard. Extraordinary Life and Work of Monsieur Gustave Eiffel, the Engineer Who Built the Statue of Liberty . . . Paris: Graphite, 1984.

———. Gustave Eiffel: Une Entreprise Exemplaire. Paris: Institute, 1989.

McCabe, James D. The Illustrated History of the Centennial Exhibition: Philadelphia 1876. Philadelphia: National Publishing, 1975.

Middleton, Robin, and David Watkin. Neoclassical and Nineteenth-Century Architecture. Vol. 2, The Diffusion and Development of Classicism and the Gothic Revival. Milan: Electa, 1980.

Miller, Iris. Washington in Maps, 1606–2000. New York: Rizzoli International, 2002.

Mills, Robert. Guide to the Capitol of the United States, Embracing Every Information Useful to the Visitor, Whether on Business or Pleasure. Washington, D.C., 1834.

Montgomery, Charles F., and Patricia E. Kane, eds. American Art, 1750–1800: Towards Independence. Boston: New York Graphic Society, 1976.

Moreno, Barry. The Statue of Liberty Encyclopedia. New York: Simon and Schuster, 2000.

Murdock, Myrtle Cheney. Constantino Brumidi: Michelangelo of the United States Capitol. Washington, D.C.: Monumental Press, 1950.

Padover, Saul K., ed. Thomas Jefferson and the National Capitol, 1783–1818. Washington, D.C.: GPO, 1946.

Paine, Thomas. Thomas Paine: Collected Writings. Edited by Eric Foner. New York: Library of America, 1995.

Paris, William Francklyn. "Richard Morris Hunt: First Secretary and Third President of the Institute." Pts. 1, 2, and 3. Journal of the American Insti-

tute of Architects 24 (December 1955): 243–49; 25 (January 1956): 14–19; 25 (February 1956): 74–80.

Pauli, Hertha, and E. B. Ashton. *I Lift My Lamp: The Way of a Symbol.* New York: Appleton-Century-Crofts, 1948.

Peterson, Merrill D. *John Brown: The Legend Revisited.* Charlottesville: University of Virginia Press, 2002.

Philp, Mark. *Paine.* Oxford: Oxford University Press, 1989.

Poetical Tributes to the Memory of Abraham Lincoln. Philadelphia: J. B. Lippincott, 1865.

Pringle, Henry F. *Theodore Roosevelt: A Biography.* New York: Harcourt Brace Jovanovich, 1956.

Provoyeur, Pierre, and June Hargrove, eds. *Liberty: The French–American Statue in Art and History.* New York: Harper and Row, 1986.

Reed, Henry Hope. *The United States Capitol: Its Architecture and Decoration.* New York: W. W. Norton, 2005.

Rice, Howard C., Jr., and Anne S. K. Brown, eds. *The American Campaigns of Rochambeau's Army, 1780, 1781, 1782, 1783.* Translated by Rice and Brown. 2 vols. Princeton: Princeton University Press; Providence: Brown University Press, 1972.

Richard, Carl J. *The Founders and the Classics.* Cambridge: Harvard University Press, 1994.

Richard Morris Hunt, architecte, 1827–1895: La tradition française en Amerique. Paris: Caisse national des monuments historiques et des sites, 1989.

Robb, Graham. *Victor Hugo.* New York: W. W. Norton, 1998.

Robbins, Miss. "Edward Laboulaye." *Appletons' Journal of Popular Literature, Science, and Art.* September 4, 1869.

Romer, John, and Elizabeth Romer. *The Seven Wonders of the World.* London: Seven Dials, Cassell, 1995.

Roosevelt, Franklin D. *The Public Papers and Addresses of Franklin D. Roosevelt.* 1940 Vol., *War—and Aid to Democracies.* New York: Macmillan, 1941.

Rosenbaum, Julia B. *Visions of Belonging: New England Art and the Making of American Identity.* Ithaca: Cornell University Press, 2006.

Rudler, and Delmas. "Exposition universelle de 1878." *Encyclopédie d'Architecture* 7 (1878): 32–39.

Rush, Benjamin. "The Influence of Physical Causes upon the Moral Faculty." In *The Selected Writings of Benjamin Rush,* edited by Dagobert D. Runes. New York: Philosophical Library, 1947.

Sandburg, Carl. *Abraham Lincoln: The Prairie Years.* Vol. 2. New York: Harcourt, Brace, 1926.

———. *Abraham Lincoln: The War Years.* Vol. 2. New York: Harcourt, Brace, 1939.

Schivelbusch, Wolfgang. *The Culture of Defeat: On National Trauma, Mourning, and Recovery.* Translated by Jefferson Chase. New York: Metropolitan Books, 2003.

Schor, Esther. *Emma Lazarus.* Jewish Encounters. New York: Schocken, 2006.

Schurz, Carl. *Speeches of Carl Schurz.* Philadelphia: J. B. Lippincott, 1865.

Scott, Pamela. *Temple of Liberty: Building the Capitol for a New Nation.* New York: Oxford University Press, 1995.

Sharp, Lewis I. *John Quincy Adams Ward: Dean of American Sculpture.* London, Ontario: Associated University Presses; Newark: University of Delaware Press, 1985.

Sloane, Joseph C. *French Painting between the Past and the Present: Artists, Critics, and Traditions, from 1848 to 1870.* Princeton: Princeton University Press, 1951.

Special Report of the Anti-Slavery Conference. London: Committee of the British and Foreign Anti-Slavery Society, [1868].

Spiering, Frank. *Bearer of a Million Dreams.* Ottowa, Ill.: Jameson Books, 1986.

Spivey, Nigel Jonathan. *Understanding Greek Sculpture: Ancient Meanings, Modern Readings.* London: Thames and Hudson, 1996.

Stedman, Edmund Clarence. "Liberty Enlightening the World." *Harper's Weekly,* October 30, 1886.

———. "Poetry in America." *Scribner's Monthly,* August 1881.

Stein, Susan R., ed. *The Architecture of Richard Morris Hunt.* Chicago: University of Chicago Press, 1986.

Stevenson, Elizabeth. *Park Maker: A Life of Frederick Law Olmstead.* New York: Macmillan, 1977.

Stiles, Ezra. *The Literary Diary of Ezra Stiles.* Vol. 2, *March 14, 1776–December 31, 1781.* Edited by Franklin Bowditch Dexter. New York: Charles Scribner's Sons, 1901.

Stokes, Margaret. "The Corona Radiata and the Crown of Thorns." *The Art-Journal* 44 (September 1882): 265–67.

Stone, John, and Stephen Mennell, eds. *Alexis de Tocqueville on Democracy, Revolution, and Society: Selected Writings.* Chicago: University of Chicago Press, 1980.

Sullivan, Louis H. *The Autobiography of an Idea.* New York: Dover, 1956.

Summerson, John. *The Classical Language of Architecture.* London: Methuen, 1964.

Sutherland, Cara A. *The Statue of Liberty.* New York: Barnes and Noble, 2003.

Swinney, Everette. "Enforcing the Fifteenth Amendment, 1870–1877." *The Journal of Southern History* 28 (May 1962): 202–18.

Thayer, Theodore. *Yorktown: Campaign of Strategic Options.* Edited by Harold M. Hyman. Philadelphia: J. B. Lippincott, 1975.

Thoreau, Henry David. *A Plea for Captain John Brown.* Boston: David R. Godine, 1969.

Tocqueville, Alexis, de. *The Old Régime and the French Revolution.* Translated by Stuart Gilbert. 1858. New York: Doubleday, 1955.

Torchia, Robert Wilson. *The Collections of the Union League of Philadelphia.* Vol. 1, *Portraits of the Presidents of the United States of America.* Philadelphia: Union League of Philadelphia, 2005.

Tower, Charlemagne. *The Marquis de La Fayette in the American Revolution.* 2 vols. Philadelphia: J. B. Lippincott, 1895.

Townsend, James B. "The Statue of 'Liberty.'" *Frank Leslie's Popular Monthly*, August 1885.

Trachtenberg, Marvin. *The Statue of Liberty*. New York: Penguin Books, 1986. First published 1976 by Viking Penguin.

Trautz, Martin. "Maurice Koechlin: Der eigentliche Erfinder des Eiffelturms." *Deutsche Bauzeitung* 136 (April 2002): 105–10.

Trefousse, Hans L. *Carl Schurz: A Biography*. New York: Fordham University Press, 1998.

Trevelyan, George Macaulay. *Garibaldi's Defense of the Roman Republic*. London: Longman's, Green, 1912.

U.S. Centennial Commission. *Report of the Director-General*. Vol. 1. Philadelphia: J. B. Lippincott, 1879.

U.S. Congress. *Appendix to the Congressional Globe*. 34th Cong., 1st sess., May 19, 1856.

———. *Appendix to the Congressional Globe*. 41st Cong., 3rd sess., March 3, 1871.

———. *Appendix to the Congressional Globe*. 42nd Cong., 2nd sess., May 30, 1872.

———. *Congressional Globe*. Senate. 37th Cong., 1st sess., July 25, 1861.

———. *Congressional Globe*. Senate. 42nd Cong., 2nd sess., February 29, 1872.

———. *House Journal*. 2nd Cong., 1st sess., March 24, 1792.

———. *House Journal*. 23rd Cong., 2nd sess., December 31, 1834.

———. *House Journal*, 36th Cong., 1st sess., February 9, 1860.

———. *House Journal*. 37th Cong., 1st sess., July 5, 1861.

U.S. Congress. *Senate Journal*. 41st Cong., 3rd sess., March 3, 1871.

U.S. Congress, House of Representatives. *Annals of Congress*. 18th Cong., 1st sess., January 20, 1824.

U.S. Congress, Senate. Committee on Foreign Relations. *Compilation of Reports of Committee on Foreign Relations, 1789–1901*. Vol. 4. 56th Cong., 2nd sess., 1901.

———. *Register of Debates in Congress*. 18th Cong., 2nd sess., December 21, 1824.

———. *Register of Debates in Congress*. 21st Cong., 1st sess., January 27, 1830.

———. Select Committee on the Harper's Ferry Invasion. *Report*. 36th Cong., 1st sess., 1860.

U.S. Department of State. *Appendix to Diplomatic Correspondence of 1865, Assassination of Abraham Lincoln*. Washington, D.C., 1867.

Van Brunt, Henry. "Richard Morris Hunt, 1828–1895." *Journal of the American Institute of Architects* 8 (October 1947): 180–87.

Viollet-le-Duc, Eugène-Emmanuel. *The Architectural Theory of Viollet-le-Duc: Readings and Commentary*. Edited by Millard F. Hearn. Cambridge: MIT Press, 1990.

———. "Introduction." *Encyclopédie d'Architecture* 1 (1872): 1.

———. *Lectures on Architecture*. Translated by Benjamin Bucknall. 2 vols. 1881. Reprint, New York: Dover, 1987.

———. "Pompéi." *Encyclopédie d'Architecture* 2 (1873): 129–31.

Vitruvius [Marcus Pollio]. *The Ten Books on Architecture.* Translated by Morris Hicky Morgan. 1914. Reprint, New York: Dover, 1960.

"Vol. XVI of 'L'Art.'" *Scribner's Monthly,* August 1879.

Ware, William R. *The American Vignola.* New York: W. W. Norton, 1977.

Washburne, Elihu B. *Recollections of a Minister to France, 1869–1877.* 2 vols. New York: Charles Scribner's Sons, 1889.

Washington, George. *The Papers of George Washington.* Confederation Series. Edited by W. W. Abbot and Dorothy Twohig. Vol. 4. Charlottesville: University Press of Virginia, 1995.

———. *The Papers of George Washington.* Presidential Series. Edited by Dorothy Twohig. Vol. 2. Charlottesville: University Press of Virginia, 1987.

———. *The Papers of George Washington.* Presidential Series. Edited by Dorothy Twohig. Vols. 5 and 6. Charlottesville: University Press of Virginia, 1996.

Wawro, Geoffrey. *The Franco-Prussian War.* Cambridge: Cambridge University Press, 2003.

Webster, Daniel. *The Private Correspondence of Daniel Webster.* Edited by Fletcher Webster. Vol. 1. Boston: Little, Brown, 1857.

Wharton, Francis, ed. *The Revolutionary Diplomatic Correspondence of the United States.* Vol. 4. Washington, D.C.: GPO, 1889.

Willcox, William B., ed. *The American Rebellion: Sir Henry Clinton's Narrative of His Campaigns, 1775–1782.* New Haven: Yale University Press, 1954.

Wills, Garry. *Inventing America: Jefferson's Declaration of Independence.* Garden City: Doubleday, 1978.

———. *Lincoln at Gettysburg: The Words That Remade America.* New York: Simon and Schuster, 1992.

Wilson, Woodrow. *Constitutional Government in the United States.* New York: Columbia University Press, 1908.

Wolanin, Barbara A. *Constantino Brumidi: Artist of the Capitol.* Washington, D.C.: GPO, 1998.

Woods, David Walker. *John Witherspoon.* New York: Fleming H. Revell, 1906.

Wordsworth, William. *The Prelude: The Four Texts (1798, 1799, 1805, 1850).* Edited by Jonathan Wordsworth. London: Penguin Books, 1995.

Wright, Gordon. *France in Modern Times: From the Enlightenment to the Present.* 4th ed. New York: W. W. Norton, 1981.

Wrigley, Richard. *The Politics of Appearances: Representations of Dress in Revolutionary France.* Oxford: Berg, 2002.

Yellin, Jean Fagan. "Caps and Chains: Hiram Powers' Statue of 'Liberty.'" *American Quarterly* 38 (Winter 1986): 798–826.

Young, Alfred F. *The Democratic Republicans of New York: The Origins, 1763–1797.* Chapel Hill: University of North Carolina Press, 1967.

Young, Bette Roth. *Emma Lazarus in Her World: Life and Letters.* Philadelphia: Jewish Publication Society, 1995.

Index

226 · *Index*